State-Sponsored Activism

In *State-Sponsored Activism*, Rich explores AIDS policy in Brazil as a lens to offer new insight into state–society relations in democratic and post-neoliberal Latin America. In contrast to the dominant view that these dual transitions produced an atomized civil society and an impenetrable technocratic state, Rich finds a new model of interest politics, driven by previously marginalized state and societal actors. Through a rich examination of the Brazilian AIDS movement, one of the most influential movements in twenty-first century Latin America, this book traces the construction of a powerful new advocacy coalition between activist bureaucrats and bureaucratized activists. In so doing, *State-Sponsored Activism* illustrates a model whereby corporatism – active government involvement in civic mobilization – has persisted in contemporary Latin America, with important implications for representation and policymaking.

Jessica A.J. Rich is Assistant Professor in the Department of Political Science at Marquette University. She has also held positions as a visiting fellow at the London School of Economics, and as a postdoctoral fellow at Tulane University's Center for Inter-American Policy and Research.

State-Sponsored Activism

Bureaucrats and Social Movements in Democratic Brazil

JESSICA A. J. RICH
Marquette University

CAMBRIDGE
UNIVERSITY PRESS

CAMBRIDGE
UNIVERSITY PRESS

University Printing House, Cambridge CB2 8BS, United Kingdom

One Liberty Plaza, 20th Floor, New York, NY 10006, USA

477 Williamstown Road, Port Melbourne, VIC 3207, Australia

314-321, 3rd Floor, Plot 3, Splendor Forum, Jasola District Centre, New Delhi - 110025, India

79 Anson Road, #06-04/06, Singapore 079906

Cambridge University Press is part of the University of Cambridge.

It furthers the University's mission by disseminating knowledge in the pursuit of education, learning and research at the highest international levels of excellence.

www.cambridge.org
Information on this title: www.cambridge.org/9781108456807
DOI: 10.1017/9781108626453

First published 2019
First paperback edition 2021

A catalogue record for this publication is available from the British Library

ISBN 978-1-108-47088-9 Hardback
ISBN 978-1-108-45680-7 Paperback

Contents

Figures

Illustrations

Acknowledgments

I find it both gratifying and daunting to acknowledge the dizzying array of people who contributed to this book. First, I am grateful beyond words to the civic activists and government workers who inspired and made possible my research. Despite their busy schedules, they gave me long interviews (often more than once); they invited me to participate in their meetings and conferences; they supplied me with key documents; and perhaps most importantly, they made me feel welcome and important. Too many people helped me along the way for me to be able to fit a mention of everyone into these few pages, but I value all of your contributions. Thanks in particular to Willian Amaral, Ernandes Costa, Rubens Duda, Gilvane Casimiro, Kátia Edmundo, Américo Nunes, Richard Parker, Roberto Pereira, Rodrigo Pinheiro, Veriano Terto Jr., and Márcio Villard. My desire not to have wasted your time is what drove me to complete the project. In addition, this book would not have been possible without my four brilliant research assistants, some of whom have already moved on to their own exciting projects. Alline Torres and Paula Vedovelli provided perfect transcriptions of my interviews. Pedro Andrada assisted enthusiastically with the survey in São Paulo. And Elis Andrade played a key role in just about every fieldwork endeavor.

In Brazil, I also benefitted enormously from a vibrant and generous academic community. I am grateful to IESP in Rio de Janeiro and CEBRAP in São Paulo for providing me with institutional homes, and to their teams of scholars for engaging me in fascinating discussions about Brazilian politics. Thanks in particular to Renato Boschi for inviting into the fold of his academic tribe, and for supporting my project with his enthusiasm. Rebecca Abers supported me in a myriad of ways throughout the process. Toward the end of the project, I was fortunate to be introduced to Laura Murray, who not only generously shared her rich scholarship on sex workers with me but also gave me encouragement, contacts, and new ideas. Igor Brandão and Rafael Viana shared their brilliant theses with me and patiently answered my endless array of questions about waste-picking and low-income housing. Their scholarship is the basis for two of the case studies in Chapter 8. Wendel Antunes Cintra graciously helped me translate the survey, exhibiting far more rigor and patience than I had myself. For intellectual and moral support, I also depended on Elena Martinez Barahona, Flavia Campos, Matthew Flynn, Guilherme Macedo, Paulo Mario Martins, Ed Pereira, Tricia Perry, Andrés del Rio Roldan, Laura Schieber, and Javier Vadell. Most importantly, Barbara Gomes Lamas and Daniela Tranches de Melo first welcomed me into their home and generously invited this gringa to all their scholarly and social gatherings. Without them, fieldwork would have been a much lonelier experience; and I am honored to count them among my friends-for-life.

I began the study leading to this book while a graduate student in the Department of Political Science of the University of California at Berkeley, where I was blessed with advisers who allowed me the freedom to invent something new while holding me to the highest standards. Each of the five brilliant members of my dissertation committee inspired large pieces of the project, and I cannot imagine this book without every one of them. Beyond their specific insights, they also imparted key lessons that I will carry with me through my career. Christopher Ansell showed me how to present complicated arguments in plain English. Laura Stoker helped me improve my writing through her painstaking, spot-on comments. While Ann Swidler technically served as my "outside" adviser, she guided me as though she were one of my committee chairs. From the start of this dissertation, Ann provided immeasurable support through her thoughtful feedback and her expressions of enthusiasm, and by describing my project to me in words far more exciting and poetic than my own.

I owe my greatest intellectual debt to Ruth Berins Collier and David Collier. Their mentorship made me the scholar I am today, and they set an example for the kind of scholar and colleague I want to be. Ruth taught me intellectual rigor by never settling for anything less than outstanding work, and by dedicating vast amounts of time helping me achieve that. Not infrequently, I would enter Ruth's office with a "quick question", only to leave two hours later with ten pages of notes addressing critical issues in my project. David taught me to focus my research on the issues that matter for people's welfare, rather than on standard political science questions. He also taught me to be a member of an academic community through his myriad of advice ranging from the prosaic to the profound, and through his constant encouragement of peer collaboration. Through their attentiveness and support, and through the support network of scholars they cultivated, Ruth and David largely made my graduate school experience. I look forward to continuing to learn from them in the years to come.

One of the most important ways in which Ruth and David shaped my academic experience is through the community of scholars they created, in particular, the graduate students in the Latin American politics group who came before me and continue to guide me, especially Diana Kapizsewski. I am also indebted to the rest of my fellow Latin American politics students, who helped me through graduate school with their feedback, their encouragement, and most importantly, their friendship. Among those I am lucky enough to consider colleagues and friends are Benjamin Allen, Mauricio Benitez-Iturbe, Taylor Boas, Christopher Chambers-Ju, Miguel Defigueiredo, Tasha Fairfield, Candelaria Garay, Samuel Handlin, Veronica Herrera, Danny idalgo, Maiah Jaskoski, Benjamin Lessing, Olivia Miljanic, Simeon Nichter, Brian Palmer-Rubin, and Wendy Sinek. Lindsay Mayka and Neal Richardson deserve special acknowledgment for helping me through a tough year with sumptuous and lively feasts, and by showing me through example how to balance work and pleasure.

I am also deeply grateful for my other Berkeley peers, who made graduate school a collaborative effort, and who showed me that smart people need not be dull. I would like to thank, in particular, Boris Barkanov, Jordan Branch, Jennifer Bussell, Naomi Choi, Thad Dunning, Brent Durbin, Rebecca Hamlin, Amy Lerman, Mike Murakami, Claire Perez, Regine Spector, and Zach Zwald – as well as the non-academics who rounded out the crew, Inseeyah Barma, Nate Martinez, Erin Rowley, and Indira Windiasti. Special thanks go to Rebecca Chen, an exceptional roommate, cheerleader, and friend. During my last year of graduate school, Jody Laporte served as my dissertation, job, and life coach. Even busier than I was, she always made time to proof-read my writing, talk me through difficult decisions, and give words of encouragement (occasionally in all-caps). Without her, I certainly would not have maintained my sanity during the writing process.

Various friends outside Berkeley's Political Science department brightened the more difficult days. Kartik Hansen served as my confidant and my one-man technical support crew. Paco Martorell, among his many contributions, kept me fed during my first year of graduate school. Erica Mohan knew just when to make me come out and play. Geoffrey Barton supplied me with the cookies, ice cream, and sympathy that saw me through the last grueling months. Thanks also to Alisa Dichter, Melissa Disney, Todd Disney, Margaret Flores, Kristy Graves, and Katie Wolford, who made me feel accomplished just for being me.

The book version of this project began to take shape at Tulane University's Center for Inter-American Policy and Research (CIPR), where I was lucky enough to spend two years as a post-doctoral fellow. Ludovico Feoli created a vibrant community of social scientists and served as a gracious host. Thomas Reese of the Stone Center for Latin American Studies built a strong inter-disciplinary community. Kelly Jones kept things running with both exceptional efficiency and exceptional cheer. Eduardo Silva shared his wisdom and advice, and made me feel so welcome. Arachu Castro, Martin Dimitrov, Aaron Schneider, and Mark Vail were integral parts of this welcoming community. I am also deeply grateful to Robert Kaufman, Ken Roberts, and Ben Ross Schneider, who dedicated a few days out of their busy weeks to fly down to New Orleans and participate in my book workshop. Together with Ruth Berins Collier and Eduardo Silva, they gave me detailed and constructive feedback on the first draft of the manuscript. The book's theoretical core was born from their input. And thanks to their combination of kindness and thoroughness, the workshop was both intellectually stimulating and fun. I was also fortunate to meet the kind and wise Manuel Alcántara during my time at Tulane. Thanks to his generosity, I spent six weeks at the University of Salamanca, where the article version of Chapter 6 took shape. I cannot imagine better post-doctoral colleagues than Matthew Johnson and Federico Rossi.

The quickest way to build close bonds of friendship is through crisis. My crisis in New Orleans was fortunately relatively minor: a hurricane that struck shortly after my arrival and left my apartment uninhabitable for several weeks. Thanks to this rather unwelcome introduction to the city, I came to know quite suddenly the couches, air mattresses, and deep wells of generosity of those who have since become close friends: Ana Margarida Fernandes Esteves, Christine Hebl, Matthew Johnson, Mattea Musso, Federico Rossi, and Kristin Wintersteen. My life in New Orleans was both intellectually rich and well-rounded because of these friendships, as well as those of Michael Brumbaugh, João Gonçalves, Virginia Oliveros, Jason Pollentier, and Jessi Taylor. Thanks especially to Mattea for cucorífica creative adventures, to Kristin for anxiety empathy, and to Virginia for making me come out and play.

It has been a joy to be a member of Marquette University's Department of Political Science. My colleagues are not only deeply committed to research and teaching, but they are also kind and supportive and make me look forward to going into the office. Risa Brooks, Mike McCarthy, Barrett McCormick, and Duane Swank provided constructive feedback on key chapters and related articles. Thank you as well to Rich Friman for support of my project through the Center for Transnational Justice. As department chair, Lowell Barrington supported this book in a thousand ways both large and small. My Political Science colleagues Julia Azari, Mark Berlin, Mónica Unda Gutiérrez, Paul Nolette, Brian Palmer-Rubin, Phil Rocco, and Amber Wichowsky kept me sane during the process. Thanks to Noelle Brigden for taking the office next door, and for providing me with endless supplies of feedback, snacks, and moral support. I cannot imagine how my life would be had we not moved into Wehr Physics Building together. My broader Milwaukee family came together without any precipitating crisis, and since my arrival has helped me balance work with pleasure. Renee Calkins, Jeffrey Coleman, Lafayette Crump, Tara Daly, Antonio Furguiele, Sarah Hamilton, Nicole Hendrickson, Bryan Johnston, John Martin, Laura Mele, Elmer Moore Jr., Travis Reed, and Ellen Wagner, each in their own ways, have provided me with important intellectual and personal support.

During the final stretch of finishing this book, I took up residence for a few months at the Department of International Development in the London School of Economics and Political Science (LSE). My hope was that, by transferring myself to a gloomy winter that was six time zones away from my day-to-day concerns, I would leave myself nothing to do but write and perhaps visit a few museums. How wrong was I. The vibrant intellectual community

I found in greater London gave me far more talks to attend and give than I had anticipated, and new sources of intellectual sustenance. I especially want to thank Cathy Boone, Kathy Hochstetler, Peter Kingstone, Martin Lodge, Dann Naseemullah, Anthony Pereira, Tim Power, and Ken Shadlen for inviting me into the fold. Victoria Whitlow gave me creative sustenance during my time abroad, and Shermeen Al Shirawi provided me with a beautiful and welcoming home.

I also benefitted greatly from a larger community of scholar and mentors, who through their wisdom and guidance shaped not only this project but also my broader way of thinking. I have the strongest admiration and respect for Alfred Montero, my undergraduate thesis adviser at Carleton College, first mentor, and continued collaborator. Kevin O'Brien gave me new words for thinking about my project and new ways of thinking about research design. Kent Eaton, Ken Foster, Mimi Keck, James McGuire, and Irfan Nooruddin provided me with generous feedback and encouragement at key moments. Rose Skelton was a perfect writing-retreat host.

Financial resources are essential for doing fieldwork. This project would not have been possible without the generous support of the Inter-American Foundation, Harvard University's Hauser Center for Nonprofit Research, UC Berkeley's Institute of International Studies and Center for Latin American Studies, Tulane University's Newcomb College and Stone Center for Latin American Studies, and Marquette University's Center for Transnational Justice and Center for Peacemaking.

Most of all, I am grateful for my family, who has supported me in all my endeavors. Thanks first to my late grandmother, Kitty Jolicoeur, for telling me everything I do is great, and for reminding me not to work too hard. Thanks also to my Aunty Rocky, Aunty Sue, Uncle Paul, and Aunt Alice for their affection. Thanks to Casey Bruno for taking an interest in my intellectual endeavors. Thanks to my stepmother, Magnhild Lien, and my stepfather, Mike Doyle, for—among their countless contributions—preparing all my welcome-home meals. Finally, thanks to my father and mother, Harvey Eric Rich and Pamela Mary Jolicoeur, for making me who I am. My father is my biggest and loudest champion, even when he tries to play it cool. My mother influences me profoundly every day, even though she is no longer here. I could not imagine more perfect parents, and I dedicate this book to them.

I

Introduction

In 1996, Senate President José Sarney introduced a bill guaranteeing all Brazilians access to AIDS treatment. This bill, eventually known as Sarney's Law, set Brazil on a path that would lead it to become a global standard bearer for HIV/AIDS policy in the developing world. This was a tortuous path, which led Brazil into prolonged conflict with world superpowers before it eventually emerged as a darling of the global health community. At the time, Brazil was brazenly rejecting global norms for AIDS policy, which focused narrowly on HIV prevention, by adopting social justice as a guiding principle and by codifying this expensive health benefit as a legal right. Powerful institutions such as the World Bank had deemed that AIDS treatment was an inefficient use of limited funds for containing the epidemic. Brazil, in bucking the advice of the international development community to concentrate its resources on prevention, was forced to finance its AIDS treatment program entirely on its own. Ultimately, the global development community adopted Brazil's emphasis on AIDS treatment access as a key complement to HIV prevention. And ultimately, Brazil became seen as a global trendsetter for AIDS policy norms.

While the story of Brazil's initial AIDS policy adoption has been told before,[1] the story of how Brazil's progressive AIDS policies were successfully maintained and implemented over the course of the two decades that followed the initial path to policy adoption is remarkable. In order to transform national policy guidelines into concrete government programs – such as those promoting condoms, needle exchanges, or even human-rights protections for HIV-positive Brazilians – national policymakers had to overcome the constant threat of political opposition from radical religious conservatives in the legislative

---

[1] In Portuguese, see Daniel and Parker (1993); Galvão (2000); Parker (1997); Teixeira (1997). In English, see Biehl (2007); Flynn (2015); Lieberman (2009); Nunn (2009); Parker (2003, 2009).

branch, as well as from governors and mayors in the executive branch who were responsible for administering most government AIDS programs (Biehl 2007). Such political challenges to policy implementation are further high-lighted when we compare this success on AIDS policy with Brazil's record on implementing programs in the general public health system (usually referred to by the acronym SUS). Once considered to be a broad arena of successful policy adoption on par with that of AIDS policy, SUS programs fared worse over time than AIDS programs on almost all major indicators – such as access to care, quality of services, and government investment (World Bank 2005a, 2007). By 2010, Brazilians commonly spoke about national AIDS policy as "the SUS that actually worked" and as "the rich cousin of public health." Brazil's relative success on AIDS policy implementation, overlooked by most scholarship, was thus far from predetermined.

How, then, did Brazil sustain its AIDS policy success whereas other, com-parable policy successes faltered over time? Social-movement advocacy has been highlighted in historiographic accounts as a driving influence on the initial adoption of AIDS policy in Brazil, but the widely accepted view attributes Brazil's continued success in implementing national AIDS policy to the political will and technical capacity of politicians and the bureaucrats they appointed to govern the national AIDS program. Whereas the initial adoption of AIDS policy in Brazil is viewed as a political act, driven forward in part by social-movement activism, the implementation of AIDS policy in Brazil is more commonly viewed as a technical challenge, driven forward by experts in government. But look-ing exclusively to committed politicians and bureaucrats, while certainly a key factor, fails to explain how these bureaucrats succeeded in pushing forward their AIDS policy goals despite the many political obstacles they faced. How did they overcome efforts by the Evangelical caucus to impose a different vision of AIDS policy norms? How did they ensure that recalcitrant governors and mayors would implement their policies? The process of AIDS policy implementation, in other words, was as inextricably linked to politics as was the process of policy adoption.

One does not need to scratch too far beneath the surface to discover a key underlying factor behind the sustainability of Brazil's national AIDS program: continued advocacy by Brazil's Movement to Combat HIV/AIDS (hereafter referred to as the AIDS movement). Behind nearly all of the judicial decisions that reinforced Brazil's national AIDS policies were lawsuits that had been filed by members of the AIDS movement. Behind almost all legislation strengthening benefits and protection for people affected by AIDS were congressional AIDS caucuses – organized by members of the movement. When the media publi-cized instances of AIDS policy malfeasance, it was often members of the move-ment who had brought the issue to the attention of the press. What's more, the political advocacy of the AIDS movement expanded significantly over the course of the twenty years following their initial policy success. Whereas the activism of the 1980s was concentrated in the small handful of states where the epidemic had first taken hold, this later phase of activism extended to all twenty-six states of Brazil – including states in which civil society has historically been weak and fragmented. Thus, the continued advocacy of the AIDS movement was a necessary condition for Brazil's acclaimed policy success – suggesting more broadly that, while we tend to think of social movements as bringing change, they are also required to sustain those changes.

Focusing on what happened after Sarney's Law was passed and providing key insights into the necessary condition for sustained policy success, this book explains the expansion and endurance of Brazil's AIDS movement from 1998 to 2010. This expansion and endurance confounds three of the core propositions within traditional approaches to understanding social movements. Firstly, traditional scholarship suggests that social movements tend to dissolve or hibernate once their initial campaign succeeds (McAdam and Scott 2005: 39). Yet Brazil's AIDS movement underwent a period of major expansion only *after* the national government had built a globally pioneering AIDS program and committed to strong benefits and protection for HIV-positive Brazilians. Secondly, traditional scholarship suggests that a strong and cohesive civil society is a necessary precondition for such social-movement mobilization (Putnam et al. 1993; Wampler 2007; Wampler and Avritzer 2004). Yet the expansion of the AIDS movement extended to regions dominated by rural oligarchs, clientelistic politics, and histories of weak civic organization. Thirdly, traditional scholarship argues that those movements that survive over time tend to become coopted by government (Michels 1949; Piven and Cloward 1979). Yet Brazil's AIDS activists continued to make independent demands on government and to use public pressure tactics to achieve their goals even as they developed close relationships with policymakers inside government. This unexpected trajectory – the expansion of independent civic activism into increasingly poor and isolated communities just as the government was meeting the movement's demands – cannot be explained by traditional theories.

The ultimate composition and character of Brazil's AIDS movement also confounds the dominant theoretical approaches to understanding civic organization and mobilization in Latin America. Civil society in Latin America has traditionally been analyzed through the lens of one of two conceptual frameworks: corporatism and pluralism. Under corporatism, the framework used to characterize civil society in the twentieth century, state actors sought to coopt organized labor into a relationship of subservience and quiescence by providing unions with subsidies in exchange for their acceptance of state controls on their behavior (Collier and Collier 1979, 1991; Schmitter 1974; Stepan 1978). Thanks to state support, civil society organizations in this era were able to build enduring national coalitions, but they were also quiescent – restricted from pushing for radical political reform and, to some degree, from using public pressure tactics to achieve their goals. Under pluralism, the system used to characterize civil society at the beginning of the twenty-first century (Oxhorn and Ducatenzeiler 1998; Oxhorn 2006), state actors are seen as adopting a hands-off approach to society, leaving organized interests to flourish or flounder on their own (Dahl 1961; Truman 1951). As a result, civil society in the contemporary period is seen as autonomous from the state, but weakly organized. While sometimes successful in achieving political reform, contemporary grassroots coalitions are seen as dependent on protest to achieve reform, and organizationally they are characterized as loosely structured and unstable (Arce 2008; Arce and Bellinger 2007; Chalmers et al. 1997; Collier and Handlin 2009b: 80–1; Roberts 2008: 342; Rossi 2015; Shadlen 2002; Silva 2009). The outcome of Brazil's AIDS movement, not predicted by either of these existing approaches, is the growth of an enduring national social movement that is organized into a stable coalition that makes independent demands on the state and combines insider strategies with public pressure tactics for achieving its goals.

The central role that civic advocacy played in sustaining Brazil's AIDS policy success, thus, raises two questions of relevance for social scientists and policymakers alike: How does civil society develop the capacity to organize and advocate for collective political goals? And, furthermore, what explains the endurance of civic activism once the initial success of setting policy has passed? The remainder of this chapter previews my answer to each of these questions – first in the context of Brazil's AIDS movement and then in comparison to existing theories of state and society.

THE ARGUMENT

The argument of this book is that Brazil's AIDS movement was able to endure and even expand over time because the movement was cultivated by national government bureaucrats who depended on activism to help them pursue their policy goals. These bureaucrats gave civil-society organizations in new communities and regions of Brazil resources and opportunities to help them participate in the AIDS policy process. Some of these resources and opportunities they gave directly to new grassroots groups; others were used to help established organizations build a national advocacy coalition with newer grassroots groups. Together, by providing resources for new groups and supporting bottom–up efforts at coalition building, national bureaucrats played a key role in helping Brazil's AIDS movement to expand and endure over time.

While the initial mobilization of the AIDS movement was largely a grassroots effort, in the 2000s it was government bureaucrats who led vast numbers of new civic organizations across Brazil to start working on AIDS policy by providing them funding for HIV/AIDS-related projects. As a result of these efforts, the population of grassroots AIDS organizations ballooned from around a dozen groups in a few major metropolises to over a thousand organizations distributed across all twenty-six states. It was also government bureaucrats who provided these new grassroots AIDS organizations with institutional opportunities for accessing the state by inviting them to participate in government policymaking circles. By opening space for grassroots groups to participate in AIDS policy discussions inside government, bureaucrats were providing new organizations with a significant opportunity to influence AIDS policy from the inside.

But bottom–up efforts by Brazil's established AIDS advocacy groups to expand the movement were crucial as well. It was the older generation of pre-existing AIDS advocacy groups who provided the new generation of civic AIDS organizations with the incentives and skills they needed in order to use their government access for political advocacy. They did this by building out the structure of the AIDS movement into a national federation of independent advocacy organizations with local branches in all twenty-six states of Brazil – what I call a federative coalition – and by engaging new grassroots AIDS organizations to participate in it. It was through this national coalition structure that pre-existing advocacy groups inculcated these grassroots AIDS associations with expertise and skills as policy advocates, and with a shared sense of the broader mission and goals of the AIDS movement. Alone, neither state actors nor established civic advocacy groups could have succeeded in building up an organized nationwide movement. But together, with the combination of resources and political opportunities provided by bureaucrats on the inside, and incentives and skills provided by grassroots advocacy groups on the outside, a new generation of AIDS advocacy organizations emerged that cut across class, race, gender, and geographic divides in Brazil.

What, then, motivated bureaucrats and advocacy groups to collaborate in expanding the AIDS movement? On the surface, neither of these groups had incentives to do so. Within traditional approaches to analyzing civil society, state actors are generally thought to lack incentives to help build independent movements because their very essence is to serve as a check on the power of the state. If truly autonomous, then a stronger and more mobilized civil society – defined here as the set of voluntary associations in society that are independent from the state – has greater potential capacity to hinder state actors in the pursuit of their goals, even if a mobilized civil society can sometimes act in support of state actors. For this reason, state actors are often depicted in traditional social-movements literature as attempting to coopt or weaken civil society (Michels 1949; Piven and Cloward 1979). Established civic groups are also thought to lack incentives for helping to expand civil society. According to traditional approaches, growth in the number of civil-society organizations tends to threaten established civic groups by increasing competition for funding and influence (Cooley and Ron 2002; Kriesi 1996: 159; McCarthy and Zald 1977). For this reason, established civic organizations are often depicted in traditional scholarship as attempting to crowd out newer and weaker organizations from the political arena.

In contrast to traditional approaches, I argue that bureaucrats in Brazil's AIDS policy sector expanded independent civic organization and mobilization to help them combat opposition to their AIDS policy goals from other state actors. In a heterogeneous state, composed of multiple branches and many agencies, bureaucrats often encounter obstacles to advancing their policy preferences not only from within society, but also from within the state. While national bureaucrats enjoy great leeway to design national policy, they often depend on legislators to approve their budgets. Similarly, legislators can propose new laws that contradict the policy guidelines previously developed by bureaucrats. National bureaucrats may also encounter political obstacles to their policy goals within the executive branch, such as when governors or mayors refuse to obey national policy guidelines. In order to advance their policy preferences, then, bureaucrats need to ensure collaboration from all these different parts of government.

By the time AIDS bureaucrats had begun to seek new allies in civil society, two dynamics related to Latin America's dual transition – democratization and neoliberal reform – had increased the complexity of the Brazilian state and, thus, the likelihood of intra-state conflict. Firstly, democratization had ushered in a new class of bureaucrats tasked with building government programs for formerly marginalized interests. Because their objective was transformative – to include new segments of the population into the welfare system – these bureaucrats had different interests from those in pre-existing state agencies. As the size of this new policymaking elite grew, so did the likelihood of intra-state conflict. AIDS-sector bureaucrats formed part of the new policymaking elite, representing new interests inside the state.

Secondly, decentralization – part of the second wave of neoliberal reforms in Latin America – had made national bureaucrats dependent on subnational actors to ensure that the policies they designed were implemented. In the early 2000s, when responsibility for AIDS policy was decentralized to the state and local levels, recalcitrant governors and mayors began to pose strong obstacles to the ability of federal AIDS bureaucrats to achieve their policy aims. It was at this point that AIDS-sector bureaucrats began to make an effort to build AIDS movements in new regions of Brazil, using state funding as inducements to encourage a wider variety of grassroots groups across Brazil to work on AIDS and offering them access to government policymaking spaces by creating new participatory institutions. In other words, national AIDS bureaucrats sought to mobilize grassroots organization outside the state in order to increase their leverage to advance their own AIDS policy goals over other actors inside the state.

In turn, this effort by national bureaucrats to cultivate new civic AIDS groups provided an additional, unintentional impetus for established advocacy groups to incorporate them into the political movement. The civil-society organizations that had taken on AIDS projects in response to state inducements tended to be relatively apolitical with respect to AIDS policy, prioritizing service provision over making demands on the state. Most of these new AIDS organizations had small budgets and limited staff. Moreover, they typically worked on multiple issues at once and had often organized initially to confront some other key social issue. In other words, they lacked incentives to invest in advocacy. Left to their own devices, these grassroots groups likely would have stayed out of policy discussions, leaving the relatively small group of established advocacy organizations to continue driving the political arm of the movement. Yet national bureaucrats, by providing access to policymaking spaces through participatory institutions, had provided a level of political relevance to these civil-society organizations that they would not have achieved on their own. This opening of access to inside influence over policy decisions by politically unskilled and uninterested "civil society representatives" threatened to reverse the past political and policy achievements of Brazil's established AIDS advocacy organizations and to diminish the coherence of the movement. It was as a defensive response to this threat that established activist groups reorganized the structure of the AIDS movement into a federative coalition as a way to incorporate these new groups into the movement and, in doing so, develop them into active and effective policy advocates who shared a common understanding of AIDS policy priorities.

At the same time, as federal bureaucrats unintentionally motivated pre-existing AIDS organizations to broaden their civic advocacy coalition, federal bureaucrats also provided the financial resources that allowed them to do so. AIDS-sector bureaucrats gave crucial support for this bottom–up effort to build a national coalition by providing funding for nearly all local, regional, and national meetings of the movement. This support extended from small amounts of financial and material resources to sustain the monthly meetings of AIDS associations that took place at the state level, to relative large amounts of funding for large-scale biannual events (*encontros*) that brought together the leaders of grassroots AIDS associations at the regional and national levels. By paying for space, food, lodging, and transportation, national bureaucrats provided critical assistance in helping AIDS associations overcome otherwise insurmountable costs to the development of formal, institutionalized structures for nationwide coordination. While all of these meetings and conferences were organized autonomously by members of the movement, almost all of them were funded at least in part by the national AIDS program.

Brazil's AIDS-sector bureaucrats were motivated to support civic coalition-building for the same reason they subsidized individual advocacy groups: because it supported their ultimate goal of increasing their leverage over AIDS policy opponents inside the state. The organization of the movement into a national coalition made it cheaper and more efficient for bureaucrats to invite them into their policymaking circles by eliminating the effort and potential controversy involved in choosing which interlocutors to represent the movement. Such a coalition also strengthened the political leverage that AIDS-sector bureaucrats could gain by collaborating with activists. By developing policies in collaboration with activists who clearly represented a broad national activist base, they could make strong claims that their policy recommendations were developed in consensus with civil society and, thus, represented the public interest.

The outcome of this combination of top–down and bottom–up dynamics was a nationwide social-movement coalition that was able to combine institutional strategies with outside pressure tactics to achieve its policy goals. The privileged access to government circles that AIDS activists enjoyed, as well as the hierarchical and centralized structure of the movement, helped activists incorporate insider strategies – such as lobbying and negotiation – into their repertoire. But AIDS activists also used government resources to simultaneously pursue contentious strategies for policy influence – sometimes even with the explicit encouragement of bureaucrats themselves. In contrast to the ephemeral social-movement networks held up by many scholars as characteristic of twenty-first century movements, this was an institutionalized, nationwide movement of NGOs, which used its close ties to government insiders to wield ongoing influence over AIDS policy while maintaining the autonomy that such privileged interests were forced to relinquish in the prior era of state corporatism.

ALTERNATIVE EXPLANATIONS

Alternative approaches to understanding civic mobilization focus more narrowly on civil-society organizations and activist leaders as the main protagonists. As I describe in Chapter 2, the widely accepted view within scholarship on Latin America suggests that state actors withdrew in the 1980s and 1990s from engaging civil society. Instead, subsequent scholarship has adopted traditional social-movement frameworks to analyze civil society in Latin America, pointing to instances in which new political opportunities and grievances have helped civil society to organize and make demands on government despite the retreat of the state. Each of these existing approaches to understanding civil society has provided important insights and, as I elaborate in Chapter 3, they also contribute substantially to explaining the initial rise of Brazil's AIDS movement in the 1980s and early 1990s. However, as I show next, none of these traditional approaches can explain the subsequent endurance and expansion of the AIDS movement throughout the following decades. As I argue more broadly in Chapter 2, without taking into account the role of state actors as a potential source of incentives and support, existing explanations are unable to explain the emergence of new forms of interest organization at the turn of the twenty-first century that are both autonomous and enduring.

Grievances

Some have argued that neoliberal economic reforms provided new grievances to inspire grassroots mobilization in the 1980s and 1990s (Kingstone, Young, and Aubrey 2013; Rossi 2015, 2017; Silva 2009). As Silva (2009) describes, governments destroyed citizen livelihoods in the process of neoliberal reform by dismantling key social programs while unemployment skyrocketed (23–6).

At the same time, national governments shut the working classes out of the political process by destroying the corporatist institutional channels they had previously used to make demands on government (29). As a result, a wide swath of citizens felt a broad sense of economic and political exclusion from these reforms. Conversely, neoliberal economic reforms threatened indigenous communities who had unintentionally been granted relative autonomy from state control under the corporatist system (Yashar 2005: 55–70). In the corporatist era, indigenous communities had enjoyed benefits such as labor freedoms, land titles, and political representation, whereas other communities had operated beyond the reaches of the state with relative freedom. In the neoliberal era, however, the state dismantled many of its earlier protections and benefits for indigenous peasants at the same time as it increased its presence in indigenous territories and promoted colonization by domestic and international companies. These grievances – either a sense of exclusion as in the case of urban factory workers or a sense of a loss of autonomy in the case of indigenous communities – motivated diverse groups in society to band together for policy reform campaigns.

In the case of Brazil's AIDS movement, grievances go a long way toward explaining the initial wave of mobilization around AIDS in Brazil, but they are less useful in explaining the subsequent endurance and expansion of the movement in the 2000s. As I describe in Chapter 3, AIDS activists in the 1980s and early 1990s faced multiple forms of state-sanctioned stigma and discrimination. Activists in the 1980s were further aggrieved by inadequate healthcare for those who were already ill. Yet the subsequent endurance and expansion of the movement occurred only after the national government had responded favorably to the movement's demands – only after the Brazilian government had included AIDS activists in politics by building a strong national AIDS program that focused on combatting stigma and discrimination, and only after the government had guaranteed free healthcare access for AIDS patients. More broadly, explanations that focus on grievances are unable to explain how movements can persist after the initial moment of success.

Political Opportunities

Other authors have focused on how the region-wide transition to democracy provided new political opportunities for citizens to make demands on government. At the most fundamental level, the reinstatement of civil rights, such as freedom of assembly, allowed citizens the space to gather and to develop strategies for influencing policy (Yashar 2005). National constitutions were drafted that incorporated explicit social rights in the text, legally obligating states to provide citizens access to social-welfare programs (Dagnino, Olivera, and Panfichi 2006; Elkins, Ginsburg, and Simmons 2013). These constitutions provided citizens and citizens' groups across much of Latin America with the legal foundation to make social-welfare demands on government. Experiments with new policymaking institutions also provided opportunities for new groups of citizens to make demands on government. In particular, the concept of participatory governance, in which citizens collaborate directly with government insiders in the policy process, caught on among government and international policymakers in the 1990s and 2000s. As a result, a significant number of countries set up new policymaking bodies that incorporated citizens and citizen groups into budgeting and social policy decisions (Cameron, Herschberg, and Sharpe 2012; Dagnino, Olivera, and Panfichi 2006; Goldfrank 2011; Mayka 2019b; Wampler and McNulty 2011). Moreover, the international community's growing interest and involvement in new issues, such as ethno-racial rights, provided new opportunities for domestic activists in Latin America to leverage in pushing for change (Paschel 2016).

While political-opportunities approaches help shed light on the initial mobilization of Brazil's AIDS movement, they are less helpful in explaining how the movement endured over time. Brazil's AIDS movement was one of the vast numbers of social movements to emerge during the period of democratic transition. Just like activists from Brazil's other movements of the 1980s, Brazil's AIDS activists used this opening in the political opportunity structure to their advantage. As I describe in Chapter 3, they used civil-liberties protections to organize provocative, performance art-based street protests that criticized the weak government investment in combatting the epidemic (Daniel and Parker, 1993; Galvão, 2000; Parker, 1997, 2003, and 2009). Because of the early democratization of the public health sector, early AIDS activists pushed their agenda in the halls of government as well. After the new constitution of 1988 entered into effect, activists took advantage of the full reinstatement of democratic institutions by pursuing policy reforms through the courts and the legislature. Certainly, then, political opportunities – provided by the period of democratic transition and by the particular characteristics of the public health sector – helped make the initial demands of AIDS activists more effective. Yet it was not until the 2000s, well after the political opportunities associated with Brazil's democratic opening first emerged, that the AIDS movement spread to a wider range of groups that cut across traditional cleavages such class, race, gender, religion and geography.

Resources

Although not a focus of recent scholarship, we might also look to resources as a potential factor in the endurance and expansion of Brazil's AIDS movement. As a large body of literature has shown, resources are important for activists to be able to turn their grievances into action and to take advantage of the political opportunities presented to them (McCarthy and Zald 1977). Traditionally, scholarship in the context of Latin America placed a strong emphasis on how financial resources provided by the state shaped labor mobilization (Collier and Collier 1991). By contrast, current scholarship tends to focus on the prospects for mobilization in the absence of traditional resources – in a neoliberal context of declining membership dues and government subsidies.

A separate body of scholarship has analyzed how resources from the international aid community affect civil-society organizations. As further studies have highlighted, an exceptionally large number of civic groups at the start of the twenty-first century depended on international donor agencies as sources of financial support (Bano 2008; Cooley and Ron 2002; Jalali 2013; Watkins, Cotts, Swidler, and Hannan 2012). Yet, in contrast to the mobilizing emphasis in scholarship on government funding for labor organization, these more recent studies argue that international donor funding tends to hinder civic organizations from political mobilization and from building national advocacy coalitions. Some have suggested that donor funding can fragment civic alliances by forcing civil-society organizations to compete with each other to secure donor funding (Kriesi 1996; McCarthy and Zald 1977). Others have argued that donor funding hinders organizations from engaging in long-term strategic planning by providing only short-term financial support (Cooley and Ron 2002; Watkins, Cotts, Swidler, and Hannan 2012).[2] At the same time, donor funding is thought to limit the autonomy of civic organizations in determining how to invest their own financial resources through the strict limitations imposed on how they can spend grant funds.[3] In other words, most contemporary nonprofit organizations – with small, inflexible operational budgets and a lean, often-volunteer staff – have few, if any, resources to divert toward supporting building advocacy coalitions (Phillips 1991; Weir 1999).

As I show in Chapter 3, international donor funding contributed to the initial emergence of Brazil's AIDS movement, but did not play a direct role in the ultimate expansion and endurance of the movement. At the outset, international foundations played a crucial role in supporting AIDS activism in Brazil by helping advocates to build professionalized NGOs that could launch sophisticated national and international campaigns. While global funding for AIDS NGOs (and for civil-society organizations in general) is now widespread, AIDS activists groups in Brazil were among the first to receive international funding. In this early experimental phase, grants were more generous and spending restrictions loose. By the late 1980s, foreign foundations were furnishing the few dozen AIDS NGOs in Brazil with enough funding to comfortably hire full-time staff, rent office spaces, purchase supplies, and travel as needed.

---

[2] In contrast to the guaranteed subsidies for labor organization in the twentieth century, donor funding for civil society takes the form of short-term grants for civil-society projects – money given for the completion of a particular service project that is usually intended to last one to two years. At the end of every grant cycle, recipient organizations must reapply for funding. When their applications fail, civil-society organizations experience sudden and sometimes major budget cuts. This budgetary uncertainty inhibits long-term strategic planning.

[3] Permitted uses of donor funding are generally restricted to expenses directly related to implementing the funded project; not even salaries for a permanent administrative staff are considered allowable expenses.

However, when the movement started to expand in the 2000s, international funding for Brazil's AIDS advocacy groups was on the wane. A perverse result of their efficacy, foreign foundations – deciding the AIDS problem in Brazil had been solved – shifted their funding toward NGOs in needier regions such as Sub-Saharan Africa. Therefore, the timing of the movement's expansion is the opposite of what we would expect if resources from foreign foundations were a determining factor. More broadly, traditional frameworks for analyzing social movements cannot account for how grassroots constituencies could acquire the resources necessary to build lasting coalitions.

Lastly, we might look to political parties as an explanation for how Brazil's AIDS movement could acquire the resources to endure and even expand over time. In the context of Brazil, recent scholarship has argued that the left-wing Workers' Party, which captured the presidency from 2003 to 2016, was the first political party to mobilize civil-society organizations as political support. From the start, the Workers' Party was what political scientists call a "movement-based" party, born out of social-movement organizations that had mobilized during Brazil's democratic transition (Hochstetler 2008; Hunter 2010). As Samuels and Zucco (2018) show, the Workers' Party cultivated relationships with local civil-society organizations as a strategy for building a loyal following. Others have suggested that, after taking over the presidency in 2003, the Workers' Party provided resources and access to civil-society organizations nationally as a strategy to maintain partisan loyalty and to mobilize support for government policies (Bruera 2013). Certainly, party-based explanations for new forms of national civic organization in Brazil are intuitive, given the natural affinity between the Workers' Party and civil society.

Yet party-based explanations cannot account for the trajectory of Brazil's AIDS movement either. Like many other social movements across Brazil, the AIDS movement began receiving state subsidies and access in the 1980s and 1990s, under centrist and right-of-center administrations. Centrist and right-of-center administrations of the 1990s were also the first to create new national policies and government programs in response to social-movement demands (Garay 2016) – including the national AIDS program. Moreover, the relationship between civil-society organizations and the Workers' Party deteriorated in many cases over the course of Luiz Inácio Lula da Silva's two administrations and into the Dilma administration (Hochstetler 2008). In the case of the AIDS movement, activists had closer relationships to government in the Centrist Cardoso administration than they did under any of the Workers' Party administrations (Cartaxo 2018).

This book does not make the case that political parties had no effect on civic organization and mobilization in Brazil. I argue, instead, that state support for new forms of civic organization and mobilization is broader than a Workers' Party phenomenon. This difference is captured by the Brazilian distinction between *políticas de governo* and *políticas de estado* – government policies versus state policies. Whereas government policies are tied narrowly to partisan administrations and are, thus, short-lived, state policies are non-partisan, tied instead to unelected bureaucrats who work across administrations. This difference is important in part for what it implies about the endurance of new forms of national civic organization and mobilization now that the Left is out of power. At the same time, this difference is important because of its implications for civic autonomy. Political parties seeking to mobilize civil society for electoral support will attempt to control the organizations they mobilize so as to prevent them from hindering governability when the party is in power. By contrast, bureaucrats who mobilize civil society to combat opposition to their policy goals from other actors inside the state depend on the perceived autonomy of their civil-society allies as a source of power and will, thus, accept more independent forms of collective action – even against their own policies.

CONTRIBUTIONS

In this book I seek to advance broad debates on social movements and state-society relations, in Brazil and beyond. In this section, I provide a preview of my contributions to each of these fields of study. For those readers interested in the theoretical material, in Chapter 2 I elaborate my argument for why a reformulated approach to understanding civic organization and mobilization is so needed. In Chapter 8, I further expand on the core contributions of the book for students of social movements and state-society relations in Latin America.

A Contribution to Explaining Social-Movement Endurance

First, by arguing that state actors are protagonists in the expansion of civic organization and mobilization in Brazil, I help to answer a universal question of relevance to social scientists and policymakers alike: how do social movements survive over time? Civic advocacy is essential for democracy to flourish. Less understood, however, is how civic advocacy coalitions develop. Much of the scholarship on social movements focuses on the initial period of mobilization. State actors, in this perspective, have little impact on social-movement organization. Others view state actors as a general threat to civil society, seeking to repress or coopt new instances of civic organization in order to maximize their control over society (Michels 1949; Piven and Cloward 1979). Both of these perspectives offer rather bleak prospects for autonomous movements to institutionalize into enduring advocacy coalitions.

In contrast to traditional approaches, this book offers a more optimistic perspective to the question of social-movement survival by revealing contexts in which state actors can help to cultivate civil society. In doing so, I fill a gap in scholarship on social movements, which tends to pit the state in opposition to society. This tendency is based on a conceptualization of the state as a relatively cohesive entity in which the dominant cleavage is between state and society. In the traditional perspective, grievances against the state are seen as the driving force behind many social movements, and the resources that social movements use to mobilize are often seen as emanating from society and leveraged against the state. Conversely, state actors are generally seen as taking one of three stances toward civil society: cooptation, repression, or turning their backs to civil society. According to most theories of social movements, then, a main goal is to push back against the state, and a main goal of state actors is to prevent civil society's capacity to pose a threat. To be sure, much scholarship acknowledges variation in the degree to which state actors hinder civic mobilization; however, this variation is generally conceptualized as more versus less repressive, or closed versus open – variables centered on hindrance rather than on support (McAdam 1982; Meyer 2004; Tarrow 1998). This traditional approach to understanding movements fails to explain cases such as Brazil's AIDS movement, in which state actors actively helped the movement to grow, and even encouraged activists to make demands on government.

To explain this paradox, I draw on recent theories of the state, which – in contrast to the state-versus-society perspective underlying traditional theories of civil society – approach civil society as an important political resource for state actors. In this perspective, the state is not a cohesive entity, seeking to control society, but rather a diverse set of institutions and actors, with diverse objectives. According to this approach, state actors sometimes depend on a strong civil society to help them control other areas of the state and may, thus, seek to cultivate allies in civil society when they face opposition to their policy goals from other actors within the state (Evans 1996). Some scholars in this vein have pointed out various means through which state actors have sought to build allies in civil society, such as by giving them information, funding, training, or access to policymaking circles (Fox 1993; Page 2011; Rich 2013; Tendler 1997; Schneider 2004). Others have focused on the outcomes of such societal support for state capacity (Abers and Keck 2013; Carpenter 2001; Evans 1996; Hochstetler and Keck 2007). Thus far, however, existing scholarship has generally given little attention to the outcomes of such state-society relations for civil society itself.[4]

Yet the Brazilian AIDS policy case shows that the reverse can also be true: bureaucrats can help social movements endure. In this book, I extend recent theories of the state by analyzing the impact of such alliances between state and societal actors on the strength and character of civil society. Contrary to the assumption underlying existing theories of the state, I find that one of the most important ways such efforts by state actors affect the strength and character of civil society in the long run is not through their direct support of grassroots advocacy, but rather through the way this support shapes the nature of relationships within civil society itself. I argue that state actors can cultivate

---

[4] Two exceptions to this trend are Fox (1993), who analyzes the effect of state support for community associations in authoritarian Mexico and Schneider (2004), who analyzes the effect of state support for business associations across Latin America.

social movements not just through their direct patronage, but also through indirect influence – shaping the incentives and opportunities for civil society to build encompassing national coalitions. By shaping civic organization itself, state efforts to cultivate allies in civil society have lasting repercussions that contribute to the capacity and propensity of civil society to mobilize around new issues in the future.

A New Model of State-Society Relations

By arguing that state actors in Brazil are helping civil-society organizations to mobilize relatively autonomous political advocacy coalitions, this book introduces a new pattern of state–society relations – what I call civic corporatism. This model challenges the dominant view on state-society relations in Brazil by proposing that the state has not retreated from shaping civil society, and further, that the new model of state–society relations in Brazil bears little resemblance to pluralism. Far from the hands-off approach by the state that characterizes pluralism, government actors in the model of civic corporatism structure and subsidize civil society; and as a result of this structuring and subsidy, many social movements are institutionalized and vertically integrated into encompassing national movement structures.

By the same token, the model of state–society relations I describe does not conform to traditional variants of corporatism, because such groups are relatively autonomous from the state, and because the interests that mobilize with state support extend far beyond urban workers. In contrast to the strong control of civil society that went hand-in-hand with state corporatism, government actors exert comparatively weak control over these contemporary movements, unable to prevent activists from protesting and from publicly criticizing the very bureaucrats who subsidize their activities. On the contrary, state actors in some instances support, and sometimes actively encourage, protest against state institutions. Moreover, whereas corporatism in the past centered on workers and employers, state support for civic mobilization in the contemporary period centers on groups that mobilized during the great "civic awakening" period of Brazil's prolonged transition to democracy, including post-material interests such as feminist groups, LGBT rights groups, indigenous and afro-descendent groups, and environmental groups, as well as material interests that do not fit directly under the rubric of workplace issues, such as public health and sanitation, education, and safety (Collier and Handlin 2009a: 18; Roberts 2008; Rossi 2017; Rossi and Silva 2018).

For scholars interested in contemporary Brazilian politics, the civic corporatism model of state–society relations elaborated in this book underscores both dramatic changes and the surprising continuities since democratic transition. While there is no longer a centralized state that seeks to control organized labor, there are important pieces of the fragmented Brazilian state that maintain a strong hand in structuring and mobilizing a more broadly defined civil society. This broad phenomenon is manifested in the term "societal control" (*controle social*), one of the most prevalent terms in Brazilian political vocabulary, and one whose meaning has been dramatically altered over the course of the past four decades. During the era of centralized, corporatist governance in Brazil, the concept of "societal control" centered on state control of society, often through repressive tactics. In the 2000s, Brazilians continue to invoke the term "societal control" in common parlance. Yet its definition has been inverted. The term "societal control" now connotes control by civil society over the state, describing state actors' new strategy of utilizing organized civil society to monitor state agencies in many policy sectors at all levels of government to act as a check on the power of bureaucrats and politicians.

A New Explanation for Brazil's AIDS Policy Success

This book also provides new insight into Brazil's AIDS policy success by revealing the central role of civic advocacy in sustaining the policy model. Because of Brazil's global prominence as an AIDS policy success story, various explanations for why and how Brazil's AIDS policy developed have already been put forth. One approach has focused on the absence of rigid ethnic and racial cleavages in Brazil, which encouraged diverse citizens and politicians in the 1980s to make policies that promoted empathy and solidarity with the victims rather than making policies that blamed and discriminated against a particular ethnic or racial group (Lieberman 2009). Another approach highlights the role of gay activists in the 1980s, who were able to use their organizational experience and connections to shape the government's response to the epidemic (Parker 1997, 2003; Galvão 2000). A third approach points to the role of activists inside the state in the 1990s, who took advantage of Brazil's democratic transition to fight for robust AIDS policies from the inside (Flynn 2015; Nunn 2009; Parker 2009). Many have also highlighted the role of the World Bank, which provided three large loans for AIDS programs in Brazil at a critical time. Each of these existing accounts has contributed important insights to advance our understanding of Brazil's AIDS policy success. Yet they also share a common limitation: none are able to explain why Brazil's AIDS policy model persisted over time whereas similar national policies within Brazil were either never fully implemented or later reversed. This book fills a critical gap in our understanding of Brazil's AIDS policy success by highlighting the role of activists outside the state, together with activists inside the state, in upholding the policy model.

This argument also takes a less sanguine perspective on Brazil's AIDS policy success than most accounts. By analyzing the trajectory of Brazil AIDS policy model after its initial creation, this book reveals the many counter pressures constantly threatening to reverse AIDS policy and the comparatively weak capacity of government actors to combat these challenges on their own. (See also Biehl and Eskerod 2007.) I show how civic activism outside the state was essential for them to uphold the policy model they built. At the same time, the book suggests that continued government support from sympathetic bureaucrats was essential for the AIDS movement to maintain its size and strength.

RESEARCH METHODS: CASE SELECTION AND DATA COLLECTION

I was first motivated to conduct this study because of an empirical interest in the NGO boom that spread across Brazil and much of Latin America during the 1990s and early 2000s. I had spent about six months in the northeast of Brazil in 2001, on the eve of Lula da Silva's historic first election to the presidency. This period was a turning point in the history of Brazilian politics – the end of an era of centrist, two-party politics and the start of the sixteen-year reign of the Leftist Workers' Party. It was also a time of great optimism. Like in many Latin American countries, the economy was beginning to grow and civil society was flourishing. New nonprofit organizations had spread across the country, together with new pockets of government funding for NGOs to develop social programs. Many of these organizations had developed political arms, and new forms of national coordination across NGOs had started to emerge.[5] It seemed as though, post-democratization, a dizzying variety of new groups in society were organizing and gaining a voice in politics for the first time. Yet research on the NGO boom was scarce. Several large-n studies and edited volumes had highlighted broad trends in the region, but notably absent were studies that identified the causal relationships and causal pathways driving these trends. In the absence of careful analysis, discussions about the political implications of such trends were subject to a polarized debate: between the optimists, who viewed recent changes through the lens of civil-society empowerment, and the pessimists, who interpreted recent trends as merely a twenty-first century reboot of traditional patterns of civil-society cooptation. This study of Brazil's AIDS movement is, in part, an attempt to explain such recent trends in social mobilization.

But this study was also driven by broader theoretical motivations. With respect to existing theories of social movements and civil society, Brazil's AIDS movement represents a deviant case. Whereas traditional theories of social movements predict that they will hibernate or dissolve over time, Brazil's AIDS movement endured and even expanded. Whereas theories of state corporatism predict that enduring movements will be coopted by government, Brazil's AIDS movement remained relatively independent from state controls. Deviant cases are useful for heuristic purposes because the outcome is not what traditional theories would expect. Careful, process-tracing analysis of the state and social-movement actors who drove Brazil's AIDS movement thus allows me to identify

[5] For example, the Brazilian Association of NGOs (ABONG) had been founded in 1991 and was growing rapidly in size and prominence over the following decade.

new variables (state support), causal mechanisms, and causal paths through which state actors influence civic organization and mobilization over time.

Three types of within-case comparisons increase my analytic leverage. First, I employ longitudinal analysis, analyzing change over time in the patterns of civic organization that emerged within a single policy sector. By exploring change within a single sector of policy, I am able to assess some policy-specific explanations for the changes in patterns that I observed. By examining similar patterns of state–society relations across different administrations and across periods of economic growth and recession, I am also able to assess – and ultimately eliminate – alternative political and economic explanations for the outcomes I observed. Second, I employ a subnational comparison of social mobilization and state–society relations across six Brazilian states, allowing me to account for the effects of local political and societal factors on the observed outcomes. Finally, I employ a large-n comparison across individual social-movement organizations, which allows me to make broader generalizations about where these organizations obtain their resources, as well as to analyze the effect of organizations' resources, members, and histories on their goals and activities.

The subnational comparison of political advocacy was initially the central component of my research design. However, like many researchers, I had embarked on this project carrying different expectations about what I would find than what I actually did. Initially, I expected the outcome of this project to be a story about the effects of decentralized governance and participatory institutions on political organization and participation. The literature makes it clear that subnational differences are now determining factors in shaping civic participation and representation in politics, and the widely accepted view suggests that national politics matters much less. The literature also makes it clear that participatory institutions are important new spaces for civic participation in politics, deemphasizing activity that occurs outside those spaces. Taking my cue from the literature, I expected to add to the existing view. I hypothesized that what drove civic AIDS advocacy was largely a story of local partisan politics – about governors and mayors seeking to either help or hinder grassroots AIDS organizations based on their electoral needs, and about local grassroots actors who cultivated their political strategies and their relationships to each other based on the opportunities and constraints emerging from the local political environment.

Starting from this premise, I initially set out to explain variation across states in the composition and strategies of AIDS advocacy groups based on the local characteristics of partisan politics and of civil society. In order to compare the effect of local partisan political domination by the left versus the right, I spent most of my fieldwork time comparing the state of São Paulo, traditionally a leftist stronghold, to the state of Rio de Janeiro, traditionally a bastion of the right. Making these two states my home base was also motivated by the fact that they contain the largest populations in Brazil and, thus, the greatest number and variety of civic AIDS organizations. But, I also wanted to test for the effect of a strong versus weak civil society, and so I spent additional time and conducted interviews in the states of Alagoas, Bahia, Espírito Santo, and Pará – all of which had weaker traditions of civic activism than São Paulo and Rio de Janeiro, although they varied among themselves. In order to capture the perspectives of national bureaucrats, I conducted interviews in the capital city of Brasília, and in order to capture the perspective of international lending community, I conducted interviews in Washington, D.C. with the main project leaders of the three major World Bank loans for AIDS in Brazil. As it turns out, I could have conducted much of this fieldwork never having left the states of Rio and São Paulo, because – as will be made clear in later chapters – there I was able to find NGO leaders and bureaucrats from across Brazil, who came to participate in a constant stream of meetings and events held in these two states.

I then set out to uncover as much as I could about the leaders of AIDS advocacy groups – their goals, their activities, and their interactions both with each other and with government. Rich historiographies of the early rise of the movement had been published, mostly by activists themselves, but very little data existed on the movement in the 2000s. Given the general lack of publicly available information, I based my data collection strategy on a combination of semi-structured interviews, participant observation, and anonymous survey questions. By the end of my fieldwork, I had conducted over two hundred interviews with the leaders of civic AIDS organizations and bureaucrats, as well as a few politicians; and I had observed over sixty meetings and events involving AIDS advocacy leaders or AIDS-sector bureaucrats. I tested the process-tracing information I gained from my interviews and observations against a broader set of informants by designing an internet-based survey of the directors of one hundred and twenty-three AIDS-related associations in the states of Rio de Janeiro and São Paulo, which I call the Brazilian Survey of AIDS NGOs. Finally, I used a government catalog of HIV/AIDS civil society organizations to construct a national database of civic AIDS organizations active in the years 2001 and 2002, which was the period after federal funding for civic AIDS projects had produced a boom in the number of service-providing organizations across Brazil, but before the federal AIDS bureaucracy had begun to focus their resources on mobilizing these organizations as political advocates. (For more information on the survey data used in the project, see Appendix.)

Combining the perspective of grassroots advocates with those of bureaucrats, and then witnessing their unfiltered interactions, proved revelatory. What I found is that it was not politicians, but rather bureaucrats who most directly shaped the opportunities and constraints for civic advocacy. I also found that, while local bureaucrats were officially responsible for engaging with civic AIDS organizations, national bureaucrats were in practice just as engaged with these organizations – and in some states, even more so. Moreover, national bureaucrats justified their engagement with local civic organizations in explicitly political terms, explaining to me how they were attempting to foster grassroots political advocacy. I found that, while participatory institutions were important spaces for civic engagement, the activities that occurred inside such institutions were strongly shaped by interactions that occurred outside such spaces; conversely, I found that the activity inside participatory institutions often led to civic engagement in other political spaces. Finally, I found that, while the composition and character of civic AIDS advocacy was far from uniform across states, such subnational differences were far weaker than I had expected.

ROADMAP

The book unfolds as follows. In Chapter 2, I build the conceptual approach that I use to explain the trajectory of AIDS advocacy in Brazil. This chapter holds the book's core theoretical contribution and argument for why a reformulated approach to analyzing civic organization and mobilization is so needed. The following chapters are then organized around an examination of three periods of transformation. In Chapter 3, I explain the period of social mobilization around AIDS policy that emerged prior to the era of state-sponsored activism. This early AIDS movement was remarkable not only for its policy success, but also because it represented a new form of social activism in Brazil. In contrast to prior eras of mass mobilization, this movement was composed mainly of NGOs, and in contrast to the combative movements of the past, AIDS activists incorporated institutional strategies for influencing government at the same time as they organized their public-pressure campaigns. But at the same time as the AIDS movement constituted a new form of social mobilization in Brazil, it was also a somewhat conventional story of social-movement success – explained in large part by traditional approaches that focus on the role of grievances, resources, and political opportunities. In contrast to the diverse, nationwide AIDS movement of the 2000s, the movement in this early period was concentrated among a handful of urban groups who were relatively well endowed with financial and political resources, and among cosmopolitan men who were socially marginalized, but experienced and well connected.

Chapter 4 describes the period of broad transformations in the 1980s and 1990s that lay the foundation for state-sponsored activism to emerge: democratization and neoliberal reform. In general, the processes of democratization and neoliberal reform have been attributed to the unraveling of the corporatist system of state-society relations. I show, however, how the very processes that undercut the corporatist system also gave rise to a new system of state-society relations. The process of democratization produced new state actors who were motivated to support civic organization and mobilization. Democratization also created institutional channels for these new state actors to engage civil society as allies by restructuring the policymaking process around participatory governance institutions. Neoliberal reforms produced the resources for these state actors to use in mobilizing allies in civil society by institutionalizing the practice of outsourcing government service delivery to civic organizations. A broad implication of this argument, which I explore in the conclusion to this book, is that the combination of democratization and neoliberal reforms did not destroy but rather *transformed* the incentives and resources that sustained corporatism.

The remaining empirical chapters, Chapters 5–7, describe the development of state-sponsored activism in Brazil's AIDS policy sector in the first decade of the 2000s. Chapter 5 focuses on why and how federal bureaucrats sought to expand the AIDS movement into poorer and more rural regions of Brazil. I argue that bureaucrats in the national AIDS program were motivated to expand independent civic organization and mobilization in the early 2000s, when AIDS policy was decentralized, because the increased AIDS policy authority of mayors and governors threatened to undermine the national policy model they had built. I then describe how these federal bureaucrats provided new grassroots organizations across Brazil with resources and opportunities to access the political arena. Chapter 6 argues that although the efforts of federal bureaucrats led directly to a dramatic increase in the number of civic organizations working on AIDS projects, established civic advocacy groups were key figures in mobilizing these new AIDS organizations as political advocates. They were motivated to reach out to these weakly skilled new organizations because of the threat they posed to the reputation and coherence of the movement in a context of participatory governance, and they converted these new service-providing groups into members of the political AIDS movement by building a national federation of advocacy organizations and incorporating these new groups into it. Chapter 7 draws together the preceding chapters by describing the diverse composition of the AIDS movement in 2010 and the hybrid set of strategies they used to influence government policy, blending institutional with contentious strategies for reform.

The concluding chapter to this book discusses the broad implications of this Brazil-focused study for our approach to understanding state–society relations in Latin America. First, I show how the concept of state-sponsored activism offers new insight into the effects of democratization and neoliberal reform on state–society relations. Conventional approaches argue that the dual transition toward democracy and neoliberalism undermined the corporatist model of state-society relations of the twentieth century by diminishing the incentives and the resources that had sustained it. By contrast, the concept of state-sponsored activism suggests that the dual transition in Latin America produced new incentives and resources for state actors to build bargains with actors in society even as it destroyed old ones. Second, I show how the concept of state-sponsored activism introduces a new model of state-society relations – one that is neither corporatist nor pluralist in its main contours. These two broad implications of my study suggest that the concept of state-sponsored activism may shed light on other contemporary social movements that bridge the traditional outsider-insider divide. I end the book by speaking to broader themes in good governance and democracy promotion, highlighting ways that bureaucrats in government and in international agencies can foster political advocacy among NGOs.

2

A New Approach to Studying Civil Society

Brazil's AIDS movement developed in two waves. The first wave of the movement occurred during Brazil's period of democratic opening in the early 1980s when, like in the United States and Western Europe, the nascent HIV epidemic devastated tight-knit, urban gay communities in Rio de Janeiro and São Paulo. At this early point, the AIDS movement was concentrated in a handful of Brazil's largest cities among activist leaders who were stigmatized and suffered from discrimination, but who were also relatively well-educated and experienced in political advocacy. These early AIDS activists – motivated by grievances, leveraging their socioeconomic resources, and taking advantage of new political opportunities associated with democratic transition – successfully prompted the national government into building an effective national AIDS program, and into changing what was an initially fear-based, stigma-inducing approach toward HIV prevention to a human-rights based approach that emphasized solidarity and care for the afflicted (Biehl 2007: 1087; Galvão 2000: 35–112; Parker 2003, 2009; Teixeira 1997: 56). While contingent factors certainly played a role, traditional theoretical approaches to civil society that highlight the causal influence of grievances, socioeconomic resources, and political opportunities go a long way toward explaining the initial rise and success of the AIDS movement in Brazil.

As I described in Chapter 1, however, traditional theoretical approaches are unable to account for the second wave of the movement between 1998 and 2010, during which the AIDS movement ballooned from a few dozen civic advocacy groups to more than a thousand associations. Unlike the initial mobilization of the AIDS movement among cosmopolitans, this expansion of the movement occurred largely in less-developed regions; and the movement's new grassroots leaders hailed from a diverse range of socioeconomic backgrounds. By 2010, the AIDS movement reflected the face of Brazil, cutting across class, race, gender, and regional divides. Moreover, the expansion of the movement occurred just as the AIDS crisis was ending in Brazil – after the central government had built a globally pioneering national AIDS program and had committed to providing all HIV-positive Brazilians with antiretroviral drug therapy. This unexpected trajectory – the expansion of civic activism into increasingly poor and isolated communities just as the government was meeting the movement's demands – cannot be explained by existing accounts that attribute the early mobilization of AIDS activists in Brazil to grievances, resources, or political opportunities.

To help us understand the unexpected durability and expansion of Brazil's AIDS movement, I show how state actors can play a role in helping new organizations within civil society overcome socioeconomic challenges to mobilization, as well as in expanding the number of strategies available to them for achieving political influence. This argument fills a gap in traditional theories of civil society, which tend to adopt a zero-sum approach to state–society relations. This zero-sum approach to state–society relations is based on a conceptualization of the state as a cohesive unit, which implies that when societal actors threaten the power of any one actor inside the state they pose a threat to state power in general. According to such approaches, state actors who support civic mobilization also wish to maintain their control over civil society, to prevent such a threat. It is, therefore, assumed within most of the literature that civic organizations lacking independent resources face a fundamental tradeoff between accepting support from the state in order to help sustain themselves over time, and maintaining autonomy from the state. While traditional approaches offer their own insights into civic mobilization, they cannot explain the emergence of new forms of social-movement organization that are both enduring and relatively autonomous from the state, such as Brazil's AIDS movement.

To develop my argument about the positive role of state actors in supporting independent forms of civic organization and mobilization, I draw from theories of the state. In contrast to traditional theories of civil society, subsequent studies of state-building and state capacity have identified mutually supportive relationships between state and society. Such virtuous relationships are possible within the framework of more recent approaches to the state because they take as a starting point a different conceptualization of the state – not as a cohesive unit but, rather, as a heterogeneous array of semi-autonomous organizations and individuals. This theoretical framework helps to explain why actors inside the state would support independent civic mobilization by introducing the possibility that state actors may sometimes be motivated to support independent civic mobilization not in order to control civil society but, rather, in order to control other actors inside the state. In this book, I draw on theories of the state to formulate my own explanations for why state actors would play a role in supporting independent civic organization and mobilization. I then build on such recent approaches, which focus on explaining state capacity, by analyzing the way in which such relationships affect the character and strength of civil society. In doing so, I find, surprisingly, that one of the most important ways that such efforts by state actors affect the strength and character of civil society in the long-run is not through their direct support of grassroots advocacy but, rather, through the way this support shapes horizontal relationships among organizations within civil society.

TRADITIONAL APPROACHES TO CIVIL SOCIETY: A ZERO-SUM PERSPECTIVE ON STATE–SOCIETY RELATIONS

Whereas traditional approaches focus on a variety of questions and, thus, offer somewhat different perspectives on civil society among themselves, they all tend to divide organized societal interests into two categories: enduring-but-coopted grassroots coalitions and autonomous-but-fleeting grass-roots coalitions. Coopted societal interests, which mobilize with state support, form stable national coalitions but are seen as restricted from pushing for radical political reform or pursuing contentious tactics by their dependence on government support. Autonomous societal interests, which mobilize without support from the state, are expected to rely mainly on public pressure tactics to achieve their goals. While sometimes successful in achieving political reform, autonomous grassroots coalitions are expected to be only loosely structured and unstable, often falling apart after the end of a campaign. What is not predicted by either of these existing approaches to civil society is the pattern represented by Brazil's AIDS movement: the growth of relatively independent societal interests that are organized into stable, enduring coalitions and that combine insider strategies with public pressure strategies for achieving their goals.

Underlying this binary, cooptation-versus-autonomy approach to understanding social movements is a state-versus-society perspective among traditional theories of civil society – which, in turn, stems from a common tendency to conceptualize the state as a relatively cohesive set of individuals and institutions. In this perspective, political parties and politicians are the main protagonists driving government decisions vis-à-vis civil society. Although nonpartisan actors such as bureaucrats also populate the state, their primary function is seen as carrying out the orders of the politicians who control their agencies. Whereas bureaucrats play an important role in implementing state policy, they are seen as subservient to the politicians who are seen as making state policy and, therefore, driving the goals and strategies of the state. According to such approaches, then, the most salient political cleavage in traditional approaches is between actors inside the state (politicians and the bureaucrats they appoint) and actors outside the state (the individuals and groups who are part of civil society).

According to such approaches, the overarching objective of state actors – both in general and vis-à-vis civil society – is to increase their own capacity to obtain and maintain political power. While state actors may also be concerned with improving the quality of governance, traditional perspectives tend to consider such goals to be subservient to the goal of controlling government – a necessary condition for accomplishing any other political goals they may have. By extension, traditional approaches to state–society relations typically portray state actors as seeking control as an overarching goal of their approach to civil society. Societal actors wish to build power and influence over the state. Conversely, state actors wish to diminish the capacity of civil society to prevent them from achieving their electoral goals. This is not to say that state and society are always in conflict within a traditional perspective. For example, actors inside the state may mobilize groups in society as sources of electoral or policy support. However, even when state and society are working in alliance, autonomous civic mobilization presents a fundamental threat to state actors as strong and autonomous groups in society may at a later time target their demands at actors within the state itself or turn their organizational strength in support of political opponents.

To achieve this goal of control, state actors are seen adopting one of three main strategies in their approach to societal actors: cooptation, repression, or turning their backs to civil society. State actors coopt civil society by offering bribes to civic associations that pose a threat in order to control their behavior through their dependence on state support; in this case, state actors can leverage the organizational capacity of coopted associations in support of their goals as well as prevent such associations from working against state goals. State actors repress civil society by punishing civic associations that pose a threat, or by fragmenting civil society to make it difficult for associations capable of posing a threat to form in the first place. State actors turn their backs to civil society by leaving civic associations to their own devices, ignoring them rather than coopting or repressing them. Which of these three options that state actors will favor depends on the nature of civil society itself and on the surrounding political and economic context. Regardless of the context, however, state actors in this framework are unlikely to support autonomous civic mobilization.

Before articulating my own explanation for the growth of enduring and autonomous organized interests, I offer a brief chronological review of the three major trends in scholarship on civic organization and mobilization that together comprise traditional approaches to civil society. Each of these approaches was developed to explain a distinct political and historical phenomenon. I first elaborate the insights that come from scholarship on state corporatism, ascendant in the 1970s, which focused on analyzing attempts by authoritarian regimes to assert control over labor organization in Latin America. This approach explained the growth of enduring-but-coopted coalitions of urban workers in an era of state-run economies, and it incorrectly predicted that civic organization would fall apart after the state retreated in the 1980s and 1990s from its prior role in supporting labor organization. I then outline the neopluralist approach, which dominated scholarship on civil society in Latin America for a brief period following the decline of state corporatism. This approach decried a supposed demobilization and fragmentation of societal interests – a result of state actors no longer helping groups in society to overcome collective-action problems.

Finally, I elaborate the insights that come from scholarship on social movements, which gained new relevance in the 2000s as an approach to explaining unexpected instances of civic organization and mobilization in the supposed absence of an active state. This approach argued that new political opportunities, new grievances, and the availability of new types of organizing structures allowed civil society to organize and make demands on government despite the retreat of the state. Without a steady stream of resources, however, contemporary civic coalitions were seen as loosely structured and unstable, often falling apart after the end of a one-time campaign. While each of these traditional approaches to understanding civil society contains its own strengths and insights, they share a common limitation – none can explain the emergence of new forms of interest organization at the turn of the twenty-first century that are both autonomous from the state and enduring, such as Brazil's AIDS movement. Without taking into account the role of state actors as a potential source of incentives and support for autonomous civic organization and mobilization, prospects for the growth and expansion of civil society into new communities are projected in the literature as rather bleak.

The Corporatist Approach

Corporatism constitutes the dominant lens through which civil society in Latin America has been understood through much of the twentieth century. Ascendant in the 1970s, the concept was first popularized by Schmitter (1971) in a study of interest organization under military rule in Brazil. According to Schmitter (1974):

Corporatism can be defined as a system of interest representation in which the constituent units are organized into a limited number of singular, compulsory, noncompetitive, hierarchically ordered and functionally differentiated categories, recognized or licensed (if not created) by the state and granted a deliberate representational monopoly within their respective categories in exchange for observing certain controls on their selection of leaders and articulation of demands and supports. (93–94: footnote 24)

In other words, the label "corporatism" is typically used to describe a pattern of civic organization and mobilization in which state actors actively structured civil society, subsidizing a small, privileged set of organized interests in society to help them build stable national coalitions and offering them an official seat in deliberations over social and economic policy in return for a degree of control over their activities. (See also Collier 1995; Collier & Collier 1979.) Later used to characterize civic organization and state–society relations across Latin America and Europe, Brazil was seen as a paradigmatic example of the corporatist system (Collier 1995: 140; Malloy 1977).

A major innovation of the corporatist approach to analyzing civic organization was to elaborate the goals and strategies of state actors vis-à-vis civil society. Mobilization and control were highlighted as the twin goals of corporatism, to confront the growing power of urban working-class interests during Latin America's period of industrialization in the early-to-mid twentieth century (Collier & Collier 1991: 48–49). Which of these two goals dominated the agenda depended on the political context. In contexts where the labor movement was already large and well-established, such as in Argentina and Mexico, populist politicians mobilized their support in order to gain power (Collier & Collier 1991: 196–270).[1] Governments pursuing nationalistic economic policies also mobilized the support of strong labor movements as leverage to confront opposition from business and in the international arena. But control was also an essential goal of corporatism, because of the labor movement's high capacity to organize opposition to government. Urban workers, because they spent long hours together on factory floors, could easily exchange ideas and grievances, and potentially develop strategies for coercing government into adopting new labor policies. Urban labor also had a high capacity for disruption, due to their ability to halt manufacturing production.

Cooptation was the main strategy used by state actors to simultaneously achieve both of the twin goals of mobilization and control (Schmitter 1974; Stepan 1978). Similar to the pattern of state–society relations I identify in this book, state actors under corporatism actively supported civic organization and offered advocacy groups privileged access to the state. But unlike the relatively autonomous civic advocacy I describe, such support in the past was explicitly used to coopt and control civil society by making labor organizations dependent on state support. Collier and Collier (1977: 493) specified the corporatist strategy by dividing it into three components: structure, subsidy, and control. State actors structured civil society into a circumscribed number of interests, integrated vertically from the municipal to the national level within areas of industry, often preventing horizontal linkages from forming across areas of industry. State actors provided subsidies to unions to ensure a financially stable structure for labor organization and to make labor organization dependent on state support for its survival. In the corporatist system, state actors then used labor's dependence on state support to control the behavior of unions. Overt forms of the state's control over civil society involved restrictions such as limits on who could organize, on what types of civic coalitions were allowed to form, and on who was allowed to lead such coalitions. Later, Collier and Collier (1979) summarized the overarching strategy adopted by state actors under corporatism by arguing that it involved a combination of inducements and constraints. Structuring and subsidy, in other words, constituted *inducements* used to convince labor leaders to accept the *constraints* that state actors wished to impose over their activities.

In the corporatist framework, the outcome of state involvement in shaping civic organization and mobilization was seen as a highly organized but

---

[1] On the connection between populism and corporatism in Argentina, see McGuire (1997, chapter 1).

deradicalized and subservient constituency of organized labor, and a fragmented civil society outside this limited scope.[2] The corporatist system was
thus seen as a way for the state to demand the political cooperation of organized labor in return for only minor or symbolic concessions (Collier & Collier
1979, 1991). State actors under corporatism were also seen as fragmenting and
weakening civil society by pitting interest organizations against one another –
separating the incentives for the interest organizations that were included in
the bargain from those organizations that were excluded. Whereas the traditional corporatist framework provides an explanation for how organized
interests in society scale up into enduring national coalitions, it also suggests a
fundamental tradeoff between stability and autonomy. What this framework
cannot explain is the development of enduring civic coalitions that are also
autonomous from the state.

Moreover, corporatism is generally seen as a relic of the twentieth century
(Chartock 2013). In the 1980s, the combination of neoliberal economic reforms
and democratization were seen as destroying the underpinnings of corporatism (Collier & Handlin 2009b: 48–60). From the perspective of state actors,
organized labor no longer constituted a potential political resource for the state
to leverage in support of its economic project. Whereas the economic development model of prior decades centered on nationalizing industries, a project
that promised real (if limited) gains for the working classes was the neoliberal
economic project centered on privatizing industries – a project that could benefit business in some cases (Kingstone 1999; Montero 2001, 2002) but cuts to
the heart of organized labor. Moreover, neoliberal reforms limited the capacity
of state actors to provide resources and subsidies for unions in return for their
political support. Further, democratization destroyed key control mechanisms
that upheld government support for state corporatism, rendering such controls
illegitimate and illegal. Post-democratization, the corporatist system promised
fewer returns for the state. For all these reasons, according to dominant thinking, state actors withdrew in the 1980s from engaging organized labor. Because
state actors no longer had either the incentives or the capacity to mobilize and
control working-class groups, state actors were seen as having turned their
backs on civil society.

---

[2] It should be noted that the outcomes of the corporatist bargaining system for civic organization
and mobilization was seen as varying significantly by country, depending on the relative strength
of the state versus civil society prior to the introduction of corporatism. Schmitter later developed subtypes of corporatism to account for such variation. Where civil society was already
strong and cohesive, such as in the Northern European context, a broad scope of societal interests was organized at the national level and given meaningful access to policy – a variant that
Schmitter (1974) labels "societal corporatism." However, where civil society was weak or fragmented, such as in Southern Europe and Latin America, what emerged was "state corporatism,"
in which a much more limited set of societal interests were co-opted into uneven bargaining
relationships with the state.

The question for social scientists then became: what were the forms of civic organization and mobilization that emerged out of the decline of corporatism and in the context of a state in retreat?

The Pluralist Approach

The first wave of scholarship on civil society that emerged in the neoliberal, or post-neoliberal, context analyzed civic organization and mobilization in the ashes of corporatism through the lens of pluralism. Pluralism, in contrast to corporatism, is a system in which the state adopts a hands-off approach to organized interests (Dahl 1961). Under pluralism, interest groups are not formally included in government policymaking spaces. However, groups in society are allowed to flourish unfettered by state regulations, without state restrictions on who can organize, or on how to structure civic associations and coalitions. Civic organization and mobilization is a bottom–up process, whereby societal interests come together at their own initiative. Moreover, they access the policymaking arena through informal channels, either through pressure tactics, such as public opinion campaigns or protest, or through other persuasive tactics, such as lobbying. Under pluralism, because it offers no one in society any formal access to the state, civil society is less prone to cooptation and repression. However, because societal interests are left to organize and fight for inclusion on their own, the system is subject to elite bias – eloquently captured by Schattschneider's famous observation that "the pluralist choir sings with an upper-class accent" (1960: 35). (See also Mills [1956]; Schlozman, Verba, & Brady [2012].)

Scholarship from the 1990s and early 2000s offered a rather negative interpretation of how civic organization and mobilization was affected by this new dynamic. Such approaches decried a decline in the quality and scope of civic organization and mobilization – a result of the state no longer helping groups in civil society to overcome collective action problems (Arce & Bellinger 2007; Kurtz 2004; Oxhorn & Ducatenzeiler 1998; Oxhorn 2006; Roberts 2005; Shadlen 2002). Representing this viewpoint, Kurtz writes:

> Although market reforms have sometimes produced economic growth, they have simultaneously often been accompanied by worsening material hardship affecting broad swaths of Latin American society. And ... despite this apparently heightened foundation for political grievances, mobilized and individual political activity have declined precipitously. Indeed, it seems that even as political channels have become more accessible to citizens during a time of democratic opening, they become ever-less utilized. (2004: 255–256)

This scholarship argued that civil society in Latin America was unable to represent its interests in the policy arena because market reforms, which went hand-in-hand with the retreat of the state, had weakened the structural bases of collective action. Oxhorn & Ducatenzeiler (1998) labeled this approach to civil society "neopluralism," to suggest that underlying this new hands-off approach to popular-sector organization was an active attempt by the state to demobilize and fragment working-class interests.

The Social-Movements Approach

Events in the 2000s posed an empirical challenge to neopluralist theories of civil society. In Latin America, two grassroots movements in particular suggested to scholars that civil society was still capable of mobilizing mass protest and of influencing policy on a national scale: the wave of anti-neoliberal protests in Argentina, Bolivia, Ecuador, and Venezuela (Kingstone, Young, & Aubrey 2013; Roberts 2008; Rossi 2015, 2017; Silva 2009); and the indigenous movements that swept the Andean countries (Lucero 2008; Yashar 2005; Van Cott 2005). These new grassroots constituencies grew out of diverse groups of citizens coming together to demand political change, and all of these campaigns achieved major political reforms. Subsequent scholarship has tried to make sense of these important instances of civic mobilization in the context of a shrinking state by adopting a social-movements framework.

As I described in Chapter 1, studies that use a social-movements approach to analyzing civil society in Latin America have pointed to factors such as political opportunities and grievances to explain how society could organize and make demands on government despite the retreat of the state. Democracy provided new political opportunities for citizens to make demands on government by organizing mass protests. Neoliberal reforms provided new grievances to inspire grassroots mobilization. Together, opportunities and grievances help to explain the rise of several new waves of protest movements since the 1980s.

An additional approach has argued that changes in the surrounding political and economic context made available new types of organizing structures for civic coalitions even as old, corporatist structures for civic organization were on the wane. This contemporary form of social-movement organization has been labeled alternately as "associative networks" (Chalmers et al. 1997: 543–582), "associational networks" (Collier & Handlin 2009a: 61–92), and "advocacy networks" (Della Porta & Diani 2006: 2; Diani 2003: 301–302; Jelin 1997; Kahler 2009: 5–6; Keck & Sikkink 1998: 8). Networks are flat in that no individual or organization has authority over any other member of the movement. The central leaders of a network have no authority to negotiate on behalf of their members, no power to control them, and no regulation over membership. Rather, they favor individual autonomy and consensus-based decision-making. Some even operate without a clearly defined leadership. Networks are decentralized in that they privilege communication and coordination at the local level over achieving national uniformity. Finally, networks are non-institutionalized in that they are commonly ad-hoc and temporary. Typically, advocacy networks emerge based on a specific political campaign, only to dissolve once the campaign ends.

The rise in salience of grassroots networks within social-movements scholarship reflects four perceived changes in grassroots coalitions (Chalmers et al. 1997: 543–582; Collier & Handlin 2009a: 61–92). First, hierarchical styles of decision-making (in which a small group of civil society leaders make decisions on behalf of a broader membership base) have been seen as replaced by "consensus-based" or "participatory" styles of decision-making. Second, permanent advocacy coalitions have been seen as being replaced by more fluid advocacy networks which come together around specific campaigns and then either dissolve or mutate. Third, national politics have been seen as giving way to "glocal" politics. Whereas twentieth-century labor campaigns centered on national-level negotiations between national confederations of societal interests and the state, twenty-first-century advocacy campaigns are likely to be national, local, or transnational – or taking place at different levels simultaneously (Chalmers et al. 1997: 555–560; Hochstetler & Keck 2007; Rossi & Von Bülow 2015; Silva 2013; Tarrow 2005; Von Bülow 2010). Fourth, whereas twentieth-century organizing was based around class and industry, twenty-first-century organizing is seen as based around the territory – the places where people live (Rossi 2015, 2017).

This type of social-movement coalition, looser and more decentralized, appeared to thrive on the very same political and economic conditions that had broken down the old, centralized model of grassroots organizing. At the domestic level, new advocacy networks emerged thanks to three additional trends in governance: the spread of democratic institutions, the decentralization of political authority, and new pockets of international donor funding for civil-society organizations. Latin America was a hub of this new wave of civil society activity, owing to its place at the nexus of major global changes in political and economic context. In the late-1970s and 1980s, the process of democratization produced a surge in social-movement activism and civic organization in many countries of the region (Alvarez 1990; Alvarez, Dagnino, & Escobar 1998; Eckstein 2001). In the early 2000s, a new wave of leftist political leadership heightened the political salience of grassroots groups (Levitsky & Roberts 2011). At the same time, the neoliberal economic paradigm dramatically increased the flow of national and international financial support to nongovernmental organizations (NGOs) for service provision (Alvarez 1999; Brysk 2000; Chalmers et al. 1997; Collier & Handlin 2009b: 53–57; Friedman & Hochstetler 2002: 21–42; Grindle 2004). Service-providing civic organizations also emerged spontaneously to meet the basic needs of poor communities, which were no longer being adequately served by the neoliberal state (Oxhorn & Ducatenzeiler 1998). Together, these three developments produced a surge not only in the number of local civic organizations across the developing world, but also in the variety of organizations (Chalmers et al. 1997; Collier & Handlin 2009b: 53–57; Friedman & Hochstetler 2002). Advocacy networks allowed this diverse array of grassroots groups to band together temporarily, over single-issue campaigns.

At the global level, the reduced cost of air travel and the massive spread of internet access allowed grassroots groups in the developing world to form loose coalitions with human rights groups in advanced industrialized countries (Della Porta et al. 2006; Keck & Sikkink 1998: 14–16; Tarrow 2005; Von Bülow 2010). Subsequent scholarship has focused on analyzing how a variety of new mass communication technologies have changed the playing field of social-movement organizing (Bennett & Segerberg 2013; Castells 1996, 2012; Juris 2008, Juris & Khasnabish 2013). According to the scholarship in this vein, activists in far-away places no longer need a centralized bureaucracy to link up with each other or to get people out onto the streets (Keck & Sikkink 1998: 8; Della Porta et al. 2006; Smith 2008; Tarrow 2005). Instead, activists can use internet list-servers to exchange information and perspectives, to debate ideas, and to coordinate campaigns (Castells 2012; Della Porta et al. 2006; Juris 2008). Similarly, they can use social media such as Facebook, Twitter, or Snapchat to inspire large numbers of people to join protests (Castells 2012; Juris & Khasnabish 2013). As a result, according to this approach, new social movements have emerged that are viral and leaderless.

This new ease of building activist networks was seen as facilitating the use of protest-based strategies for advocacy, leading to important short-term victories for revolutionary and other movements seeking short-term goals. Because of the way networks facilitate the rapid spread of information, they are particularly good structures for activists to use in mobilizing short-term public opinion or political pressure campaigns. Due to the absence of long-term commitment requirements or centralized authority, activists can use networks to quickly attract a wide array of participants to cooperate on a particular political campaign – to march on the streets and join in other public acts of defiance – even if they differ greatly in their goals and philosophies (Bennett & Segerberg 2013). As scholarship on transnational activism has shown, the scope of these temporary coalitions can now be quite broad, sometimes even spanning continents (Della Porta et al. 2006; Smith 2008; Tarrow 2005). Scholarship on advocacy networks thus explains, in part, how contemporary waves of protest movements have developed and achieved dramatic short-term political change, even toppling regimes such as in the Arab Spring uprisings (Howard & Hussain 2013; Zayani 2015).

By showing how new actors and models have emerged to replace old models of civic organization and mobilization, social-movements approaches to analyzing civil society have thus explained the surprising emergence of mass mobilization in a context of a state that has retreated from structuring and subsidizing civic organization. In the social-movements framework, ephemeral-but-autonomous protest movements have arisen in the wake of enduring-but-coopted coalitions of organized interests.

What social-movements approaches have not been able to explain are the rise of movements that are capable of both protesting and negotiating with state actors. To be sure, there are some studies that acknowledge complex combinations of strategies among social movements and interest groups (Amenta 2008; Hansen 1991; Paschel 2016). However, the suggestion in most contemporary social-movements frameworks is that new movements maximize their mobilizational capacity to the exclusion of capacities to work with state actors. As scholars such as Sidney Tarrow have shown, activists in networked movements often have a difficult time lobbying and negotiating with government because they have trouble developing concrete programs and because they lack leaders who are empowered to negotiate on behalf of their broader membership (Tarrow 2005: 176). This is not only because networks tend to reject hierarchy in principle, but also because the composition of their membership is diverse and ever changing. For a social movement to achieve ongoing influence over government policy decisions, however, activist leaders must be capable not only of protesting, but also of lobbying and negotiating with government officials.

From this social-movements perspective, Brazil's AIDS movement and other recent grassroots movements in Latin America stand as a paradox. While largely overlooked by mainstream scholarship, there exist a variety of social movements that use street protest as a central strategy, but which also negotiate with government over national policy reform. Across the Andes, indigenous groups have not only launched mass protests, but also lobbied states to grant them decision-making power over development issues that affect their communities (Brysk 2000; Lucero 2008; Yashar 2005). In Argentina, unemployed workers have both protested and bargained with government over important welfare benefits (Garay 2007; Rossi 2015). In Brazil, civic movements have both organized regular protests and collaborated with government on policy not only on HIV/AIDS, but also in areas such as environmental protection, education, black rights, LGBT rights, women's rights, and land reform (Alvarez 1990; Ewig 1999; Hochstetler 2000; Paschel 2016; Tarlau 2013; Thayer 2010; Wolford 2010). These movements appear to be autonomous from government, able to independently criticize the state, and organize protests, but they are also able to use inside channels for influencing government policy decisions. Many of these movements are also enduring, having survived over the course of various campaigns and several decades.

Traditional frameworks for analyzing civil society – existing corporatism, pluralism, and social-movements approaches – cannot explain such autonomous and enduring movements because they cannot account for how grassroots movements could acquire the resources necessary to build lasting coalitions without also falling subject to cooptation. I argue in the following section that traditional approaches are limited in their explanations for civil-society development by virtue of their implicit conceptualization of the state as a relatively cohesive unit, driven by politicians. Within this conceptualization of the state, there are only three main approaches that state actors are likely to adopt vis-à-vis civil society: cooptation, repression, or turning their backs to civil society. Whereas the dominant approach to civil society in the corporatist era was seen as a combination of cooptation and repression, the approach emphasized by more recent scholarship on civil society has been to either ignore or attempt to fragment grassroots groups. Neither approach can explain why state actors would help to strengthen autonomous civic organization and mobilization.

THE ARGUMENT

This book highlights a different approach to civil society among certain sectors of the state: to harness the power of new civil-society constituencies in support of social policy reforms by mobilizing autonomous national advocacy coalitions. The protagonists of this approach are not politicians but, rather, bureaucrats who seek to use civil-society organizations as leverage over other actors inside the state. The outcomes of such an approach are national coalitions of new civic interests who have access to the state and support from the state, but who also use protest to make demands on the state. Overlooked by most contemporary literature, this type of relationship between state and society exists side-by-side with more repressive and contentious relationships.

The rest of this chapter elaborates my argument that the role of state actors is a key variable explaining civic organization and mobilization among new interests in society. In building the argument, I first draw from theories of the state to lay out a new approach to understanding the motivations and objectives of state actors – conceptualizing them not as a relatively cohesive group but, rather, as a heterogeneous array of individuals and agencies who may have conflicting goals. I then extend this concept of a heterogeneous state to outline several specific motivations that may lead some state actors to support the growth and mobilization of new grassroots constituencies. Finally, I use the case of Brazil's AIDS movement to analyze the consequences of such state actions for civil society. In doing so, I elaborate the mechanisms by which state actors foster new forms of civic organization and mobilization.

A New Conceptualization of the State

In contrast to traditional approaches to understanding civil society, studies that focus on analyzing state capacity conceptualize the state not as a cohesive entity driven by politicians but, rather, as a heterogeneous entity – as a mishmash of diverse institutions and individuals (Gupta 2012). Although such recent approaches to analyzing the state acknowledge the role of politicians, the main government actor highlighted in most analyses of civic society, they also acknowledge the potential role of bureaucrats as independent actors – i.e., as more than merely the servants of elected officials. In this approach, bureaucrats are sometimes key policymakers, who draft regulations and legislation, who apply pressure to ensure the laws they draft are passed, and who often have significant authority over administering state policies (Carpenter 2001: 6). The bureaucrats within this conceptualization of the state may also hold different objectives than politicians. Whereas electoral goals are seen as dominating the strategies of politicians, studies of the state have proposed that policy goals are seen as more common among bureaucrats (Evans 1996: 1127; Fox 1993: 29–36; Schneider 2004: 27).

In a state comprised of a diverse array of semi-independent institutions and actors, conflicts can emerge not only between state and society, but also within the state itself. Intra-state conflicts can emerge across different branches of the federal government, such as between bureaucrats in the executive branch and elected politicians in the legislature who may seek to control bureaucracies as a source of patronage (Geddes 1990). In a federal system, conflicts can also emerge across different levels of government, such as between the national bureaucrats who design policy and the governors or mayors who are in charge of implementing policy, but who may seek to shirk their responsibility (Amengual 2016; Rich 2013). Intra-state conflicts can also emerge across different bureaucracies, such as in the case of intersectoral programs that require coordination among agencies in different ministries. Especially in a disaggregated or decentralized state, the number of actors and agencies with independent power and who may have opposing policy preferences can be quite large (Grindle 2007). When the state is conceptualized as a complex system, then, actors inside the state must not only put pressure on different segments of society, but also on different parts of government, in order to accomplish their objectives. In this perspective, the challenges that bureaucrats face in pursuing their goals come not just from powerful interests in society, but also from powerful interests inside government itself (Grindle 1980).

Across Latin America, and especially in Brazil, two dynamics increased the complexity of the state in the 1980s and 1990s. As I describe in Chapter 5, the trend toward administration decentralization – part of the second wave of market reforms – increased the relevance of subnational actors in the policy process (Kaufman & Nelson 2004; Montero & Samuels 2004). As a result of decentralizing reforms, the national bureaucrats who designed policies found themselves newly dependent on governors, mayors, and the bureaucrats they appointed, to implement their policies. This challenge was particularly acute in Brazil, which even prior to second-wave market reforms was a federal system known as an extreme case of decentralized governance due to the high level of autonomy enjoyed by governors and mayors.

As I describe in Chapter 4, the broad wave of social-movement mobilization that accompanied democratic transition in many Latin American countries, but especially in Brazil, led to the creation of new government programs and new state agencies to administer them. During democratization, groups in society who had previously been excluded from politics used their newly instated civil and political rights to make policy demands on government, and elected politicians responded by creating new government programs to benefit them (Garay 2016). The bureaucrats who were recruited to administer these programs were, thus, tasked with building national policies that supported formerly marginalized interests. This new class of bureaucrats represented new sets of interests inside the state. As the size of this new policymaking elite grew, so did the likelihood of intra-state conflict.

Several studies within recent scholarship on the state analyze the strategies that bureaucrats pursue to achieve their goals in the context of such a complex environment. Studies that adopt this approach take as a starting point that institutional design is often not enough for bureaucrats to be able to formulate and implement their own policy goals. Abers and Keck (2013), for example, argue that bureaucrats operating in complex environments such as the Brazilian state must develop what they call practical authority in order to influence how others behave (6). According to them, practical authority is something that is cultivated rather than bestowed upon bureaucrats; and it can shift from organization to organization, as well as from state to society and back (8). Carpenter (2001) argues that bureaucrats build the autonomy necessary to pursue their goals in part by cultivating an upstanding reputation among policymakers and other interests, and by cultivating political networks to support that reputation. According to him, a bureaucracy's reputation is important because it imposes two types of political costs on politicians who oppose its decisions. Whereas a general belief in an agency's expertise and capacity imposes generalized costs on any politician who attempts to restrain it, the broadband coalition behind the agency's reputation imposes specific political costs on any politician who attempts to restrain it (33). Similarly, D'Argent (2015) argues that the main tool bureaucrats use to forge the autonomy to pursue independent goals is their expertise, which not only legitimizes their role but also provides them with leverage over actors inside the state who possess less specialized knowledge and who, therefore, could not manage without them. Although the arguments of these studies vary, they all suggest that bureaucrats often look outside the state for sources of power over other actors inside the state. Evans (1996) labels such mutually reinforcing relationships between state and societal actors "state–society synergy."[3]

Although not explicitly outlined in most scholarship on the state, this perspective suggests that an overarching goal of state actors vis-à-vis civil society in some contexts may not be control, as depicted in traditional approaches to understanding civic organization and mobilization, but rather *leverage*. In the unitary-state perspective within traditional approaches to analyzing civil society, state actors seek control as an overarching objective of their approach to civil society because all actors inside the state are seen as sharing the same fundamental objectives; therefore, autonomous civic mobilization necessarily poses a threat. By extension, the range of strategies they pursue vis-à-vis civil society is limited to cooptation, repression, or turning their backs to civil

[3] For a recent study of the effect of such mutually supportive relationships between state and NGO actors on government transparency and accountability, see Brass (2016).

society. In the heterogeneous-state perspective, however, state actors may also seek a fourth strategy: to strengthen autonomous grassroots constituencies as allies outside the state in order to increase their leverage over opposition emanating from within the state.

Motivations for Bureaucrats to Support Civic Organization and Mobilization

The specific goals that may lead state actors to mobilize allies in civil society as political leverage vary widely across political and policy contexts. Such objectives can range from narrow, self-interested goals to broad, policy-oriented goals. While an exhaustive list of incentives is beyond the scope of this book, in the following section I draw from existing studies of the state to outline three specific motivations that may lead state actors to mobilize autonomous organized interests within society as allies. (See Schneider 2004 for a longer list of motivations.) First, I argue that a personal commitment to civic activism among bureaucrats increases the likelihood that bureaucrats will support civic organization and mobilization among grassroots constituencies. But, second, I argue that bureaucrats are unlikely to pursue such strategies without additional motivations centering on necessity, such as to help them pursue policy reform or to help them pursue policy implementation against opposition from within the state.

One motivation, not to be discounted, may be a personal commitment among some bureaucrats to supporting civic activism. As more recent scholarship has shown, bureaucrats' goals and strategies vis-à-vis civil society are shaped in part by their personal histories (Abers & Tatagiba 2015). Bureaucrats with past experience in activism, or who have friendships with activists, may thus approach the task of sustaining civic mobilization around their area of policy as a goal in itself (Fox 1993: 163). Such "activist bureaucrats" tend to enter the state during periods of broad civic mobilization, when presidents incorporate activists into the fold of state agencies as a way to alleviate civic unrest. During the 1960s era of civil rights activism, for example, President Lyndon Johnson brought in outside scholars and other civic reformers to implement the new national anti-poverty policies (Davis & Hawes 1967). In the context of Mexico, Fox (1993) describes how "the post-1968 generation of radical reformist policymakers had pursued the 'long march through the institutions,' like many of their compatriots around the world" (163). In Brazil, a broad movement of civic activists into state bureaucracies occurred in the 1990s, when a series of new state agencies were created in response to the societal demands that had been organized during the great civic awakening period of the 1980s that had accompanied democratization (Abers & von Bülow 2011; Abers, Serafim & Tatagiba 2011; Steinberg 2001: 349). In this sense, state–society relations are mutually constitutive; social movements that are able to penetrate the state are in turn more likely to be supported by state actors.

On its own, however, a personal affinity for activism is unlikely to drive bureaucrats to cultivate allies in civil society. For bureaucrats to mobilize and engage civic organizations in a policy alliance, they must make significant investments of time and money. These investments constitute major strategic and budgetary decisions and, therefore, must necessarily reflect a general priority among top bureaucratic officials. Moreover, even the most civic-minded bureaucrats may not seek to build alliances with civil society groups if they do not depend on civil society as leverage to accomplish some kind of policy goal. Because civic participation in policy development is inherently an inefficient and volatile process, bureaucrats tend to limit civil society input over policy in order to increase the efficiency and rationality of their operations (Greenstone & Peterson 1973: 219). In other words, without some element of necessity, bureaucrats are unlikely to build alliances with civic actors.

But when bureaucrats are unable to accomplish their objectives autonomously, they may be motivated to make the hard investments involved in mobilizing members of civil society as allies, in order to provide a needed "power boost" (Needleman & Needleman 1974: 103). One such objective may be the pursuit of policy reform. Reform-minded bureaucrats often face opposition to their goals from economic or political elites who have vested interests in maintaining the status quo. Progressive tax reforms, for example, are likely to be opposed by elites who want to retain their earnings (Fairfield 2015). Land reform is likely to be opposed by rural elites who want to retain control over property. More generally, any reform involving a redistribution of wealth from the rich to the working class or the poor is likely to be opposed by those in society who have the greatest capacity to influence politics and policy through their economic or political power. Reforms may be opposed by political elites based on ideological principles as well – such as opposition to legalizing abortion or to marriage equality reforms by religious conservatives in the legislature.

One strategy bureaucrats can use in circumventing elite opposition to policy reform is to use grassroots organizations to rally public opinion in support of reform (Evans 1996: 1128). Steinberg (2001: 347) describes how environmental reformers in the Bolivian government in the 1990s mobilized the support of environmental NGOs to help them overcome opposition from the timber industry to their proposed legislation (Steinberg 2001: 347). In the context of Brazil, Abers (2000) shows how governors in the state of Rio Grande do Sul mobilized formerly excluded grassroots groups to participate in local politics in order to increase their capacity to push forward policy reforms. Even in China, bureaucrats have sometimes cultivated civil-society allies as leverage to push forward policy reforms. According to Spires (2011):

Some environmental NGOs, for example, are allowed to exist, even when technically illegal, because they help bolster the case of a local Environmental Protection Bureau (EPB). As one government official explains, "The EPB needs NGOs to voice their concerns. Without them, when the EPB tries to tell other government officials or units to take some action to protect the environment, the response is always 'But is there really a need for that?' So the EPB wants NGOs to speak loudly, because then it can say 'Well, of course. See, society is demanding it.' It's more persuasive when NGOs give voice to these problems, because many government agencies are extremely concerned about meeting demands voiced by society. If they don't respond to these needs, things might get out of control." (33)

In the United States, Page (2011) shows how public-sector prison-guard unions strategically used grassroots victims' rights associations to monitor prison policy, to mobilize outside public pressure in favor of its policy goals, and to legitimate the union's policy proposals and preferences as representing the interests of victims' families (82, 91). In a wide range of contexts, then, from democracies to authoritarian regimes, bureaucrats may seek to mobilize organizations in civil society as allies to pursue policy reform over opponents inside government.

Similarly, bureaucrats may be driven to cultivate allies among civil society to help them pursue policy implementation. Even when bureaucrats succeed in making new policies, they face the implementation challenge of getting these actors to comply with the new policies. When these new policies are targeted at the private sector, they may face resistance from business elites who oppose new restrictions on their behavior (Schneider 2004: 29). Decentralizing reforms that transfer responsibility for social-sector programs to state and municipal governments may be opposed by governors or mayors who prefer to spend their budgets in ways more directly useful toward increasing local support for their reelection (Grindle 2004). Often, the regulatory powers of national bureaucrats are weaker than their policymaking powers. As a consequence, national bureaucrats are often less capable of ensuring that their policies are implemented than they are of putting new policies on the books in the first place. This challenge is particularly salient in Brazil, known as a case of "strong" or "robust" federalism, in which governors wield a large amount of influence over national politics (Abrucio 1998; Arretche 2002; Samuels & Abrucio 2000; Souza 1997).

Civil society groups can help federal bureaucrats enforce policy implementation by calling public attention to local government malfeasance, using strategies that lie outside the scope of the legal authority that federal bureaucrats possess (Rich 2013: 3). Unlike government officials, civic groups can use public pressure tactics, such as street marches, public petitions, and calls to the press. Civic groups can also use a wider range of institutional channels, such as the courts and legislative lobbying, to pressure politicians into investing in social sector services. Civil-society groups may also help enforce policy implementation by providing bureaucrats with additional information about the on-the-ground dynamics of policy processes and outcomes (Rich 2013: 3; Schneider 2004: 29). Whereas national bureaucrats are unable to maintain constant surveillance of state and local behavior – especially in a large country like Brazil, with 26 states and 5,570 municipalities – local civic groups are better situated to keep track of policy implementation. Thus, when national bureaucrats mobilize local civic groups as policy allies, they may increase their capacity to monitor local policy and to develop effective strategies for enforcement. Fox (1994) calls this dynamic, whereby national bureaucrats mobilize autonomous civil-society organizations to counteract the power of regional elites, a "sandwich strategy" for reform.

In summary, bureaucrats tend to support grassroots mobilization when they rely on assistance from civil society to overcome elite opposition to their policy goals. In a heterogeneous state, bureaucrats must gain the compliance of a wide variety of individuals and agencies in government in order to advance their policy goals. Yet bureaucrats are limited in the direct strategies they may pursue in order to ensure the compliance of all these actors – limited by the purview of their authority as government actors under the law, and limited by the types of institutional and human resources they possess. Groups in society are less limited by the law in the types of strategies they can use to exert pressure on government actors, and they have different types of institutional and human resources they can use to pursue such strategies. Government bureaucrats may, therefore, be motivated to mobilize allies among civil society as leverage to increase their control over other actors inside government.

The Mechanisms through Which State Support Shapes Civic Organization and Mobilization

Outlining the motivations for state actors to support autonomous grassroots mobilization still leaves the question of what strategies they use to cultivate allies in civil society, as well as how such support shapes the opportunities and incentives for civic organization and mobilization. The implication in existing studies of the state is that bureaucrats foster new forms of civic mobilization by providing grassroots associations with a combination of opportunities and resources. Some studies have shown how state actors used participatory governance bodies to provide new opportunities for grassroots associations to voice their demands and concerns (Abers 2000; Abers & Keck 2013; Avritzer 2009; Goldfrank 2011; Wampler 2007). Others have shown how state actors provided resources to assist grassroots associations in organizing, and in launching campaigns to monitor and sanction politicians (Fox 1993; Page 2011; Tendler 1997). Existing studies thus suggest that the route from state support to civic mobilization is relatively straightforward. (See Figure 2.1.)

What these studies tend to overlook, however, is that the way opportunities and material resources affect political participation also depends on the capacity and incentives of civic organizations. While participatory governance institutions open a new point of access to the state for civic groups, civic associations must have the political capacity to be able to pursue their goals by participating through this channel. If this goal is political advocacy, then they must be capable of figuring out who is to blame for policy failures, as well as of pursing solutions to policy failure through participatory governance institutions. This requires not only political skills, but also a certain degree of policy

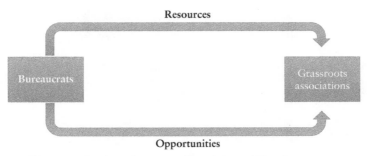

FIGURE 2.1. *Direct mechanisms for promoting civic mobilization*

expertise. Moreover, an association must have compelling incentives to be willing to invest some of its limited resources into building the skills and expertise to participate in the political process. Building skills requires resources – in the form of a staff member who dedicates time to gaining an understanding of how the policy process functions. It is largely because of this gap between opportunities and material resources on the one hand, and capacity and incentives on the other, that the vast amounts of global financial and technical support for NGOs across the developing world has largely failed to mobilize new civil society constituencies (Watkins, Swidler, & Hannan 2012). How, then, do civic associations acquire the capacity and the incentives to participate in the political arena?

My study of Brazil's AIDS movement suggests that state actors provide grassroots associations with the capacity and the incentives to engage in political advocacy not through direct channels but, rather, by encouraging the development of national civic coalitions that allow experienced civic advocates to spread the capacity and the incentives for advocacy to new grassroots leaders. (See Figure 2.2.) Whereas government bureaucrats are experts in policy-making, it is the leaders of civic advocacy groups who are experts in political demand-making. Experienced civic advocates are, thus, better positioned than government bureaucrats to build the capacity for political participation among new grassroots associations. Moreover, whereas government bureaucrats can offer access to policymaking spaces, it is the leaders of already established civic advocacy groups who can incentivize new civic leaders to use such access to advocate for policy reform, rather than for particularistic benefits. In other words, grassroots associations tend to acquire the capacity and the incentives to participate in the political arena not from government bureaucrats but, rather, through their relationships with other civic associations.

The way established civic groups spread the capacity and incentives for advocacy to new civic groups is through institutionalized grassroots coalitions. Established grassroots advocates pass skills and expertise to new grassroots leaders by using regular meetings and conferences that constitute the backbone

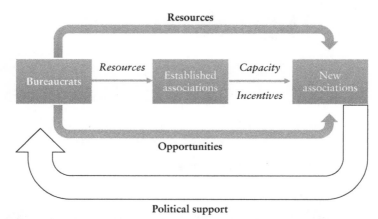

FIGURE 2.2. *Direct and indirect mechanisms for promoting civic mobilization*

of such coalitions to disseminate skills and expertise. This exchange of skills and expertise can occur organically, such as when new leaders participate in communal discussions about political challenges and strategies for overcoming them, or when they observe and participate in the process of constructing the movement's national platform. Established leaders can also intentionally use coalition meetings to spread skills and expertise to new leaders, such as when they include capacity-building workshops on their conference agendas.

The leaders of established civic groups provide new grassroots leaders with incentives to invest in advocacy by offering them opportunities for career advancement as activists through the structure of institutionalized activist coalitions. As grassroots leaders gain experience and skills, they can be promoted over time to increasingly important leadership positions within the movement. Moreover, as grassroots leaders move up the career ladder from state to national movement representatives, the professional training they receive, in tandem with their increasing immersion in professional networks, inculcate them with a shared set of values and norms – in a process that DiMaggio and Powell (1983) label normative isomorphism. By the time activists make it to the top of the movement's leadership hierarchy, they all possess a significant degree of technical expertise in policy, strong experience in participating on government committees, and a common understanding of the movement's core mission and values.

At the same time, government bureaucrats can play a key role in promoting and facilitating such horizontal coalition-building among grassroots organizations. While there are likely a variety of ways that bureaucrats can promote civic coalition-building, this study suggests that negative incentives are an important mechanism. At least at the outset, bureaucrats can provoke established grassroots groups into building coalitions with newer associations by posing a common threat – thereby motivating grassroots associations to band together in defense. This finding echoes that of Schneider (2004), who in a historical study of business organization in Latin America found that the initial impetus toward coalition-building often came from threats – sometimes from labor, and sometimes from the state. The case of Brazil's AIDS movement, a twenty-first-century coalition of grassroots associations, suggests that participatory governance institutions can also pose such a threat, even as they also pose new opportunities for civic influence over policy. In the context of unregulated access to the state, such as under the pluralist model, activist groups can ignore newer NGOs – crowding out less-skilled groups from the political arena. However, the participatory governance structure of policymaking provides a level of political relevance to these new civic organizations that they would not have achieved on their own; by opening space for privileged access to the state, such collaborative policymaking bodies provide opportunities for political influence to civic organizations who lack advocacy skills, or even broad political goals. This opening of access to inside influence over policy decisions by politically unskilled "civil society representatives" with narrow interests threatens to reverse the past political and policy achievements of established advocacy organizations. Established activist groups may choose to respond to this threat by mobilizing newer civic organizations as political allies.

While government bureaucrats may motivate grassroots coalition-building at the outset via threat, such coalitions are unlikely to take hold or survive over time unless government bureaucrats also subsidize them. Schneider (2004) shows that one important form of subsidy state actors can provide is selective incentives to help civic organizations overcome collective-action problems. By providing members of business associations with exclusive access to public funding or policymaking, he argues, state actors force individual business leaders to participate in, and support, business coalitions in order to reap the benefits of such collective action (31). But building a strong national coalition across a geographically dispersed set of organizations also requires resources – in terms of funding to cover the cost of regular meetings, and in terms of time to coordinate events and other common activities. Whereas for-profit business organizations are able to use some of their own resources to cooperate with other groups and achieve shared political goals, nonprofit civic associations – with small operational budgets and a lean, often-volunteer staff – have few if any resources to divert toward supporting collaboration with other associations. This resource mobilization challenge has been highlighted by some as a key reason why some social movements have failed to come together at the national level in anything more than loose networks (Phillips 1991: 768; Weir 1999).

I argue that state actors can mitigate the resource mobilization challenge to civic coalition-building by providing resources to sustain national advocacy alliances. By paying for the space, food, lodging, and transportation to state-level, regional, and national meetings, national bureaucrats can provide critical assistance in helping NGOs overcome otherwise insurmountable costs to the development of formalized, regularized structures for inter-associational coordination. Together, by motivating established civic organizations to build encompassing coalitions that include newer organizations and by providing established civic groups with the resources necessary to build and maintain such coalitions, national bureaucrats can lead social movements to expand into new communities, as well as to help them to endure over time.

CULTIVATING ACTIVISM IN BRAZIL'S AIDS POLICY SECTOR

At first, Eduardo Barbosa had a difficult time navigating the transition from activist to bureaucrat. When he accepted the call to join Brazil's national AIDS program, some members of the movement criticized him for selling out, although others were supportive of his decision. In general, he said, this was a very intense period of time, filled with discussions about how to differentiate between the role he used to occupy in civil society and the role he was going to occupy in government. Eduardo remembered several questions that were repeated as common themes of his conversations with activists during that transition period.

To what degree should we consider your move to be government cooptation, and to what degree should we consider it to be building government capacity, based on societal demands? How can an activist from the movement collaborate from inside government?[4]

Other issues entered into the discussion during this period as well, such as how to ensure that new leaders emerged to continue the work of the movement in the future and how to help these new leaders build the capacity for advocacy. "In the same way that people like me leave to work in another space," he explained, "there have to be other people to take our places in the spaces we used to occupy."

Eduardo started working for Brazil's national AIDS program (NAP) in 2004 when the incoming director, Pedro Chequer, asked him to launch a new bureaucratic unit he was organizing called the Sector for Relationships with Civil Society and Human Rights (the CSHR unit). By the time I interviewed him at the end of 2008, Eduardo had already built the CSHR unit into an efficient fourteen member team. Many of the team members he hired into the unit during his tenure had been activists as well, although some were career bureaucrats. Outside the CSHR unit, few bureaucrats in the national AIDS program had previously been activists, but many were doctors or public health specialists who had entered the national program in order to advance their AIDS policy goals rather than to pursue lifelong careers in government. At the point of our interview, Eduardo himself was actually no longer a member

---

[4] Interview with Eduardo Barbosa, Adjunct Director of Brazil's National AIDS Program and former director of the Civil Society Unit, November 18, 2008.

of the CSHR unit; he had recently been promoted to Vice Director of the entire national program.

When I asked Eduardo about his main objectives as director of the CSHR unit, he articulated a three-point mission:

[T]o keep the AIDS movement independent from the national AIDS program; but at the same time to make sure the movement has all the possible information at its disposal to use for advocacy, for societal control (meaning for society to control government); and to [financially] subsidize the movement so that it can grow stronger – in order to increase the movement's political influence and sustain the AIDS policy framework that [Brazil] deserves.[5]

Eduardo then stopped and recapped the mission in a one-sentence summary, this time emphasizing local-level politics, telling me: "what's important for the Program is that social movements be strengthened, subsidized, so that they have local influence over politics – especially today, within a context of decentralized policy."[6]

Eduardo's reflections raise several questions about the relationship between bureaucrats in Brazil's national AIDS program and activists in Brazil's national AIDS movement. What made the incoming director of the National AIDS Program in 2004 – a doctor who was never a member of the AIDS movement – organize a unit dedicated to building relationships with civil society? What made local-level activism so central to the mission of the CSHR unit? What made the objectives of the CSHR unit so central to the mission of the NAP that its coordinator was eventually promoted to second-in-command of the entire program? What were the strategies that bureaucrats in the CSHR unit pursued to strengthen the AIDS movement and increase the unit's influence over government at national and the local levels? And finally, what was the impact of such government support on the character and the composition of the movement itself?

The following discussion offers an overview of state–society relations in Brazil's AIDS policy sector. I describe both why and how bureaucrats in Brazil's national AIDS program strove to strengthen grassroots advocacy. I then outline the effects of such efforts on the character and the composition of the AIDS movement.

Motivations for Bureaucratic Support

The bureaucrats who populated Brazil's national AIDS program were unified around the same basic set of AIDS policy principles and goals, but they were also a heterogeneous crew. Some were activist-types; some were doctors or public-health specialists; others were career bureaucrats. All of them were

---

[5] Ibid.
[6] Ibid.

driven to strengthen independent activism in order to help sustain their AIDS policy achievements, albeit with different degrees of enthusiasm and for somewhat different specific reasons.

On the frontline of grassroots mobilization were bureaucrats like Eduardo who had been directly plucked from the AIDS movement to join the government's national AIDS program. These bureaucrats had obvious sympathies with activists outside the state and most of them worked in the CSHR unit, specifically tasked with supporting social-movement activism. They were the type of bureaucrats that Jonathan Fox calls "radical reformers" (1993: 163) – those with strong beliefs in social justice and links to community organizers. These bureaucrats were key players in cultivating civic activism because of the value they placed on independent social movements and because of their ability to work with activists. But at the same time, none of these bureaucrats expressed a direct interest in supporting activism during their interviews with me. Rather, all of them framed their goals vis-à-vis civil society in terms of helping promote the policy goals of the national AIDS program.

The support of other types of bureaucrats was key to state-sponsored activism as well. Without the support of a larger number of bureaucrats within the NAP, the CSHR unit would never have existed or been given such a strong degree of independent authority within the NAP. These other bureaucrats in the national AIDS program were supporting players in state-sponsored activism. Some of these bureaucrats had personal connections to activists through their prior experiences working to combat HIV, but had never been AIDS-movement activists themselves. Some were career bureaucrats and had no experience with the AIDS movement prior to entering the NAP. These bureaucrats were motivated to support grassroots activism in order to promote their own policy goals. National bureaucrats used grassroots organizations to confront various sources of opposition to their policy reform goals. Because AIDS strikes at the heart of core religious taboos, such as promiscuous sex and drug use, developing aggressive new national policies such as those promoting condoms, needle exchanges, or even human-rights protections for HIV-positive Brazilians involved the constant threat of opposition by conservative political forces in the legislative branch of government, as well as in the executive branch at other levels of government. Beginning in the mid-1990s, bureaucrats in the national AIDS program began to seek political alliances with civic organizations as crucial support to face each of these challenges to promoting their AIDS policy goals.

In the early 2000s, another policy-centered motivation emerged for bureaucrats in Brazil's AIDS policy sector to cultivate new allies in civil society; to help them ensure the policies they had designed were implemented at the state and local levels. After responsibility for AIDS policy administration was decentralized to the state and municipal levels beginning in 2003, bureaucrats in the national AIDS program found they had little control over the implementation over national AIDS policies. Their strategy for overcoming this implementation challenge was to mobilize new civic organizations to monitor the actions of local politicians in politically corrupt or conservative states and pressure them to conform to national policy guidelines.

What, then, were the methods these bureaucrats pursued for mobilizing new allies in civil society? In the 1990s, the task of seeking alliances with AIDS advocacy groups was relatively straightforward. Such groups had been around for longer than the national AIDS program itself and were already involved in political advocacy. The strategy bureaucrats pursued at that time was to build new relationships and channels of communication with their counterparts in civil society, in addition to subsidizing some of their political activities. In the 2000s, however, the challenge of mobilizing grassroots allies in new regions of Brazil was more complicated. In some areas, there were few civic AIDS organizations if at all, and those few that existed were often inexperienced in advocacy. Mobilizing grassroots organizations in new regions of Brazil as AIDS activists required a more complicated strategy.

The Mechanisms of Support

National bureaucrats helped to expand Brazil's AIDS movement through a combination of direct and indirect forms of support. Bureaucrats directly provided grassroots organizations in new communities and regions of Brazil with a combination of resources and opportunities that would facilitate their participation in the AIDS policy process. They indirectly helped new grassroots groups to acquire the capacity and the incentives to engage in advocacy by promoting the development of national coalitions that brought them into regular contact with already established civic advocacy groups. As a combined strategy, by providing a combination of resources and political opportunities for new grassroots groups and by supporting bottom-up efforts at coalition building, national bureaucrats played a key role in helping Brazil's AIDS movement to expand and endure over time.

Resources and Opportunities

The direct mechanism through which national bureaucrats helped to expand Brazil's AIDS movement was by providing grassroots organizations in new communities and regions with a combination of resources and opportunities that would facilitate their participation in the AIDS policy process. Resources centered on giving project funding – money for grassroots groups to run AIDS service projects – to grassroots groups in new communities. This money was supplied by a large World Bank loan given to Brazil in 1992 to help finance HIV prevention projects, but the money was distributed according to the preferences of Brazilian bureaucrats who worked in the NAP. Although much of this project funding was oriented toward service provision for NGOs to run HIV prevention programs in marginalized communities, some of this money was distributed for projects oriented toward advocacy – such as "legal aid" funding for NGOs to hire a lawyer to help them prosecute private and public entities that fail to provide HIV-positive citizens with the protections or benefits that were mandated by national policy. And, while national bureaucrats distributed some of this funding to established AIDS groups to support their ongoing work, they also used this project funding to encourage existing grassroots groups in new parts of Brazil to incorporate AIDS policies into their mission. This money was disseminated widely, targeted to reach groups working with new communities and in new regions of Brazil. Although project funding typically involved meager amounts of money, it helped small grassroots organizations – who often suffered a precarious existence – to keep their doors open. Project funding also brought awareness about AIDS as an issue to new groups. As a result of these funds, the number of civic AIDS organizations in Brazil ballooned from a few dozen organizations in the late 1980s to over a thousand organizations in 2003. The population of grassroots organizations working on AIDS projects also expanded to a more diverse range of groups – cutting across class, ethnic, and regional divides.

National bureaucrats also offered these new grassroots AIDS organizations access to policymaking circles. They accomplished this by creating a variety of councils, committees, and working groups that brought government policymakers and activists together to discuss various dimensions of AIDS policy, and by designating certain numbers of seats on them for activists from each region of Brazil. By participating in these policymaking fora, grassroots groups earned a direct channel for voicing their policy preferences to the government. They also received privileged information about new policy directions. By opening space for grassroots groups to participate in AIDS policy discussions inside government, bureaucrats were providing new organizations with an opportunity to influence the state's AIDS policy.

Yet, on their own, these direct forms of support had only a limited effect in terms of mobilizing new grassroots groups to join the political arm of the movement. Whereas the AIDS associations that had organized from the bottom up in the 1980s were focused on political advocacy, the associations that had organized around AIDS in response to inducements by state actors tended to be relatively apolitical with respect to AIDS, prioritizing service provision over making claims on government. One reason this top–down support was insufficient to mobilize new groups to participate in AIDS advocacy was because these organizations lacked the political capacity and the incentives to invest themselves in AIDS advocacy. Most of these new AIDS NGOs had small budgets and limited staff. What time and energy they did have was largely dedicated to managing their service provision projects, preparing reports for funders, and applying for new sources of funding. Moreover, these new AIDS NGOs typically worked on multiple issues at once and had often organized initially to confront some other key social issue. In other words, they lacked incentives to dedicate their precious human resources to gaining the in-depth knowledge about the mechanics of AIDS policy development and implementation that would be required to make them effective policy advocates.

However, bureaucrats also provided less visible, but crucial, indirect forms of support to expand the AIDS movement into new regions of Brazil by supporting established AIDS advocacy groups in their efforts to develop these new grassroots AIDS associations into political advocates. They did this by providing funds for established advocacy organizations to expand and institutionalize a national coalition of AIDS NGOs. They also provided additional funds to established organizations to train the leaders of new grassroots groups in political advocacy. This horizontal/bottom–up effort to expand the AIDS movement was both incentivized and shaped by government bureaucrats. It also, in turn, had an independent effect on the movement.

Capacity and Incentives

Established activist groups turned these new AIDS organizations into active and effective policy advocates by imbuing them with the capacity and the incentives for advocacy. Established AIDS advocacy groups did this by adding new institutional layers to the existing structure of the AIDS movement and engaging new service-providing groups to participate in it. First, beginning in 2003, activists from São Paulo and Rio de Janeiro attempted to increase local-level coordination among activists by encouraging activists in other states to adopt the NGO forum model. They did this by organizing training sessions to explain the process of building a forum and by providing organizational materials for activists in other states to copy. Later, after NGO fora had begun to flourish, activists added a regional-level layer to the coalition, called the Regional NGO Meeting (ERONG). This regional-level tier constituted a conference held every two years just prior to the national-level conference, in which activists from each region would coordinate among themselves before they came together for the national-level meeting of the movement. The idea, in essence, was to build outposts in new states of Brazil and knit them together into regional-level and national-level umbrella organizations. This structure accommodated regional diversity, but it also encouraged coordination and a certain degree of assimilation.

This new multilayered national coalition played a key role in providing new grassroots AIDS organizations with both the capacity and the incentives to dedicate themselves in part to AIDS policy advocacy. These groups gained the capacity to do advocacy through their participation in the many meetings and conferences that formed the backbone of the coalition, through their interactions with established AIDS advocacy groups. While much of this exchange of skills and expertise occurred spontaneously during casual conversations that occurred over meals or coffee breaks, skill-building was also an explicit emphasis of coalition meetings at all levels of the movement. At the state level, forum members frequently organized conferences and seminars about themes related to explaining policy process. At regional and national conferences, workshops were offered to train new grassroots leaders as political advocates and as effective organizational leaders. For example, "capacity building" sessions were regular features of coalition conferences, and they covered topics such as strategies for increasing the AIDS movement's representation in state and local policy circles, or strategies for promoting progressive state and local AIDS policies.

Through this national coalition, experienced AIDS activist groups also provided the new generation of AIDS associations with incentives to participate in political advocacy, both by giving them opportunities for career advancement and by inculcating them with new political values. The structure of the national AIDS advocacy coalition also gave the leaders of new civic AIDS organizations incentives to invest their time in political advocacy by providing them with significant opportunities for career advancement as AIDS activists. Although most positions within the movement were unpaid, the structure of the coalition provided ample and increasing opportunities for state, regional, and especially national leaders to network, travel, and otherwise build their professional reputations. National movement leaders travelled regularly to the capital of Brasilia and abroad, met with politicians and global AIDS policy leaders, and made appearances in the national and international press.

The national conferences and meetings that structured the alliance also facilitated the development of shared political values by bringing new organizational leaders into extended periods of close contact with experienced activists. Through these interactions with experienced AIDS activists, new grassroots leaders were often moved by the movement's compelling narrative of successful opposition to oppression and through the personal success stories of overcoming fear and discrimination that the older generation of activists shared with them. Another important lesson that came from attending national AIDS movement gatherings is that the label "AIDS activist" carried a strong degree of cachet, garnering admiration and respect, both in Brazil and around the world.

The Role of State Actors in Promoting Civic Coalition-Building

While the effort to mobilize new grassroots organizations as political advocates was led by established AIDS advocacy organizations, it was in response to encouragement by government bureaucrats. At first, this encouragement was unintentional. The policies that had been designed to engage new groups in AIDS policy discussions were perceived by established activist groups as a threat to the coherence and strength of the movement. This had the unintended consequence of encouraging the established AIDS organizations to incorporate these new groups into a political coalition. Later, government bureaucrats intentionally encouraged established AIDS advocacy groups to strengthen their coalition with these more diverse range of grassroots groups by supporting their efforts with financial and material resources.

In the case of Brazil's AIDS movement, experienced activist groups were motivated to reach out and engage Brazil's new service-providing organizations as allies and fellow political advocates because of the perceived threat that the influx of grassroots AIDS groups that had taken on AIDS projects in response to state inducements would detract from the goals of the national AIDS movement. It was not project-funding itself that posed a threat to established AIDS social movement organizations (SMOs). If a large number of new groups had begun to work on HIV prevention while staying out of policy discussion, then the relatively small group of established advocacy organizations could have continued to drive the political arm of the movement just as they had been doing before. However, by extending access to policymaking fora to grassroots groups from all over Brazil, bureaucrats in the NAP had provided a level of political relevance to these new grassroots AIDS organizations that they would not have achieved on their own. This opening of access to inside influence over policy decisions by politically unskilled and narrowly self-interested "civil society representatives" threatened to reverse the past political and policy achievements of Brazil's established AIDS advocacy organizations and to diminish the coherence of the movement.

But at the same time as the threat that incentivized these established AIDS organizations to build the coalition came from federal AIDS bureaucrats, the financial support that allowed them to build the alliance *also* came from federal AIDS bureaucrats. A principle challenge to building and maintaining an encompassing coalition of civic AIDS organizations was the continuous outflow of resources required to cover the costs of regular meetings and conferences. Significant amounts of funding were needed to cover costs such as event space, food, and conference materials; and transportation and lodging had to be purchased for grassroots leaders to be able to attend them. Whereas for-profit business had large budgets for discretionary spending and labor unions could rely on membership fees for such expenses, civic AIDS organizations had little to no flexible income of their own to use for coalition building.

In response to this funding challenge, activist groups sought financial support from bureaucrats in the National AIDS Program. When activists came up with the idea to develop NGO fora in new states they turned to federal bureaucrats to pay for the expense of travelling around the country to conduct training sessions. As new fora were created, the leaders of such efforts also sought support from federal bureaucrats, who regularly helped them with small amounts of materials and expenses needed to hold meetings. When activists developed the concept of the ERONG, they turned to federal bureaucrats for funding as well, who responded by incorporating funding for the ERONGs as a new line item in their yearly budgets. Federal AIDS bureaucrats also came up with their own pockets of funding to help established advocacy groups build political alliances with new grassroots AIDS organizations – such as for the "networks" project, developed in 2009, which funded one established advocacy AIDS group in each region of Brazil to develop advocacy training programs for newer grassroots groups.

Bureaucrats in the NAP were willing to provide such funding because they also felt threatened by the sudden increase in the number of AIDS NGOs and because they shared an interest in building a strong and cohesive national movement. In addition to the threat perceived by Brazil's established AIDS organizations, bureaucrats faced another challenge resulting from the sudden ballooning of the number of AIDS NGOs. Before the movement coalition was organized into a federation, the diverse array of associations claiming to represent the interests of AIDS activists had led to confusion for federal bureaucrats who were looking to incorporate civil society representatives into collaborative policy committees. In the absence of NGO fora, government officials used to have to invest a significant amount of effort simply in figuring out which AIDS movement representative to select for negotiation or collaborative problem-solving. Selecting a single AIDS movement representative would also lead to complaints from other associations left out of the process. By contrast, the organization of the movement into NGO fora facilitated government efforts to involve the AIDS movement in policymaking decisions by eliminating the effort and potential controversy involved in choosing which interlocutors to represent the movement.

The Composition and Character of Brazil's AIDS Movement

The ultimate outcome of such state-sponsored activism was a new type of social movement in Brazil. In contrast to the urban labor movements of the corporatist era in the twentieth century, Brazil's AIDS movement was a diverse movement that cut across class, ethnic, and geographic cleavages. Moreover, the AIDS movement employed a hybrid strategy for influencing policy, relying in equal measure on inside collaboration with government policymakers and contentious behavior. This pattern of demand-making among AIDS associations in Brazil does not fit existing models of corporatism, pluralism, or social movements – neither in the basic attributes of the organizations that have mobilized nor in the strategies that they employ to influence policy.

In contrast to the small range of mobilization among urban factory workers in the corporatist era, Brazil AIDS movement encompassed a wide range of groups that cut across traditional cleavages such as class, race, gender, religion, and geography to mobilize and influence policy. In Brazil's AIDS policy sector, politically mobilized AIDS organizations were from the industrialized regions of the South and Southeast, as well as from the poorer and rural areas of the North and Northeast. Within each region, these AIDS organizations hailed from both middle-class communities and poor neighborhoods (known as *favelas*). They claimed to represent a number of distinct identities, including: gay, lesbian, and transgendered individuals; prostitutes; injection drug users; people with disabilities; women; children; afro-Brazilians; indigenous Brazilians; members of geographic communities; and, of course, people living with HIV/AIDS (PLWHA).

Brazil's AIDS movement also bridged the mainstream scholarly divide between SMOs and interest groups by relying equally on outside and inside strategies to make claims on government. In Brazil's AIDS policy sector, civic associations used, on the one hand, a variety of contentious strategies for making demands on state actors. Frequently, they utilized media tactics to pressure government, either by directly calling the attention of the press to policy problems or by staging dramatic small-scale protests, designed for a television audience. On the other hand, AIDS organizations also utilized a wide range of institutional channels of access to state actors, suggesting they had developed into savvy, politically connected organizations in the style of American interest groups. AIDS associations collaborated with government officials on nearly all key policy decisions through participatory state policymaking institutions – known typically as "councils," "commissions," or "committees." These associations also engaged the legislative process and the courts to influence policy. Brazil's civic AIDS organizations, thus, relied as much on the insider lobbying strategies associated with formal interest groups as they did on the "unruly" strategies associated with social movements. At the same time, the wealthiest, most professionalized AIDS organizations in Brazil were just as likely as poor, community-based associations to participate in contentious activities – suggesting that protest in Brazil may be turning into a routine political strategy for a wide range of groups. Conversely, a significant number of poor community-based organizations participated on government committees as a strategy for influencing policy – suggesting that the popular majority in Latin America has gained a new channel of access to the political arena.

Moreover, Brazil's AIDS movement used this dual tactic – contentious behavior in addition to collaboration with government – despite deep financial and personal ties to state actors. The vast majority of the nearly 1,000 nongovernmental AIDS groups in Brazil in 2010 relied on some form of governmental financial support for organizational survival. Smaller associations often depended almost entirely on governmental contracts or on material assistance such as electronic equipment, basic supplies, and travel allowances. Even the largest and wealthiest AIDS associations relied on government to finance key meetings and conferences. In addition, the personal ties between grassroots AIDS advocates and bureaucrats were extensive. One might have expected these friendship bonds to dampen the criticisms leveled against the government. Instead of co-opting these activists into silence, however, the strong linkages that tied the leaders of Brazil's AIDS movement to state actors actually encouraged them to shout louder.

Brazil's AIDS movement thus represents a new form of political organizing and interest intermediation in Latin America – in which social movements are sustained by their connections to the government, even while they make aggressive demands on the government. The set of demand-making strategies utilized by Brazil's AIDS movement suggests that new relationships are forming between associations and state actors in Latin America, which are neither primarily cooptive nor primarily combative. The socioeconomic and geographic diversity of organizations in this model has important implications for interest representation in Brazil as well. In a country renowned for its extreme socioeconomic and political inequalities, the presence of a large body of advocacy organizations that cuts across class and other social and economic cleavages suggests that direct access to power may be expanding within certain policy and political realms.

This book, thus, contributes both to theories of civil society and to theories of the state by analyzing how state support affects what happens inside the "black box" of civic organization and mobilization. Using a fine-grained analysis of Brazil's AIDS movement, the chapters that follow provide insight, first, into the motivations that may drive government bureaucrats to foster the growth of civil society and, second, into how this support affects the largely hidden processes by which social movements form and adopt organizational structures, and formulate goals and strategies.

3

Grievances, Resources, and Opportunities: The Initial Success of Brazil's AIDS Movement

The AIDS epidemic arrived in Brazil much like it arrived in the United States – perceived by the public as a "gay cancer." Men who had already been fighting stigma and discrimination based on their sexual identity were suddenly faced with a much more complicated threat. Previously, during the era of free love in the 1970s, gay rights activists had made inroads into reframing gay and straight sex as equivalent acts of love and pleasure. In the 1980s, the AIDS epidemic seemed to provide gruesome evidence against their thesis by handing down a death sentence to men who engaged in acts of "sodomy." The battle against HIV/AIDS thus had to be fought on two fronts at once. The first front was educational and social – organizing safe sex campaigns to teach and encourage people to protect themselves. The second front was political – to pressure the government into controlling the supply of blood donations, providing adequate medical services for infected citizens, promoting messages of compassion and solidarity with those who were afflicted, and protecting gay men and HIV-positive citizens from acts of discrimination. In organizing their campaigns, gay men were joined by hemophiliacs and other groups targeted by the epidemic.

While the threats posed by AIDS were common to a number of countries, it was relatively uncommon for grassroots AIDS movements to mobilize a response – and even less common for them to succeed in pushing their agendas on both of these fronts. In this chapter, I attribute the extraordinary success of Brazil's AIDS activists to the coincidence of two factors. First, AIDS activists had resources. At first, these resources took the form of activist skills and powerful social connections to draw on in organizing their social-movement campaigns. Later, these skills and connections helped them to attract financial resources to build professionalized social-movement organizations. Second, AIDS activists mobilized during an unprecedented opening in the political opportunity structure for public health advocacy groups to make their voices heard in government. Brazil in the 1980s was in the middle of a prolonged process of transition to democracy, and the public health sector was already run by policy experts who were dedicated to improving preventive healthcare. As a result, many municipal and state-level AIDS programs were run by sympathetic bureaucrats who shared a broad commitment to fighting the epidemic.

Brazil's early AIDS activists leveraged their resources and political opportunities to launch a broad AIDS policy campaign that took place both in the halls of government and on the streets. They took advantage of the favorable political opportunity structure by using institutional channels to influence government – collaborating with local public health officials, arguing cases in the courts, and lobbying politicians. But they also organized street marches and protests, designed to bring media attention to their cause and their criticisms of government policy. And, although the causes of policy reform are notoriously complex and hard to disentangle, most agree that it was in no small part a result of this broad effort that, in the early 1990s, Brazil built a strong national AIDS program that emphasized social justice as a guiding principle – a principle that, in turn, laid the foundation for the series of government policies to follow. This pro-active and human-rights focused response to AIDS stood out in stark contrast to the tardy and stigmatizing responses to AIDS that were much more common across the world at the time.

Beyond its remarkable policy successes, Brazil's early AIDS movement is significant because it constituted a new form of social mobilization in Brazil. Unlike prior generations of activism, this was a movement of organizations – of NGOs – not of individuals. These organizations drew much of their financial resources from foreign funders, and only relatively little from individual donations. Also, unlike prior generations of activism in Brazil, which had pushed their policy agendas primarily through contestation, the AIDS movement used institutional channels to influence policy at the same time as it used public pressure tactics. This was a new type of social movement for Brazil and it set the stage for a broad new generation of social movements that would follow on its heels – movements composed of NGOs, which used institutional channels to advance their policy agendas in addition to public pressure tactics.[1]

At the same time as the AIDS movement constituted a new form of social mobilization in Brazil, it was also a somewhat conventional story of social-movement success – explained in large part by traditional approaches that focus on the role of grievances,[2] resources,[3] and political opportunities.[4] The sudden emergence of a public health emergency, together with the national

---

[1] Recent scholarship that discusses such movements includes Garay (2016) and Paschel (2016).
[2] Classical approaches to the role of grievances in mobilization include Gurr (1970) and Smelser (1962).
[3] For more on the role of resources in mobilization, see McCarthy and Zald (1977).
[4] Important examples of political opportunities approaches include Amenta (2008) and Tarrow (1998).

government's fear-based, stigma-inducing reaction to the epidemic, provided a strong set of *grievances* that encouraged groups who were targeted as a result of the epidemic to band together in response. These groups, which included relatively large numbers of educated, cosmopolitan men, also had social and financial *resources* available to them that they could leverage to organize, to formulate strategies, and to pressure government into responding. Finally, the coincidence in timing of the early AIDS movement with Brazil's democratic transition meant that activists were also able to take advantage of new *political opportunities* to build allies in government, and to push their agenda from inside the halls of government at the same time as they took to the streets. As I discuss in Chapters 5–7, it was only in the 2000s that the AIDS movement took a more unexpected trajectory – expanding into increasingly isolated and resource poor communities.

The rest of this chapter explains the remarkable mobilization and success of the AIDS movement in 1980s Brazil – the period prior to the development of state-sponsored activism. In this chapter, I first show how the combination of grievances, resources, and political opportunities led to the mobilization and organizations of a movement of NGOs. I then describe the combination of institutional and contentious strategies adopted by the movement to advance their policy agendas. Finally, I link civic activism to the development of progressive AIDS policies and capable government AIDS programs.

THREATS AND GRIEVANCES

In 1980s Brazil, the immediate threat posed by the sudden arrival of the AIDS epidemic was what first brought together gay men, hemophiliacs, and public health experts. Shortly thereafter, the government's lackluster initial response to the epidemic also engendered two shared grievances among this diverse community of concerned citizens – inadequate medical services for the sick, and government-sanctioned discrimination against people suspected of carrying HIV Ultimately, these grievances inspired those who were affected by the epidemic to transform their collective action into a political advocacy campaign.

The Threat of an Exploding Epidemic

Gay men and hemophiliacs felt the immediate threat of the HIV/AIDS epidemic most acutely. (See Castilho and Chequer 1997: 19; Daniel and Parker 1991: 17–18; Galvão 2000: 52–9, 173–4; Trevisan 1986: 429–75.) Numerous stories were recounted to me during my interviews that spoke to incredible physical suffering and the loss of countless friends. The immediate concern that brought these groups together was the physical threat to their existence posed by the spread of HIV.

Although there was no one to blame for the spread of HIV among gay men, these groups blamed government for the spread of HIV among hemophiliacs.

As Silvia Ramos, founding director of ABIA (one of Brazil's earliest AIDS NGOs), recollected:

ABIA's first fight was for public policy reform in the area of blood banks. At that time in Rio de Janeiro, blood was sold by totally unscrupulous entrepreneurs, who would buy blood in extremely poor neighborhoods, and very sick people would give blood because they would get money when they gave blood...

There was a total lack of control. So it was very common for people to get hepatitis, and other diseases transmitted by blood...

Hemophiliacs used a type of product called "krill." Krill was a blood derivative that helped with coagulation. So if I'm a hemophiliac and I start to bleed, I don't need to take various bags of blood – I just need to take the coagulant. Each dose of that coagulant contains blood from 300 people... So each time a hemophiliac took a blood coagulant he was exposed to 300 people.

There was no public policy to control the blood supply. And there were greedy and dishonest business people who were in charge of this area. They were true mafias. And they were the people who owned the blood banks in Brazil and in Rio.[5]

Because of Brazil's total lack of regulation over blood banks, nearly all hemophiliacs in São Paulo and Rio de Janeiro contracted HIV in the 1980s.

Public health experts in Brazil were also grievously concerned about the HIV/AIDS epidemic in Brazil. Their main worry was that the incipient epidemic was in fact poised to "explode" out of its niche communities and into the broad population, causing widespread devastation (World Bank 1998: 1; Trevisan 1986: 440–41). Whereas seven AIDS cases had been reported nationally in 1982, the first year with official statistics (Castilho and Chequer 1997), 800 AIDS cases had been reported by 1989 in the state of Rio de Janeiro alone. It was also generally acknowledged that these officially recorded numbers represented less than half the true number of AIDS cases (Boletím ABIA 6, February 1989: 13–14). This gross underestimate of AIDS cases in Brazil was generally acknowledged to be an outcome of faulty recording by public health workers, failures of communication between different health bureaucracies, and the stigma of the virus, which led infected individuals to avoid hospitals for fear of being publicly revealed.

Public health experts were also concerned that the number of total AIDS cases in Brazil represented only a small fraction of the number of HIV-infected individuals in the population. Because the HIV virus lies dormant in the human system for long periods, often years, before producing serious signs of illness, recent infections often go undetected. This was especially true in the early years of AIDS, when the methods of HIV testing were more complicated and, therefore, less accessible, and when individual incentives to get tested were low due to the nonexistence of an AIDS treatment. Public health experts thus feared

---

[5] Interview with Silvia Ramos, founding member and first director of the Brazilian Interdisciplinary Association for AIDS (*ABIA*), September 3, 2008.

that the fairly rapid increase in HIV infections over the course of the 1980s represented only the gradual beginning of a steep exponential growth curve. By the late 1980s, the medical establishment in Brazil had produced a series of dire reports, such as the oft-cited prediction that by the year 2000, over two million people in Brazil would be infected with HIV.[6] Health experts, gay men, and hemophiliacs were, thus, drawn together to confront the challenge of developing HIV prevention campaigns tackling such taboo subjects as anal sex, prostitution, and drug use.

Inadequate Treatment and Care for AIDS Patients

This shared feeling of threat quickly developed into a shared feeling of grievance as these early AIDS advocates witnessed the lack of a serious government effort to provide adequate treatment and care for the sick. In part, the challenge of improving services for AIDS patients was technical, due to the lack of medical knowledge in the early 1980s about how the virus spread within the body. But the lack of services for AIDS patients was also perceived as a public policy failure, stemming from a broken healthcare system and the refusal by many medical professionals to treat AIDS patients. Whereas HIV prevention was seen as a collective challenge that bridged the state–society divide, AIDS treatment was seen as a government obligation – and the lack of treatment as a government failure.

The AIDS policy failure most commonly mentioned in published texts and among informants was insufficient hospital beds for AIDS patients. In the state of Rio, for example, only 75 hospital beds were available for the 800 officially notified AIDS patients in 1989 (Boletím ABIA, February 1989: 17). This problem was exacerbated by lengthy hospital stays, which was in turn caused by a lack of other medical resources. According to an interview with the director of Rio's state AIDS program, published in 1989:

[B]y taking so long to produce an [AIDS] diagnosis, by not making medications available [in clinics], patients stay in their hospital beds for a very long time, which aggravates the crisis ... The length of an [AIDS] patient's stay in a hospital bed today ranges from 20 to 35 days, because diagnosis is slow and because there aren't medications. (*Boletím ABIA*, February 1989: 16, author's translation)

The absence of hospital beds for AIDS patients left a strikingly large number of gravely ill individuals denied entrance into hospitals. Without anywhere else to go, they sometimes lay at emergency room doors for hours until someone intervened (Daniel and Parker 1991: 21). According to a founding member of *ABIA*, "[P]eople had nowhere to call. And so they used to call *ABIA* saying: 'Look, my husband is here at the door of the hospital, and he is dying

---

[6] See, for example, *The Economist* July 28, 2005.

of AIDS, and no one wants to attend to him, and the nurses don't want to come for him', and so on."[7]

Even when AIDS patients were admitted to hospitals, they were often treated poorly as a result of fear and prejudice among medical professionals. Among many examples, Trevisan (1986: 441) recalls a nurse reporting "how doctors made jokes in front of terrified patients, saying things like: 'You screwed around, didn't you? Now deal with it!'" In response to such poor treatment, sympathetic doctors and nurses used to redirect hospital patients to civic AIDS associations where they would receive better palliative and psychological care.[8]

Government-Sanctioned Stigma and Discrimination

These early AIDS advocates were further aggrieved by the prevalence of government-sanctioned discrimination against people with HIV, as well as against the broader communities who were publicly associated with the virus. Like in the United States and Europe, the public perception of HIV in 1980s Brazil was that it targeted a relatively wealthy group of "out" gay men (Galvão 2000: 52–7; Daniel and Parker 1991: 17; Parker 1993: 33–4).[9] The perception of HIV as concentrated among "promiscuous" gay "playboys" added an extra layer of stigma against gay men. It also gave rise to new acts of discrimination against homosexuals in Brazil (Facchini 2005: 84). Such discrimination was often sanctioned by the government, and sometimes directly perpetuated by government actors.[10] Police raids on gay establishments were legitimated as public health operations. Doctors would diagnose men they deemed to be "obvious homosexuals" as HIV positive without performing exams. Public figures even proposed quarantining gay men in their houses (Trevisan 1986 441–2; Daniel and Parker 1991: 22). Trevisan (1986) highlights a particularly chilling newspaper report, recounting how "in [the state of] Pará, eighty miners who were considered to be homosexual had their hair, eyelashes, and eyebrows cut or shaved; afterward, they were taken by force from the place, thrown into two trucks, which displayed the sign 'Gay Transport', and left in the middle of the Transamazon [remote Amazonian highway], in the middle of the jungle" (444, author's translation).

---

[7] Interview with Silvia Ramos, founding member and first director of the Brazilian Interdisciplinary Association for AIDS (*ABIA*), September 3, 2008.

[8] Interviews with Queiroz, Director of External Relations, *Grupo PelaVIDDA, Niteroi*, August 13, 2008; Silvia Ramos.

[9] I distinguish here between gay men and MSM (men who have sex with men), a term popularly used in the global AIDS community. In contrast to a behavior, the term "gay" connotes a social and sexual identity. In 1980s Brazil, men who identified themselves as gay tended to hail from cities and on average enjoyed a higher socioeconomic status than the much larger percentage of men who engaged in sexual acts with other men, but did not identify themselves as gay. See Green (1999: 1–11); Parker (1999: 27–51); Daniel and Parker (1991: 53).

[10] For a description of the impact of the AIDS epidemic on gay men in Brazil, see Terto Jr. (1997).

Public and private discrimination against people with HIV reached beyond gay men as well. Because of its reputation as a highly contagious death sentence, HIV carried an additional layer of stigma that was independent of its association with taboo sexual behavior. Herbert Daniel, author and founder of one of Brazil's first AIDS NGOs, aptly coined the term "walking dead" to characterize the public perception of people with HIV, explaining:

What [AIDS] does is divide the world into a new "minority": that of the mortals, who are the ones who are sick with AIDS, against a majority, who are all the "others" (the healthy, or the immortals) ... This is simply to say that you don't have any more rights, because you died. Now, he who has died has no rights. Why care for or bother with someone who is dead?[11]

The stigma of HIV thus operated somewhat independently from the stigma of homosexuality in 1980s Brazil.

The public's perception of AIDS victims as "walking dead" led to further acts of public discrimination against people with HIV – similar to early rights violations in the United States and Western Europe. HIV positive children were denied admittance to schools, and basic health services were routinely denied to people known to have the virus – even in large cities such as Rio de Janeiro and São Paulo (Daniel and Parker 1991: 21–2; Galvão 2000: 177–81; Terto Jr. 1997; Trevisan 1986: 444). According to one informant from the city of Rio de Janeiro:

Dentists were practically the last ones to agree to treat people with HIV. They were the most retrograde. Betinho (a famous social activist who was HIV positive) managed to find a dentist in Ipanema. And so everyone went to Betinho's dentist. But this clinic was too small, and the dentist was able to treat hardly any [of the people who needed him], you see, and so we lost teeth. We lost teeth. I lost a tooth because of that – because the line was too long! (laughter)[12]

Discrimination was even more severe in small towns. Public ordinances were passed banning people known to have HIV from the streets, and at least one incident was reported of an HIV-positive boy being stoned and thrown out of town (Daniel and Parker 1991: 21).

The Presence of Threats and Grievances but Absence of Mobilization outside Brazil

As a large body of scholarship shows, threats and grievances are relatively common across time and space but social movements relatively rare (Olson 1965; McCarthy and Zald 1977). The gap between the potential desire for social movement mobilization and the capacity for mobilization is highlighted

---

[11] Summary of a talk given by Herbert Daniel at ILDES in July 1990. (Source: unpublished document, accessed in the ABIA center for documentation. Author's translation.)
[12] Interview with Bruno Cattoni, Co-Founder of *Grupo Pela VIDDA*, September 5, 2008.

empirically when we compare AIDS advocacy in Brazil to the absence of advocacy across most of the developing world during the early stages of the epidemic. Like in Brazil, the arrival of AIDS in the 1980s and early 1990s exacerbated stigma and discrimination against societal groups who already suffered from stigma and discrimination. Gay men, prostitutes, and injection drug users already lived at the margins of society because of their association with deviant behavior – "sodomy," sexual "promiscuity," and drug "abuse." In highly racialized societies, the AIDS epidemic played into race-based stereotypes and discrimination. AIDS threatened to lend these groups an added layer of stigma and to lend the broader public a new excuse to discriminate against them. But unlike in Brazil, in most cases the stigma associated with these groups led them not to mobilize a political response but rather to react either by denying the existence of the epidemic or by blaming other groups for the epidemic.

In countries with strong racial cleavages such as in South Africa, where discrimination against black Africans was legal until 1990, the societal response to HIV involved racial blame. As one 2006 study concluded, "Whites accuse Blacks, and Blacks accuse Whites, of having brought AIDS into South Africa" (Petros et al. 2006: 71, cited in Lieberman 2009: 150). In the United States, African Americans failed to organize a significant collective response to AIDS even as the epidemic spread among black Americans. At the time the epidemic struck the United States, black Americans had made fragile progress in the realm of racial equality. Black Americans needed to emphasize a strong, coherent public image in order to further strengthen their social and political status. According to Cohen (1999), the AIDS epidemic threatened this image; and as a consequence, African-American communities engaged in a "secondary marginalization" of "deviant" black community members – including gay men and drug users.

In most of Latin America and the Caribbean, where HIV spread initially within the homosexual community, gay men mobilized only weak or fragmented responses to AIDS. (See Frasca 2005.) In Mexico, the gay movement consciously avoided "AIDS issues," while the government avoided "gay issues," leading to weak HIV prevention programs. In Trinidad and Tobago, where homosexual relations were illegal and gender violence was common and unpunished, no AIDS movement existed at all. In Chile, where the gay movement emerged at the same time as the AIDS epidemic, there was a divided response to AIDS within the gay community, with one branch choosing to tackle the epidemic head on and the other choosing to downplay the threat of AIDS in favor of preserving their fragile progress in the realm of gay rights.

Some members of the gay community in Brazil also responded at first to the news of AIDS with strong denial of an epidemic – interpreting the news as a medical strategy to silence gays (Daniel and Parker 1993: 34; Daniel and Parker 1991: 34).[13] *Grupo Gay da Bahia (GGB)*, for example, actively opposed

---

[13] This information was corroborated in an interview I conducted with Edward Macrae, founding member of *Somos* (Brazil's first gay rights group) and Professor of Anthropology at the Federal University of Bahia, December 13, 2008.

HIV-prevention campaigns for a short period before it eventually became a leader in promoting HIV prevention campaigns.[14] *Triangulo Rosa* at first chose to ignore the problem.[15] In São Paulo, a famous Argentine poet and gay activist who was contracted by a publisher to write an informational booklet titled "What is AIDS?" wrote an "anarchical" piece opposing the idea of condom use (Macrae 1997: 232).[16] This early denial of the epidemic was facilitated by the continued (though waning) presence of the military regime, whose reputation for disseminating politically motivated misinformation made it particularly easy to write off early warnings about AIDS in Brazil.[17]

However, in contrast to the rest of the region – and to most of the developing world – in Brazil there was *also* a large and vocal group of influential gay men who publicly recognized the threat of AIDS to their community. Beginning with the emergence of the epidemic in Brazil in 1983, citizens quickly organized to lead the effort to bring attention to alarming death rates, denounce emerging forms of discrimination, carry out AIDS prevention, and spur the Brazilian government to provide treatment. Why, then, did civil society mobilize an early and politicized response to AIDS in Brazil, whereas in most of the developing world initial grassroots responses to the epidemic were absent or weak?

RESOURCES

What the communities affected by AIDS in Brazil had at their disposal that communities elsewhere did not was a diverse set of resources to use in shaping the government response to AIDS, as well as a favorable political context that made such resources more effective. Resources for social mobilization can come in the form of money or manpower, but they can also come in other forms, such as social connections or political experience. Brazil's early AIDS activists started out with social connections and political experience, which they subsequently used to attract large amounts of financial resources from foreign donors.

Political Experience and Social Connections

Brazil's early AIDS activists possessed extensive experience in political demand-making, which helped them to mobilize quickly in the face of the AIDS crisis. This experience came in part from the *Diretas Já* (Direct Elections Already)

---

[14] Interview with Julio Simões, founding member of *Somos* and Professor of Anthropology at the University of São Paulo, November 13, 2008.

[15] Interview with Julio Simões. Simões attributed this decision to the involvement of the group's director, João Antônio Mascarenhas, in a political campaign to constitutionally ban discrimination against homosexuals in Brazil.

[16] The publisher quickly withdrew the booklet from store shelves and commissioned a doctor to rewrite it.

[17] Interview with Edward Macrae.

movement, a broad wave of social mobilization that swept up a large swath of the Brazilian population in the late 1970s and early 1980s. When the military government initiated its gradual political opening in the mid-1970s, hoping to stem domestic and international criticism by granting a limited number of political freedoms, a surge in anti-government mobilization arose and grew exponentially until the completion of the regime transition in 1985. As Brazil's AIDS epidemic took root in the early 1980s, an "unprecedented generation of social movements" (Hochstetler 2000) was engaging in oppositional politics. By actively opposing the military regime, a disparate set of organizations – from neighborhood associations to labor unions, student groups, environmental, gay rights, and black activist groups – took on a highly politicized character and united under a common frame (Hochstetler 2000).

Many of these early AIDS movement leaders also had gained activist skills and experience through their participation in a short-lived gay rights movement (Galvão 2000: 58, 68; Parker 1997: 44, 2003: 147). Initially, the movement had materialized as a social support network – centering on semi-underground self-help groups, where gay men met clandestinely to discuss their personal challenges (Macrae 1990: 96; Trevisan 1986: 339). Quickly, however, these social support networks blossomed into an active political movement, taking energy from the waning power of Brazil's military regime and the widespread social mobilization that was accompanying its departure (Green 1999: 270–7; Macrae 1990: 97–100; Trevisan 1986: 343–50). Between 1978 and 1983, activists in Brazil's gay rights movement had achieved a few key advances in raising public consciousness.

The way in which these gay rights activists had framed their movement was around the goal of "homosexual liberation," defending the right of all individuals to feel pleasure (Trevisan 1986: 339–40). According to João Trevisan, founding member of *Somos*, one of the first gay rights groups in Brazil:

It was thought that the revolution should start inside the home, addressing great taboos – those such as monogamous lifestyles and possessiveness in love. Thus, group sexual relations were not uncommon ...

So we said: if we are going to study ourselves, why don't we start to know our bodies, the first and the most suppressed evidence that we are different from each other? We decided to gather with the only goal of getting naked, to touch each other indiscriminately and thus reveal the flesh that our activist relations insisted on camouflaging. Perhaps the intention was too naive, but at the time it made absolute sense, in the sense of a desire to insert everyday life into the turmoil of the transformations we dreamed about (Trevisan 1986: 349, author's translation).

With pleasure as their political goal, breaking sexual taboos took on a revolutionary character for gay rights activists.

In 1984, however, the sudden arrival of a public health epidemic that was driven by sexually transmitted disease rendered the gay rights movement's ideological frame obsolete. Gay rights activists were forced to radically redefine their priorities over the next few years. According to Perlongher, "The party of the homosexual orgy end[ed], one could have said; and with it ended ... the sexual revolution that rocked the West" (Perlongher 1993: 40, cited in Facchini 2005, author's translation). On an individual level, a significant number of the gay rights movement's leaders contracted HIV themselves. Nearly all members of the movement watched some of their closest friends and companions endure both extreme physical suffering and extreme social ostracism – even from the gay community itself. In light of the public health emergency, fighting the AIDS epidemic seemed to many key activists a more important concern than homosexual liberation. These men turned their attention from mobilizing gay rights campaigns to organizing AIDS policy campaigns, using the lessons from their experience fighting for gay rights to inform their new activist mission.

Beyond political experience, Brazil's early AIDS activists also had powerful social connections to leverage in pushing forward their campaigns and in organizing their movement. Although the early media reports about the wealth and glamour of those who had contracted HIV were sensationalized, playing into existing stereotypes about gay men (Galvão 2000: 48–60), a substantial proportion of early AIDS activists were in fact highly educated individuals with powerful social networks. A number were university professors (Daniel and Parker 1991: 27–8). Many had lived abroad in Europe, the United States, or Canada during periods of the military dictatorship. And at least two leaders of the early AIDS movement, Herbert Daniel and Herbert Betinho de Souza (known popularly as Betinho), were famous political figures. Herbert Daniel was a prominent gay rights activist who, at one point in the 1980s, ran unsuccessfully as a Green Party candidate for Rio de Janeiro's state legislature. Before that, he had been a communist militant who had participated in the famous kidnapping of the American ambassador in 1969 and was the last political exile to return to Brazil under amnesty. Betinho was an iconic public intellectual and activist, who led a variety of renowned national social movements in the 1980s and early 1990s, including the Landless Workers Movement (*MST*), the Movement For Ethics in Politics, and the Movement to Combat Hunger. In contrast to some of the movement's earliest leaders, Betinho was not gay. Rather, he joined the AIDS movement because he was a hemophiliac who, along with his two brothers, had acquired HIV through blood transfusions. He represented a second group of early AIDS movement leaders, which included women, who were not homosexuals but were affected by the epidemic for other reasons.

Financial Resources

These early AIDS activists used their social connections to attract financial resources for political organizing. For example, the director of ISER, a human rights organization that was also a founding member of the AIDS movement, would fundraise by travelling to Europe to meet with his personal contacts in large foundations. According to one informant:

Twice a year, Rubem [César Fernandes, then-director of ISER] went to Europe with a folder of projects under his arm. Full of projects ... for everything within *ISER*'s area of interest: ... prostitution, human rights, AIDS, religiosity ... He knew contacts [there], so he would arrive [in Europe] and meet with [various] groups. He would carry those projects in search of financing. And that is how fundraising work[ed].[18]

Beyond ISER, activist leaders across the spectrum of the first generation of AIDS organizations had close personal connections with international funders, as well as with each other. Several of the early Ford Foundation representatives in Brazil had even worked for brief periods at ABIA (Galvão 2000: 97). According to an early Ford Foundation representative in Brazil, the task of finding and choosing AIDS NGOs to fund was easy because everyone in the AIDS NGO community knew each other.[19]

Over the course of the 1980s, Brazilian AIDS organizations became darlings of the international aid community. By the late 1980s, a handful of European and American foundations – such as the Inter-American Foundation, The Ford Foundation, the Catholic Fund for Overseas Development, and Misereor – were providing the dozen or so AIDS groups in Brazil with large amounts of financial support (Galvão 2000: 64).[20] According to Silvia Ramos, Director of the Brazilian Interdisciplinary Association for AIDS (ABIA) during the late 1980s:

The sense I had is that they were beating down the doors to finance *ABIA* ... [T]here came a moment when there wasn't any financial difficulty. On the contrary, my sense is that ... they rang our bell, and I answered. Who is it? There, a European would arrive, an American, saying: 'I am here because I want to finance *ABIA*.'[21]

By the late 1980s, foreign foundations were furnishing Brazil's AIDS NGOs with enough funding for them to hire full-time staff, rent office space, and launch expensive campaigns.

Although domestic funding was comparatively scarce, a few public bureaucracies also provided financial resources for Brazil's early AIDS movement organizations. For example, the state-level AIDS program in São Paulo lent the AIDS movement's first official organization, GAPA, office space for meetings

---

[18] Interview with Milton Quintino, Assistant Coordinator of ARCA (Religious Support Against AIDS) 1989–1992, Coordinator 1992–1994, August 20, 2008.

[19] Interview with Peter Fry, September 30, 2008.

[20] Galvão (2000) provides a list of international sources of support for Brazilian AIDS NGOs. Multiple informant interviews provided testimony about the strikingly large amount of funding offered – oftentimes unsolicited – to their small, emerging organizations.

[21] Interview with Silvia Ramos, founding member and first director of the Brazilian Interdisciplinary Association for AIDS (*ABIA*), September 3, 2008.

(Raizer 1997).[22] The state AIDS program also provided early AIDS movement organizations with small amounts of cash to purchase supplies, such as ink and paper for flyers. Beginning in the late 1980s, government AIDS programs in several states funded advocacy groups by contracting them to manage projects such as developing HIV prevention campaigns and running hospices for AIDS patients (known in Brazil as *Casas de Apoio*). Federal bureaucracies, while a comparatively minor source of support for AIDS NGOs in the 1980s, also provided a few of Brazil's early AIDS NGOs with key financial assistance. For example, in 1987, the federal social security ministry donated five thousand US dollars for ABIA to rent a house, buy a telephone and typewriter, and hire a janitor (Parker and Terto Jr. 2001).[23] In the same year, FINEP, the federal fund for research and projects, provided ABIA with a striking US$100,000– $200,000 contract to create and maintain a database of AIDS information (Parker and Terto Jr. 2001).[24]

POLITICAL OPPORTUNITIES

Political opportunities helped Brazil's early AIDS activists make effective use of their resources. Although Brazilian political institutions in general had not yet democratized when the AIDS epidemic arrived in 1983, the health policy sector had already developed into a bastion of transparent and democratic governance in the 1970s.[25] In the arena of public health policy, military technocrats had delegated significant autonomy to state and local bureaucracies to make policy and spending decisions. Simultaneous to this transition, health policy experts had mobilized a movement to take over government health agencies with the explicit purpose of helping the poor and marginalized gain access to healthcare. As a result, state and local government health agencies were run by bureaucrats who were committed to improving policy, and who were sympathetic to civic activism. Sympathetic bureaucrats provided AIDS activists with allies inside government who were receptive to their demands, and who could provide them with insider information to use in organizing public pressure campaigns for AIDS policy reforms.

Open Government Institutions

Local bureaucrats who were at least somewhat sympathetic to societal demands could be found in a range of policy sectors throughout Brazil's period of military rule from 1964 to 1985. This relative receptiveness of local bureaucracy

---

[22] An informant interview with Paulo Teixeira corroborates this claim.

[23] My informant interview with Silvia Ramos corroborates this information.

[24] The amount of funding was listed in the source text in dollars as a range, due to the hyperinflation that led to frequent and extreme fluctuations in the Brazilian exchange rate at the time.

[25] The first direct elections for congress occurred only in 1985, and for the presidency in 1989.

to societal demands was a side effect of Brazil's decentralized political system. In Brazil, a case of "strong federalism," governors and mayors have controlled national politics from behind the scenes since independence (Abrucio 1998; Samuels and Abrucio 2000; Souza 1997). The military regime was thus forced to make key concessions to subnational politicians during their bid to take national political control. These included maintaining democratic elections for mayor and re-introducing elections for governor a full decade before Brazil's complete transition to democracy (Samuels and Abrucio 2000; Abrucio 1998; Souza 2008a; Arretche 2002). The political decentralization that undergirded military rule in Brazil empowered subnational politicians who responded to bottom-up, citizen demands for improved public services rather than to orders from above (Samuels and Abrucio 2000). Mayors' electoral sensitivity to citizen's needs thus facilitated the development of relatively autonomous, capable, and policy-oriented local bureaucracies. In the health policy sector, a national economic crisis in the late 1970s had led both mayors and national military leaders to further develop local bureaucracies that were responsive to societal demands. As a result of the crisis, poverty had increased and social tensions had turned violent in poor neighborhoods across Brazil. Mayors, searching for immediate responses to the crisis, turned to expanding health services as one of the few policy measures they could easily implement (Faleiros et al. 2006). Consequently, mayors hired health bureaucrats based on merit rather than personal connections, and ceded them a significant degree of autonomy to implement local reforms. National military rulers responded to the crisis by creating a new national governing body for public health and appointing highly trained, reform-minded health experts to key posts within it (Faleiros et al. 2006).[26] In turn, these new national health officials pushed for the further expansion of health coverage, increased local control over administering health services, and the decentralization of health program financing. The resulting fiscal decentralization of the public health sector nearly doubled state and local healthcare budgets from 1982 to 1983, and it allowed subnational health bureaucracies to play a stronger role in influencing the structure of public health programs (Faleiros et al. 2006: 70–1).

Allies inside Government

Simultaneous to the health-sector reforms that were initiated by government, a social movement for health reform had also emerged in 1970s Brazil – providing subnational bureaucracies with policy experts who were sympathetic to the demands of AIDS activists. National government investment in public health training programs in the 1970s had subsequently produced a large pool of highly-qualified public health professionals. These new doctors,

---

[26] The name of the new governing body over healthcare administration was, in Portuguese, Conasp (*Conselho Consultivo de Administração da Saúde Previdenciária*).

nurses, students, researchers, and other health professionals responded to what they saw as extreme inequities in the healthcare system by mobilizing what became known as the *sanitarista* (health reform) movement. The main goal of this movement was to expand access to healthcare for poor and marginalized communities. Their main strategy for achieving these goals was to take over government health agencies. By empowering state and local health bureaucracies, Brazil's military leaders had paradoxically encouraged health policy experts to join government – convincing them of the possibility to transform public health provision in Brazil from the inside (Weyland 1995). According to various accounts, the *sanitarista* movement achieved significant success in taking over the upper-echelons of bureaucracy, reaching positions of power within the main agencies in charge of healthcare at all three levels of government by the late 1970s (Falleti 2010; Mayka 2019b; Weyland 1995). In this way, early democratizing and decentralizing reforms in the area of health governance led to the development of subnational cadres of health bureaucrats who shared overarching goals with AIDS activists and were, thus, sympathetic to their demands, and who had the capacity and autonomy to generate aggressive policy responses to the AIDS epidemic.

Supportive Bureaucrats

These sympathetic bureaucrats supported AIDS activist groups by feeding them inside information to use as leverage in making demands on government. According to Paulo Teixeira, the architect of São Paulo's state AIDS program:

We never withheld any information and, on the contrary, we took the initiative to inform NGOs when we detected some problems (for example, a lack of hospital beds or inadequate treatment because of the structure of our services). This was always done explicitly, authorizing the NGOs to identify the source (the state AIDS program).

By the same token, when criticisms and protest from NGOs were broadcast by the press, we confirmed the information when it was correct and we recognized the criticisms when they made sense, even when it embarrassed our own state government.[27]

By informing activists on the specificities of political and bureaucratic challenges that prevented them from developing a stronger state response to AIDS, and by confirming NGO allegations of government wrongdoing that were reported in the press, bureaucrats in Brazil's state and local AIDS programs provided critical support for the political campaigns of the early AIDS movement in Brazil.

One reason these state and local bureaucrats were so supportive of NGO efforts was because they relied on activists to push forward their AIDS policy goals from the outside. From an apolitical standpoint, state-level bureaucrats relied on activist leaders to educate "at risk" groups about HIV prevention.

---

[27] Email correspondence with Paulo Teixeira, first coordinator of the State AIDS Program in São Paulo, May 13, 2010.

Stigmatized communities – in this case, gay men and intravenous drug users – tend to be particularly wary of government officials (Cohen 1999). Consequently, for bureaucrats to effectively encourage behavioral change, they needed to delegate educational campaigns to community leaders. AIDS bureaucrats also utilized activists' insider knowledge of community values and consequent knowledge of the type of message most likely to elicit a positive response.

But state-level bureaucrats also relied on civil society activists to advocate politically for resources and legislation. Public pressure was particularly important in the development of state-level AIDS programs, because government investment in preventive health services was extremely low and, consequently, various public health programs were competing for a small pool of state funding. Moreover, in most states other than São Paulo, AIDS programs emerged initially as relatively marginalized areas of the state-level bureaucracy, without the attention or the personal support of the health secretary. To overcome the strong bureaucratic and financial hurdles to the development of AIDS prevention and treatment programs, bureaucrats used activist groups to call public attention to AIDS – putting political pressure on health secretariats to support AIDS policy development.

Universally across my interviews, former AIDS-sector bureaucrats recalled depending on social-movement activism to support their own efforts inside the state. According to Álvaro Matida, the architect of Rio de Janeiro's state AIDS program:

Everybody understood that the role of civil society was to be in the ears of government, making demands and facilitating [our] AIDS responses. Take the example of civil-society pressure over hospitals and over health insurance companies. When the first AIDS cases arrived, patients needed hospital rooms and beds. The pressure that civil society organized at the time was very important in getting rooms opened for AIDS patients, and for forcing health insurers to cover AIDS patients.[28]

Like the rest of my informants, Álvaro was well aware that activism gave him leverage in his own battle to improve AIDS services.

Early activists from Rio concurred that Álvaro Matida depended on outside pressure, and that he had communicated this need to activists. As one former AIDS activist recollected:

Our fight wasn't exactly against the state government per se. It was like this: hospitals didn't have beds – there was a bed crisis – so the television station would come over to film us, and we would say, 'There are no beds! The state government isn't doing its job! The hospital doesn't have any beds!' Or, 'It's not taking in patients!' And then I'd [turn and] say: 'Álvaro, dude, sorry.' And Álvaro would say: 'No no, it's ok. It's good you're making noise, because that gives me power.' Get it? So while we didn't necessarily have an alliance with the state government, we had alliances with certain sectors of the

---

[28] Interview with Álvaro Matida, first director of Rio de Janeiro's state AIDS program, December 9, 2008.

state ... or with people [in the state]. You know, because politics is in reality like that, many of these bureaucrats depend on the pressure that civil society makes for government to give them money and such.[29]

Although this type of relationship would not scale up to the national level until the 1990s, state-level bureaucrats in the 1980s were already cultivating allies in civil society as leverage over opponents inside the state.

As I will show in the following sections, Brazil's AIDS activists of the 1980s were particularly adept at political advocacy because of their strong political connections, their high public profiles, and their extensive activist experience. In particular, these groups were known for their aggressive and clever use of the media to sway public opinion in favor of AIDS policy reform. Moreover, the public statements of a few AIDS activists like Betinho, one of Brazil's national political heroes, carried extra political weight – forcing public officials to pay attention. Consequently, state-level AIDS bureaucrats in the 1980s fostered strategic alliances with civil society groups to support AIDS policy development.

COMBINING INSTITUTIONAL AND CONTENTIOUS STRATEGIES FOR ADVANCING POLICY AGENDAS

This opening of access to the state encouraged leaders with backgrounds in contentious activism to incorporate institutional strategies for claim-making into their repertoires. In stark contrast to the combative behavior that ran across Brazilian political movements in earlier decades, AIDS advocacy groups took a decidedly pragmatic approach to achieving their policy goals. In addition to organizing street protests and media campaigns, AIDS activists worked in close partnership with state officials. After 1988, activists took advantage of reinstated democratic institutions by pursuing policy reforms through the courts and the legislature. Brazil's AIDS movement thus employed a hybrid set of tactics – utilizing contentious tactics – posited by traditional theories to be a core characteristic of social movements – but also relying heavily on "insider" tactics – one characterized by traditional social-movements scholarship to be the purview of interest groups.[30]

Institutional Strategies

Collaboration with State Officials
One of the most striking new strategies pursued by AIDS NGOs to influence policy was through direct collaboration with bureaucrats on government commissions. Government bureaucrats initiated these early efforts to engage civil

---

[29] Interview with Silvia Ramos, founding member and first director of the Brazilian Interdisciplinary Association for AIDS (*ABIA*), September 3, 2008.
[30] Tarrow (1998)

society leaders in AIDS policymaking commissions.[31] According to Teixeira, the founding director of São Paulo's statewide AIDS program:

[T]hose initial [AIDS policy] principles (of state responsibility, citizen rights, the defense of rights, and nondiscrimination) were *proposed* by the secretariat, by activists in the secretariat. But they were *endorsed* by the community. So, when we [wrote] an AIDS policy proposal ... before [we sent it to the secretary for approval] we would present it before a commission that included activists ...

[We put together a large commission], and we called activists, researchers, and people from other areas of health to comprise it. So, my group would elaborate a proposal; we would present it before the commission, which would approve it; and from there the secretary would authorize us to implement it.[32] (author's italics)

Given activists' recent experiences with state repression and cooptation, AIDS advocacy groups were at first hesitant to collaborate with government officials. In São Paulo, government bureaucrats responded to this hesitancy by leading the effort to collaborate with civil society.

In Rio de Janeiro, where activists were even more hesitant to collaborate with government officials due to a local history of contentious relations, the state AIDS program director actually launched a campaign to convince AIDS activists to join a government policy commission.[33] According to Milton Quintino, the director of an AIDS NGO active in the 1980s:

Álvaro [Matida, the state AIDS program director] ... want[ed] nongovernmental organizations to be represented [in the governmental AIDS commission]. So we [in the community of AIDS NGOs] held a meeting [about it], and the majority camp...was against [the idea]. They thought it was a cooptation strategy by the state, and that we would end up reinforcing the structures we opposed and diminishing our power to criticize, blah blah blah ... that type of conversation. [But we ended up] coming to an agreement ... and I was elected to represent nongovernmental organizations [on the government AIDS commission], along with ... a [small] group of representatives from [other NGOs].[34]

Eventually, most other states with early AIDS programs copied the AIDS NGO commission model – allotting space for civil-society organizations – that was first established in São Paulo and Rio de Janeiro.

These collaborative policymaking institutions constituted an important channel for AIDS activists to directly influence policy development at the

---

[31] Most scholarship on the AIDS movement in Brazil ignores early efforts by state bureaucrats to include civil society in policymaking committees – arguing instead that these collaborative policymaking spaces that emerged in the mid-1980s to the mid-1990s came about as a result of bottom-up civil society pressure for greater inclusion in the policymaking process.

[32] Interview with Paulo Teixeira, June 12, 2008.

[33] Multiple informant interviews.

[34] Interview with Milton Quintino, former coordinator of ARCA (Religious Group Against AIDS), August 20, 2008.

subnational level.[35] Perhaps most importantly, activist suggestions were often directly translated into policy guidelines (Parker 2003: 149; Spink 2003). In addition, collaborative commissions played a key role in legitimizing government policies by obtaining official civil society endorsement. At the same time, collaborative AIDS commissions facilitated a critical exchange of information between bureaucrats and civil society leaders about problems – both practical and political – that needed to be solved. Civil society leaders provided key information about service needs and service failures, and bureaucrats fed civil society information about political obstacles to AIDS program improvement.

Yet, as Quintino described, activists faced a philosophical dilemma in deciding to collaborate with state-level bureaucrats. On the one hand, early AIDS activists recognized that these government officials were well meaning and, moreover, that they depended on activists for support. But on the other hand, AIDS activists were wary that any form of cooperation with government would lead to cooptation – a wariness that emanated from their recent experiences with dictatorship and, for many, from their far-left political orientations such as Trotskyism and anarcho-syndicalism. Elaborating further on the dilemma, Quintino told me:

We had Álvaro, who was a really special guy, [working under] health secretaries who were in general corrupt or poorly intentioned or bad administrators. I thought we had to support Álvaro, and the others thought [we couldn't do it as activists]. That our only role was to denounce the public health situation in Rio. My worry was that we were stuck worrying about generic politics and weren't advancing on AIDS, where we had a possibility, because of Álvaro.

So we started meeting to talk about it, and in the end I ended up convincing the representative from Pela VIDDA, whose name was Stalin, who had a more "Stalinist" orientation ... (laughter)

He thought we should participate too, even though Herbert thought we shouldn't, Betinho thought we shouldn't, Ranulfo thought we shouldn't. We went to participate in the State AIDS Commission [anyway], and through it we met really good people.

The State AIDS Commission was really great. The problem was the structure of the public health system. And we ended up having important discussions. It was a very productive environment, despite all the limitations that existed, and it was a new experience, a mixed forum of government and society. So it was a new experience, although at the time results were still very modest. But it strengthened Álvaro's position within the secretariat.[36]

Ultimately, the broader group of AIDS activists in Rio chose to collaborate with sympathetic bureaucrats as a pragmatic decision that prioritized their immediate AIDS policy goals over their broader movement philosophies. This

---

[35] Most of these councils were not technically "participatory" in the sense of granting civil society formal veto power over policy guidelines.

[36] Interview with Milton Quintino, former coordinator of *ARCA* (Religious Group Against AIDS) August 20, 2008.

decision was driven in part by the public health emergency they were confronting, which heightened the need for immediate policy outcomes. As an activist from Rio recounted, Betinho used to respond to critics of his eventual collaboration with state officials by saying that to fight AIDS, he would accept an alliance with the devil himself.[37]

As the end of Betinho's quip suggests, however, activists remained wary of cooptation, and they sometimes loudly criticized well-intentioned AIDS-sector bureaucrats even as they cooperated with them and accepted their support. Jane Galvão, an AIDS activist and academic, captures this complex relationship in a 2008 book chapter she wrote to commemorate Betinho's life and role in the AIDS movement:

A favorite saying of Betinho's at that time was, "We cannot accept the theory that if the foot is too big for the shoe, we should cut the foot to size. The shoe is what needs to be changed." He strove to do just that by seeking to implement more inclusive public health policies. Betinho publicly challenged, in the media and at events, the individuals responsible for Brazil's federal AIDS program and the AIDS program in the state of Rio de Janeiro.

In 1991, Betinho and I sat together in a meeting with the coordinator of the AIDS program for the state of Rio de Janeiro. At that time I was working on AIDS-related issues through a nongovernmental organization (NGO) in Rio de Janeiro called the Institute of Religious Studies. One of the institute's projects was a program called Religious Support against AIDS, which aimed to work with different religious groups in Brazil in order to promote solidarity with people living with HIV/AIDS (PLWHA).

The coordinator seemed to us to be a very sincere man, soft-spoken and kind. However, programs for both AZT distribution and prevention were much weaker than we thought they could be, and one of the results was that very few Rio hospitals were equipped to actually receive and care for AIDS patients. As a large state, Rio was important to us in terms of strengthening HIV surveillance – monitoring the number of infections as well as the care and treatment of those who had acquired the virus. The city was the second largest in terms of AIDS cases in Brazil, a fact Betinho pointed out, and a good policy in Rio could potentially serve as an example for the rest of the country.

I sat next to Betinho as he outlined these circumstances, emphasizing his words with the rise and fall of his hands. As he spoke, his luminous green eyes bore down on the coordinator. His cane leaned against the armrest of his chair and, despite his gaunt appearance, his speech was full of vigor. He was not rude or aggressive; that was not Betinho's style. Instead, he demanded that the AIDS coordinator *do* something about the problems, making it clear through his voice where he thought responsibility lay. When the man finally cut Betinho off and responded as we had anticipated, with defensiveness, Betinho leaned back in his chair and listened. The man launched into a detailed speech about all of the obstacles that he faced, referring to budget constraints, the difficulty implementing training in hospitals, and finally his own inability to tackle the problem alone. He threw his arms up in the air, in mock helplessness, and Betinho,

---

[37] Interview with Silvia Ramos, founding member and first director of the Brazilian Interdisciplinary Association for AIDS (*ABIA*), September 3, 2008.

along with the rest of us in the room, watched him go on and on. When the man finally paused and took a deep breath, Betinho leaned his frail body forward again and trained his powerful gaze on him.

"*This,*" he said, "is why *you* are here. You are the person in charge of this program. You need to do something. The NGOs can help you, and we can collaborate, but this is *your problem.*"

As he spoke, I found myself saying *yes, yes,* along with him in my head. Betinho refused to let the man excuse away his inaction. I looked at a few of the other activists who were in the room; from the expressions on their faces, it looked as if they were having similar thoughts. This encounter was typical for Betinho: he was expressing many of our frustrations in his eloquent and powerful way, and as always he was trying to systematize discussion surrounding the problem. He saw his role as one of creating *awareness* and increased pressure, so that action would be taken at the highest levels possible. (Galvão 2008: 235–6)

This meeting took place several years after Álvaro Matida had begun to build an alliance with AIDS activists from Rio de Janeiro. It shows how movement leaders continued to exert strong pressure even on well-intentioned and supportive state-level bureaucrats, even as they collaborated with them to improve services. Activist pressure on bureaucrats was particularly acute in Rio, where public health services were – and continue to be – notoriously weak and corrupt.

Bureaucrats and other activists in Rio expressed similar memories of how their alliance with the AIDS movement slowly developed, even as activists continued to put pressure on them for better results. According to Fatima Rocha, who worked in the state AIDS program:

The way that Betinho's words resonated with the general public put a lot of pressure on us from the state health secretary. NGOs [were] wanting things to happen. And [there was] perpetual slowness [on the part of government bureaucracy]. And Álvaro killing himself to make things happen. Working I-don't-know-how-many hours per day. [But there was also a gradual] recognition [among NGOs] that, independent of the health secretary, the state AIDS program had committed people working in it. This realization that there were committed people working inside the program took some time to sink in, for NGOs. But I think the way we ended up working together bore fruit for the future.[38]

Silvia Ramos, the activist from ABIA echoed Fatima's memory of how NGOs gradually came to build alliances with state-level bureaucrats despite their strong reticence. In Silvia's words:

The 1980s is when the story of NGOs in Brazil starts. The term "NGO" at that time was not well known among Brazilians. So people would say "non-governmental organization." Well in Brazil, "non-governmental" sounds like "anti-governmental," whereas in

---

[38] Interview with Fatima Rocha, bureaucrat in Rio de Janeiro State AIDS Program, 1989–2005, Coordinator of program, 2003–2006, July 29, 2008.

English it means non-state ... So a lot of people used to think in the beginning – before NGOs became a "thing" like they are today – that the idea of a "non-governmental organization" was that you were against the government. And we would say: "No, we're not against the government" ...

Of course deep down we *were* [anti-government], because NGOs in that era were all formed by the Brazilian left. All of them. Or by former exiles, like Betinho [names others]. And as this was during the period of Brazil's transition away from dictatorship, the tradition was to be against government.

But this experience with some sectors of the state-level government ended up showing [AIDS activists] that it was in fact possible to build alliances with parts of government. As incredible as that sounds, because that was against our nature at the time. Today, to be an NGO seems like it is almost synonymous with depending on government, doesn't it? But at the time, to be an NGO meant to have independence, to be autonomous, to be critical.[39]

As both Silvia and Fatima allude to in their interviews, and as I show in the following chapters, what was for activists in the 1980s a radical decision to cooperate with some government bureaucrats at the state level ultimately developed into a new national model for state–society relations.

Judicial Advocacy

The AIDS movement also stands out for its early use of the judicial system as a strategy for pushing forward policy (Galvão 2000: 170; Parker 2003: 160; Ventura 2003). Brazil's AIDS advocacy organizations were not only the earliest groups to take advantage of the new democratic legal framework in Brazil to promote their policy goals through the courts, but they were also among the most successful (e.g., Rios 2003; Ventura 2003). GAPA, Brazil's first AIDS NGO, included legal aid as a core component of its activities during the first year of its foundation in 1985, a pattern also followed by *Grupo PelaVIDDA* in Rio de Janeiro shortly thereafter (Ventura 2003: 242). By the late 1980s, nongovernmental AIDS organizations in several states had copied GAPA's model for legal assistance (Ventura 2003: 245).[40] These early AIDS organizations quickly developed into the foremost national legal experts in the field of AIDS policy, filing claims not only on behalf of the individuals who came to them directly for help, but also at the request of unions, state bureaucracies, and businesses. Together, they filed and won a wide variety of legal claims, ranging from making the state responsible for preventing HIV contamination through blood transfusion, to making health insurance companies cover the cost of AIDS treatment, to forcing businesses to rehire and pay damages to employees they had fired due to their HIV status (Ventura 2003: 245).

These court decisions played a critical role in AIDS policy development in Brazil by laying the legal groundwork for Brazil's most progressive policy

---

[39] Interview with Silvia Ramos, founding member and first director of the Brazilian Interdisciplinary Association for AIDS (*ABIA*), September 3, 2008.

[40] For an example of the spread of the legal-aid model to other states which outlines the broad set of legal strategies used the branch of GAPA in the state of Salvador da Bahia.

guidelines. Moreover, because many of these judicial hearings received broad coverage by the media (often publicized intentionally by the AIDS movement to increase their public profile), they served as a model for other social movements in Brazil. In the following decade, filing civil lawsuits would be adopted broadly as a core activist strategy in Brazil. The AIDS movement's legal advocacy benefited other contemporary social movements in Brazil directly as well. Because the claims of AIDS advocacy organizations centered on basic questions of social rights, such as access to healthcare, education, and work, and equal treatment under the law, the legal precedents set by the AIDS movement advanced policy along a variety of social-sector issue areas. According to Ventura (2003): "No doubt these legal questions [in the area of AIDS] made a great contribution to public policies on health and assistance to carriers of deficiencies, and today there are more and more claims of the same nature presented before the judiciary" (Ventura 2003: 245).

The AIDS movement's focus on the judicial system, rather than the legislature, was driven in large part by two aspects of the surrounding institutional context. First, the legal framework set out by the 1988 constitution, which adopted a broad definition of citizenship rights and established access to healthcare as a universal right, provided a strong constitutional basis for making legal claims in the area of public health (Rios 2003; Ventura 2003). Second, the inefficiency of the Brazilian congress, in which legislative proposals often languished for years before coming up for debate, led AIDS activists to seek more efficient routes to securing human rights protections (Ventura 2003: 244).

Lobbying

Given the slowness of the legislative process, congressional lobbying remained a relatively weak component of the AIDS movement's strategic repertoire for influencing policy in the 1980s. However, on a few important occasions, early AIDS activists also pushed forward AIDS policy by directly appealing to congressional leaders. These lobbying efforts were relatively informal and unorganized, and they consisted mainly of personal appeals by the most high-profile activists – principally, Betinho – who in key moments traveled to Brasília to convince legislators of the need to pass (or block) AIDS policy legislation. For example, during the movement's campaign to develop national guidelines for controlling blood banks:

Betinho himself would go to Brasília to talk to deputies [and] senators ... to show them the insanity of the situation, of how the country had abandoned control over the blood supply. And he achieved their support to insert [a clause] into the constitution saying that Brazil would have to control blood, that blood control was a responsibility of the state and could no longer be commercialized.[41]

---

[41] Interview with Veriano Terto Jr., Director of ABIA, September 5, 2008.

This type of congressional lobbying by the AIDS movement was effective in large part because of the high personal regard among congressional politicians for activists such as Betinho.

Research and Expertise

Activists used scientific research to support their other strategies for influencing AIDS policy development from within government. AIDS activists conceptualized research as an explicitly political act, as fostering "the democratization of information," in response to government suppression of data under the prior military regime. According to a document detailing ABIA's organizational history:

[The word] democratization ... symbolized the importance of breaking governmental control over information as a fundamental question for civil society to take back control over the democratic regime. With respect to HIV/AIDS, that concept emphasized the importance of overcoming the general denial of the dimension, nature and impact of the epidemic, with the goal of developing more effective policies and answers in combatting it (Parker and Terto Jr. 2001).

AIDS NGOs thus developed cadres of trained researchers who would conduct scientific studies in areas such as the effectiveness of prevention strategies, access to AIDS services, and human rights violations against people with HIV. These groups would then hold conferences to develop their findings into concrete AIDS policy recommendations, which they would both take to bureaucrats and publicly disseminate. (See Parker and Terto Jr. 2001: 96–9.)

In addition to the direct impact of scholarly research conducted by AIDS activists on policy development in Brazil, activist-led research indirectly increased their influence over AIDS policy development in Brazil. Through their dedication to research, AIDS activists in Brazil became the leading national experts on AIDS prevention and treatment. National and state-level policymakers depended on civil society leaders for their expert advice, thus encouraging them to expand and deepen official state collaboration with civil society in drafting AIDS policy guidelines.

Contentious Strategies

This new repertoire of institutional strategies complemented, rather than replaced, the old repertoire of contentious pressure strategies as a route to influencing policy. But AIDS activists turned away from disruptive protests and toward small-scale, media-oriented protests instead – a protest tactic that relies on dramatic imagery rather than on mass mobilization.

Protest

Street protests were a central political strategy of the AIDS movement in the 1980s.[42] Regularly, activists would take advantage of commemorative

---

[42] Multiple informant interviews.

(a)   (b)

IMAGE 3.1. *World AIDS Day 1991 and 1988*

occasions to make broad political statements – such as on World AIDS Day in 1991, when activists covered an obelisk in downtown Rio de Janeiro with a gigantic condom to protest the Catholic Church's opposition to condoms as a method of HIV prevention (Parker and Terto Jr. 2001). Activists would also organize protests in response to specific challenges – such as in 1989, when HIV positive activists from the Group *Pela VIDDA* picketed the headquarters of *Varig* (a major Brazilian airline) for making negative HIV tests an employment requirement, and for secretly conducting HIV tests during job orientations (Boletim ABIA 8: August 1989; Parker and Terto Jr. 2001: 30). In 1988, activists descended on the national capital of Brasília to demand mandatory screening for blood donations, covering the Ministry of Health with banners and flooding the steps with fake blood (Massé 2009: 39, citing interview with Aurea Abbade, member of GAPA São Paulo).

Yet in contrast to prior waves of political protest under the military regime, which were strongly anti-state in character, AIDS protests were sometimes organized in *collaboration* with government officials. In the case of the campaign to ban the sale of blood in the state of Rio de Janeiro (the first stage of what would develop into a major national campaign), the government official in charge of the health surveillance department actually instigated public protests – calling both the press and AIDS activist organizations to join his team as they shut down illegal blood suppliers.[43]

Protests organized by Brazil's AIDS organizations also differed from typical protests of prior decades because they were often small in scale, geared more toward attracting media attention than toward producing mass disturbance.

The Media

More generally, AIDS organiztaions used the media – both print and television – as key channels used to influence policy, beyond simply as a means to publicize protests. One major use of the press was to directly denounce government misdeeds and pressure the government to invest more in AIDS (Parker and Terto Jr. 2001: 25). According to Ramos, of the group ABIA, "We used to go on TV and speak poorly of the health secretary, and then the secretary had to come over and invite us in for a meeting. And the secretary knew what the game was [we were playing]."[44]

In general, AIDS-sector bureaucrats recognized that this kind public criticism, even when directed at state AIDS programs, supported their ultimate goals. As Ramos continued to recollect:

Those state-level bureaucrats, because they were from the Left, had a very advanced understanding of that game, of civil-society pressure on government ... They understood that the relationship between government and civil society could take on much more complex and subtle configurations than "you're for me or you're against me."[45]

In other words, state-level AIDS bureaucrats recognized that autonomous social-movement activism supported their overarching goals even if it was occasionally a thorn in their sides.

At the same time, AIDS organizations used the media proactively. Developing their own media campaigns, they sought to combat the negative national discourse on AIDS, which was fostered by the national program's fear-based prevention campaigns. Again, according to Ramos:

So then, *Globo* [Brazil's largest television network] starts to produce the first media campaigns about AIDS based on our principles, and not on the government's principles. The principles of the government were: "Be careful, AIDS kills." And our principles were: "It is possible to prevent AIDS," "You can't get AIDS like this," "Stay away from AIDS, but not from the ill," "Create an epidemic of solidarity."[46]

---

[43] Informant interviews with Álvaro Matida; Silvia Ramos; Fatima Rocha, bureaucrat in Rio de Janeiro State AIDS Program, 1989–2005, Coordinator of program, 2003–2006, July 29, 2008.

[44] Interview with Silvia Ramos, founding member and first director of the Brazilian Interdisciplinary Association for AIDS (*ABIA*), September 3, 2008.

[45] Interview with Silvia Ramos, founding member and first director of the Brazilian Interdisciplinary Association for AIDS (*ABIA*), September 3, 2008.

[46] Interview with Silvia Ramos, founding member and first director of the Brazilian Interdisciplinary Association for AIDS (*ABIA*), September 3, 2008.

AIDS NGOs' strategy of influencing policy through the media was effective in large part because of the political prominence and public reverence for a handful of Brazil's early AIDS activist leaders, whose statements both captured the public's attention and forced politicians to respond (Parker 2003: 159–160).[47]

AIDS activists also relied heavily on personal connections with members of the media industry to publicize their human-rights based HIV prevention campaigns and political demands. In particular, a founding member of *Pela VIDDA Rio* worked (and continues to work) as a journalist for *TV Globo*, the premier television network in Brazil. Through him, activists substantially increased their media presence – via "infiltrating" the press.[48] Moreover, because NGOs had developed into premier authorities on AIDS in Brazil through their investment in research, members of the press themselves sought out AIDS NGOs to transmit information to the public via interviews – thus increasing their control over the public discourse (Parker 2003: 159; Parker and Terto Jr. 2001).

INFLUENCE OF CIVIC ACTIVISM ON BRAZIL'S EARLY
AIDS RESPONSES

There exists near universal agreement among key Brazilian policymakers and scholars alike that the power of the AIDS movement, together with activist bureaucrats in state and municipal health programs, drove the development of progressive AIDS policies and capable government AIDS programs from the mid-1980s to the early 1990s (Biehl 2007: 1087; Galvão 2000: 35–112; Parker 2003; Teixeira 1997: 56).

Policy Development

The first government AIDS responses in Brazil emerged at the state and municipal levels, due to the initial concentration of the epidemic in a handful of cities. As in all cases of new public health threats, the earliest AIDS policies in Brazil focused on emergency management. These emergency response efforts centered on building systems for monitoring the epidemic, developing guidelines to treat AIDS patients, passing legislation to safeguard the blood supply, and educating the public about HIV prevention.[49] Yet almost immediately, the strong influence of grassroots activists over policy development began to color government AIDS policies as well. Specifically, unlike the fear-based responses to AIDS across the developing world that included a wide array of discriminatory policies (such as quarantining AIDS victims), governmental responses to AIDS in Brazil emphasized instead the human rights dimension (Galvão 2000: 167–73). State and local AIDS policy commissions adopted the concept

---

[47] In addition: interviews with Fatima Rocha, Ranulfo Cardoso.
[48] Informant interview with Bruno Cattoni.
[49] Informant interviews with Ranulfo Cardoso, Álvaro Matida, Fátima Rocha, and Paulo Teixeira.

of social justice as one of their core guiding principles, and they explicitly high-lighted human rights violations as a force in perpetuating the spread of HIV (Galvão 2000: 169).

While national policy development lagged behind state and municipal responses to AIDS (Parker 2003: 146), Brazil achieved a few significant advances in national policy development and investment in AIDS during this period as well. In particular, the National AIDS Program adopted the framing of human rights and nondiscrimination that had been developed at the state and local levels (Parker 2003: 149; Teixeira 1997: 56–7). These guiding norms of the National AIDS Program led to policy advances such as national decrees outlining explicit human rights protections for AIDS patients, and a national law extending bene-fits to people with AIDS suffering from other diseases (Parker 2003: 149; Teixeira 1997: 61). All informant interviews and written accounts about the period sug-gest that the AIDS movement influenced each of these policy debates.

Developing the Bureaucratic Infrastructure

The development of bureaucratic infrastructure for government AIDS responses followed the same basic trajectory as that of AIDS policies and guidelines in Brazil – progressing first at the state and local levels, and then scaling up to the national level. The AIDS program in the state of São Paulo served as the Brazilian model, copied not only by state AIDS programs across Brazil but also by the national AIDS program itself (Parker 2003: 148–9). This diffusion of the basic organizational structure and guiding norms of São Paulo's AIDS program was driven by the shared perspectives and ideals of progressive state and municipal health officials. According to Paulo Teixeira (the key architect of São Paulo's AIDS program and a key architect of Brazil's National AIDS Program), because most bureaucrats who founded AIDS programs at the state level were from the *sanitarista* movement, an *a priori* trust existed among them that facilitated the establishment of dialogue between states.[50] In 1983, Rio Grande do Sul was the first state-level AIDS program to seek out São Paulo for help in designing its AIDS program, and it adopted Sao Paulo's model exactly, including both its organizational structure and its guiding norms; Minas Gerais, Paraná, and other states soon followed.[51] During this period of early bureau-cratic development, officials from São Paulo's AIDS program were both invited to and hosted frequent meetings and conferences to present their AIDS program model for AIDS program development across the affected state of Brazil.[52] By 1985, state AIDS programs had been established in at least eleven of Brazil's twenty-six states, in addition to a significant number of municipal AIDS pro-grams (Parker 2003: 148; Teixeira 1997: 52). Civic influence was also felt in the

---

[50] Interview with Paulo Teixeira.
[51] Interview with Paulo Teixeira.
[52] Interviews with Ranulfo Cardoso, Álvaro Matida, and Paulo Teixeira.

design of these subnational AIDS programs; as noted above, civic activists were integrally involved in developing the AIDS program in São Paulo from the start.

By contrast, the eventual development of a national-level AIDS program in Brazil was a slower and more belabored process. Although the epidemic was spreading across a significant number of Brazilian states by the late 1980s, funding and bureaucratic development for a national AIDS coordination developed in fits and starts (Galvão 2000: 123–5; Parker 2003: 150–2). During these periods of development, civic influence was felt. For example, the Ministry of Health adopted the major guidelines of São Paulo's AIDS program, which had been designed in collaboration with civic activists, when it established the National AIDS Program in 1986 (Galvão 2000: 121).[53] The Ministry also directly contracted AIDS NGOs as consultants in designing the program – lending activists a significant degree of influence over the structure for AIDS policy development in Brazil.[54] Most strikingly, a National Advisory Committee was created to incorporate civil society voices in national AIDS policy discussions (Galvão 2000; Parker 2003: 149; Spink 2003; Teixeira 1997: 58). While the National AIDS Commission offered civic associations no formal decision-making power over policy, it served in practice as a powerful opportunity for policy input: not only was it presided over by the key figures that drafted AIDS policy guidelines, but it was also relatively small in size, thus fostering deep discussion and deliberation. This institution, later renamed the National AIDS Commission, stands as a precursor to the participatory governance institutions that have swept through Latin America and dominated subsequent discourse over global development policy.[55] Yet, until the early 1990s, the national AIDS program was still a relatively neglected and underfunded area of the national healthcare bureaucracy.

Between 1992 and 1994, however, Brazil's AIDS program suddenly metamorphosed from an underfunded area of the national healthcare bureaucracy to the "rich cousin of healthcare," characterized by capable bureaucrats and a strong, collaborative relationship between the national government and civil society organizations. This is the next episode of change in the story of Brazil's AIDS movement, to which I will turn in Chapter 4.

CONCLUSION

Brazil's AIDS movement of the 1980s is important not only for its remarkable policy successes, but also because it was the harbinger of a new paradigm

---

[53] Interview with Paulo Teixeira.
[54] Interviews with Pedro Chequer, Paulo Teixera.
[55] Given that Brazil has been used as a model for global AIDS policy, based largely on the close dialogue between state officials and civil society representatives, one could also argue that the National AIDS Commission is likely the model on which the National Coordinating Mechanisms that have been mandated for all recipient countries of the Global AIDS Fund are based.

for civic advocacy across Latin America. Unlike prior generations of social-movement activism, which were mass-based, this was a movement of NGOs – a movement of semi-professional organizations with relatively small numbers of members. Also, unlike prior generations of activism, which took place primarily in the streets, the AIDS movement worked inside government institutions to influence policy at the same time as it used public-pressure tactics. While these traits made the AIDS movement stand out as unusual at the time, hybrid movements that bridge the insider–outsider divide have since spread across Latin America and beyond.

At the same time, the success of Brazil's early AIDS movement can be explained in large part by traditional social-movement approaches. Grievances, driven by the government's lackluster response to a public health emergency, drove activists to organize. Political opportunities, provided by the period of democratic transition and by the particular characteristics of local health bureaucracies, helped make their demands more effective. And resources, both social and financial, were available to them to use in organizing because of their status as relatively well-educated and politically connected cosmopolitans. It was not until the 2000s, well after the success of the movement's initial campaigns, that the AIDS movement spread to a wider range of groups that cut across traditional cleavages such class, race, gender, religion and geography. How, then, did the AIDS movement sustain political organization and mobilization after its initial success? How did the movement expand into more diverse communities – and into regions dominated by rural oligarchs, clientelistic politics, and histories of weak civic organization – over the course of the 2000s?

As I show in Chapters 5 and 6, it was only once federal bureaucrats inside government took up the fight for AIDS policy reform, and took up central roles in shaping civic organization and mobilization around AIDS, that the movement expanded into new communities. In the mid-1990s, during the transformation of Brazil's national AIDS program into a new agency of the state, policy experts and activists took up posts as government bureaucrats to run the program. These new bureaucrats were committed to advancing the national AIDS policy guidelines that had emerged as a result of civic activism in the 1980s, and they were given the budget and the formal authority to pursue their policy goals without interference from outside actors. Yet, once in government, they found that achieving their policy objectives depended on the cooperation of other actors inside the state – in the legislature, in other state agencies, and at the international level – whom they were unable to control. Unable to independently overcome the many political obstacles to advancing their AIDS policy goals, these bureaucrats looked to civil society to lend them political support from outside the state.

When federal bureaucrats later encountered new political obstacles to advancing their AIDS policy goals at lower levels of government, they sought to expand civic organization and political mobilization out from the relatively narrow range of cities where the movement had originated into new regions of Brazil. In Chapter 5, I show how in the 2000s bureaucrats in the national AIDS program faced the challenge of decentralizing control over government AIDS policy to governors and mayors, many of whom had little interest in investing in high quality AIDS services, and some of whom were religiously opposed to national AIDS policy guidelines. Lacking effective mechanisms to directly control subnational behavior, these federal bureaucrats launched a grassroots-style campaign to mobilize civic organizations in new regions of Brazil as AIDS policy advocates. They did this by spreading resources to support new organizations in all twenty-six states, as well as opportunities to access government policy circles. These efforts resulted in a boom in the number of NGOs working on AIDS projects across Brazil. Although, as Chapter 6 shows, these top-down efforts were on their own insufficient to mobilize these new civic AIDS organizations as political advocates. It was the older generation of AIDS advocacy organizations who, for their own reasons, provided the newer generation of civic AIDS organizations with the skills and the motivations for political advocacy.

Chapter 4 shows how policy experts and activists came to enter the national AIDS program in the first place, as well as how they acquired the motivation and the resources to mobilize civic organizations outside the state as policy allies. This movement of policy experts and activists into the state was part of a major transformation of Brazil's national AIDS program from what was once a backwater of the Ministry of Health into its own semi-autonomous agency of the state, funded in part by the World Bank. Those who have written about AIDS policy in Brazil hold it up as special for this reason. I show in Chapter 4, however, that the transformation of the national AIDS program was part of a broader transformation of state institutions in Latin America that were outcomes of the twin processes of democratization and neoliberal reform. In turn, these transformations in the state laid the foundation for a new model for state–society relations to emerge – what I call "civic corporatism" and describe in detail in the concluding chapter to this book.

4

Transformations in the State

Once a backwater of the healthcare bureaucracy, Brazil's national AIDS program developed from 1992 to 1994 into an autonomous and independently funded sector of the state. This restructured national AIDS program stood out as a new type of state agency in Brazil and contrasted sharply with the traditional bureaucracies of twentieth century Brazil in three ways. Firstly, policy experts and former activists ran the program, rather than traditional career bureaucrats. Secondly, civic advocacy groups were given formal influence over AIDS policy through representation on "participatory governance" policymaking committees. Thirdly, civic AIDS organizations were subsidized by government resources through project funding specially designated for civil society.

As others have described, a variety of factors specific to AIDS policy contributed to government investment in a new national bureaucracy. As I showed in Chapter 3, strong civic mobilization by gay men, hemophiliacs, and their allies played a significant role. High-ranking officials within the national political administration also personally supported the decision to develop a strong national AIDS program (Nunn 2009: 56–60; Solano 2000: 83–4). Certainly, factors unique to AIDS policy were at play in determining the timing and the strength of Brazil's investment in a new national AIDS program.

In its broad contours, however, the transformation of Brazil's national AIDS program was not unique but, rather, reflective of broader transformations in the state in Brazil and across Latin America. During the 1990s and into the 2000s, the range of social and development policies addressed by the government expanded from a relatively narrow set of worker protections to a much wider range of constituencies such as indigenous groups, black communities, women, children, and the unemployed. New state agencies were constructed to build these national policies and programs, which brought into the state a new class of bureaucrats who shared broad policy goals with activists outside the state. In many cases, social-movement activists were given formal access to the state through new "participatory governance" institutions. State subsidies for NGOs surged as national governments contracted nonprofit civic organizations to administer these new benefits and protections. This set of trends has been conceptualized by some as an "inclusionary turn" or a "second incorporation" in Latin American politics (Silva & Rossi 2018).

In this chapter, I attribute these transformations in state institutions – both in Latin America in general and in Brazil's national AIDS program in particular – to two broad regional shifts in government: democratization and neoliberal reform. Democratization gave power to new voices in society. Their demands led presidents to create new social policies, to construct new state agencies to govern them, and to hire outside experts and activists to run them.[1] The particular form that democratization took in much of Latin America, based on the principles of social democracy and participatory governance, also led executives to build institutional channels for civil society to access the state (Mayka 2019a). Neoliberal reforms led national executives to subsidize civic organizations. The broad adoption of neoliberal economic principles in Latin America, with its emphasis on a minimal state, conflicted with national government commitments to expanding social protections. To resolve the contradiction, government policymakers offered project funding for civic organizations to deliver services on behalf of the state. As the practice of outsourcing government services to local NGOs expanded and institutionalized, vast numbers of civic organizations began to receive government subsidies. The transformations in the state that resulted from the combination of democratization and neoliberal reforms are important because they involved government recognition of new identity groups, new channels of access to the policymaking process for wide swaths of civil society, an expansion of social welfare policies to reach historically excluded groups, and government subsidies for new and more diverse groups in civil society.

As I show in this chapter, these transformations in the state were also important because they gave rise to incentives and resources for state-sponsored activism to subsequently emerge. The policy experts who ran new state agencies were motivated to cultivate civic advocacy because they were committed to shared policy goals with activists outside the state, and because they were often stymied in the pursuit of their goals by actors in other sectors or branches of government. These policy experts were capable of pursuing a civil society-centered strategy for overcoming obstacles inside the state because of the participatory governance institutions that gave them an institutionalized structure for building alliances with civic activists, and because of the earmarked budget for civil society projects that gave them protected resources for subsidizing civic organization.

---

[1] On the effects of democratization on the expansion of social policy in Latin America, see Garay (2016).

This argument is important, in part, because it highlights an unexpected and positive effect of the dual transition toward democracy and neoliberalism on state–society relations in Latin America. In general, the processes of democratization and neoliberal reform have been attributed to the unraveling of the corporatist system of state-society relations.[2] I show instead that the very processes that undercut the traditional form of corporatism in Brazil in fact gave rise to a new form of corporatism – introduced in the concluding chapter of this book as "civic corporatism." The process of democratization produced new state actors who were motivated to support civic organization and mobilization. Democratization also created institutional channels for these new state actors to engage civil society as allies by restructuring the policymaking process around participatory governance institutions. Neoliberal reforms produced the resources for these state actors to use in mobilizing allies in civil society by institutionalizing the practice of outsourcing government service delivery to civic organizations. I show, in other words, that the combination of democratization and neoliberal reforms did not destroy, but rather *transformed*, the incentives and resources that sustained corporatism.

TRANSITION TO DEMOCRACY

The third wave of democratization in Latin America radically transformed the structure of incentives and opportunities for organized society to make demands on the state. At the broadest level, democratic institutions replaced authoritarian institutions, making it possible for wide swaths of society that previously had been excluded from the formal political arena to make demands on government without fear of repression. In addition, national political reformers built this Latin American version of democracy on a new philosophy of governance, which paradoxically combined the socialist principles of state intervention to create a more just and equal society with a neoliberal emphasis on the minimal state. This regional transformation in the principles of governance that undergird politics manifested itself in major institutional changes to national political systems across Latin America. In turn, these institutional changes transformed the nature of state–society relations.

Three interrelated aspects of the democratization process in Latin America were particularly important for changing the incentives and opportunities for organized society to make demands on the state. First, new social questions became politically salient as activists used their newfound political and civil rights to make policy demands on government. Second, presidents created new government programs in response to these demands and recruited a new class of bureaucrats to build and administer them. Third, these new constitutions opened channels for civic advocacy groups to access the state by redesigning the policymaking system according to the principles of participatory governance. The ultimate outcome of

---

[2] For a well-developed summary of this argument, see Collier and Handlin (2009), chapter 2.

the democratization process was the birth of new state agencies in Brazil, run by bureaucrats who shared broad policy goals with activists outside the state, and who had channels to use in building policy alliances with civic organizations.

New Social Questions

First, re-democratization brought new social questions to the table as civil society gained space to organize and make their voices heard (Garay 2016; Rossi 2015). As military regimes eased repression and reinstated civil rights, societal groups of many stripes began to organize and make policy demands (Escobar and Alvarez 1992; Eckstein 2001). In turn, the civil-society mobilization that grew out of these regime transitions helped to deepen democratic reforms. Of particular importance, civic mobilization put pressure on politicians to allow popular participation in the constitution.

In turn, rewritten national constitutions across the region dramatically expanded the definition of citizens' rights, which provided a broad range of civic activists with a new legal basis for demand-making. Far beyond the minimalist constitutions embraced by countries such as the United States, which focus narrowly on civil and political rights, the new national constitutions that were adopted in Latin America incorporated a wide range of social, economic, and cultural rights. For example, the right to equal pay for equal work is included in all South American constitutions. The right to healthcare is incorporated into all constitutions but in Argentina. Explicit references to social class are included in the constitutions of Argentina, Brazil, Colombia, and Ecuador.[3]

In contrast to civil and political rights, which are centered on protecting citizens from interference by the state (and are thus commonly referred to as "negative" rights), the social, economic, and cultural rights outlined in these new Latin American constitutions obligated states to actively intervene in defense of these rights. Often, such active intervention required national governments to invest in new social programs. For example, Article 43 of the Colombian constitution declares that, "[T]he State will gradually extend the coverage of Social Security which will include the provision of services in the form determined by law."[4] Article 45 of the Uruguayan Constitution states, "Every inhabitant of the country has the right to a decent home."[5] Article 196 of the Brazilian constitution declares that, "Health is the right of all persons and the duty of the State and is guaranteed by means of social and economic policies aimed at reducing the risk of illness and other hazards and at universal and equal access to all actions and services for the promotion, protection and recovery of health."[6]

---

[3] Information obtained from www.constituteproject.org (last accessed December 27, 2016.)

[4] For the entire text of Colombia's constitution in English, see: www.constituteproject.org/constitution/Colombia_2005.pdf (last accessed April 26, 2018).

[5] For the entire text of Uruguay's constitution in English, see: www.constituteproject.org/constitution/Uruguay_2004.pdf?lang=en (last accessed April 26, 2018).

[6] For the entire text of Brazil's constitution in English, see: www.constituteproject.org/search?lang=en&q=Brazil&status=in_force (last accessed April 26, 2018).

Subsequent "enabling" legislation translated these broad constitutional guarantees into specific government policies mandating benefits and protections for new groups in society. Between the late-1980s and the late-1990s, laws recognizing indigenous rights were adopted in sixteen out of the nineteen countries of Latin America, and laws recognizing rights for subsets of black populations in seven countries (Paschel 2016: 11). Gender quotas in the national congress were adopted in fifteen countries (Htun and Weldon 2018: 39). Laws guaranteeing access to healthcare were adopted across the region. Although the process was gradual and uneven, through the process of constitutional reform a variety of new policy issues arrived on the political agenda in the 1980s and 1990s in Latin America, and particularly in Brazil.

Civic mobilization was both cause and effect of these processes of constitutional, legislative, and policy reform. In countries where the process of democratic transition involved large-scale civic mobilization, such as Brazil, activists played central roles in drafting their constitutions. In Brazil, black activists (Paschel 2016: 88–102), feminist activists (Alvarez 1990: 251), environmental activists (Hochstetler and Keck 2007: 46–51), public health activists (Melo 2015: 112–21), and many others participated in the constitutional convention process; and all succeeded – albeit to varying degrees – in including key benefits and protections into the new document. In turn, by adopting an expansive definition of states' obligations to its citizens, the new Latin American constitutions provided citizens with a constitutional basis for making a much broader range of demands on government than ever before in modern political history.

From the perspective of national executives, the processes of democratization and constitutional reform in Latin America thus produced new "social questions" – social challenges they were forced to confront. National executives were forced to confront the policy demands that were bubbling up from below in order to attract voters, and to prevent civil unrest. National executives were also forced to confront the policy obligations that came directly from their national constitutions, and from the national laws that had followed from constitutional reform. Not unlike the social question that emerged in the early-1900s during industrialization, which incorporated labor as a new actor in Latin American politics, the social questions of the late-1900s involved new political actors who were gradually recognized and legitimated by government (Rossi 2015: 7). This time, however, a much wider range of societal groups were involved.

New Bureaucracies

The new social questions that emerged through democratization led to a second transformation in state institutions in Latin America: the construction of new national bureaucracies, run by policy experts who shared broad goals with activists outside the state. Because many of the government benefits and protections that emerged out of the constitutional reform process surrounded previously neglected issues, new or redesigned state agencies were required to enact and regulate them. National executives thus transformed existing bureaucracies and created additional state agencies in order to execute their responses to the social questions that had surfaced in the 1980s and 1990s.

Although comparative data on these new bureaucracies is still scarce, examples of this general trend abound in recent literature on social movements and public policy. Argentina's Ministry of Social Development was created in response to the "unemployment question" that had been made salient by the *Piquetero* movement (Rossi 2015: 13). Ecuador's CODENPE – a ministry-level agency in charge of development in black and indigenous communities – was created in response to indigenous mobilization (Chartock 2013: 62). In Brazil, where civic mobilization was particularly widespread, a vast array of new state agencies was created, such as the Ministry of Cities, the Ministry of Social Development, the Special Secretariat for the Promotion of Racial Equality (Paschel 2016: 132, 174) and the Special Secretariat for Women's Policies. Others were significantly redeveloped, such as the public prosecutor's office (*Ministério Público*) and the national environmental bureaucracy (Hochstetler and Keck 2007: 36–7). The development and redevelopment of central government agencies was a policy current that occurred simultaneous to, and worked occasionally in opposition to, the more high-profile trend toward decentralizing responsibility for government service provision.

In many cases, national executives recruited outside policy experts to build and manage these new arms of the state. National executives also recruited activists to join these government agencies, many of whom were policy experts themselves. In Colombia, black activists were recruited to lead the Office on Black Communities, created in 1993 (Paschel 2016: 157). Members of Argentina's unemployed workers' movement were given top posts in the Ministries of Social Development and Federal Planning (Rossi 2015: 11). Indigenous activists in Ecuador were recruited to lead the DINEIB, the national indigenous education agency created in 1988 (Chartock 2013: 63). This trend toward recruiting experts and activists to build new bureaucracies was so prevalent in Brazil that the term "*militantes no estado*" (activists in the state) entered into common parlance. A significant number of the bureaucrats in Brazil's newly developed state agencies had, thus, built long careers working on a single issue from both outside and inside government. These bureaucrats were not dependent on government employment for career advancement, and they had deep knowledge about the issue area for which they were in charge of policymaking.

In Brazil, more and more citizens who cared about expanding political inclusion also began to take civil service exams as a way of pushing forward their goals from the inside. Because these state agencies focused on building new government programs to serve non-elites, citizens who cared deeply about the social issues began to recognize that they could support traditionally marginalized groups through careers as civil servants. The bureaucrats who ran these government agencies – whether policy experts or career civil servants – held interests that differed fundamentally from the interests of bureaucrats in the pre-democratization period: to build national policies in support of formerly marginalized interests.

This process of building new national bureaucracies dramatically altered the incentives that structured state–society relations. These arms of the state were dedicated to building the policies and programs that new social movements had demanded. Consequently, the personnel who ran these state agencies shared broad goals with activists outside the state: to develop policy in support of traditionally marginalized interests. As I show in the final section of this chapter, these bureaucrats, when confronted with obstacles emanating from within government to the pursuit of their policy goals, were motivated to look to civil society for support.

New Policymaking Institutions

In Brazil, a third transformation in state institutions during democratization, the redesign of policymaking procedures around the principles of participatory governance, gave bureaucrats a structure for engaging civic activists as allies.[7] Participatory governance institutions incorporate citizens and civic organizations directly into the policy-making process by having them discuss and even vote on specific policy decisions. The most prevalent variety, participatory policy councils, involve joint state–society governance of the policy process by including civil-society representatives and employer representatives in discussions about the design and implementation of policies. Seen as a variant of direct democracy, they have been touted by leftist politicians and global intellectuals alike as a new avenue for citizens to represent their interests in government without depending on political parties as intermediaries. Participatory governance institutions also created a structure for activists and bureaucrats to develop shared norms and relationships of trust – bridging the state–society divide and creating opportunities for political alliances in times of crisis.

Although most existing scholarship depicts the spread of participatory institutions as a local-level phenomenon, participatory governance in Latin America has taken root at the national level as well (Mayka 2019a). In Brazil, national participatory institutions are abundant. As of 2016, participatory policymaking councils governed national policy in over fifty-six sectors of the state in such diverse areas as health, education, the environment, women's rights, energy policy, urban policy, crime and punishment, foreign trade, sports, and culture (Mayka 2019b). Other types of participatory institutions have spread as well, such as national public policy conferences, which are convoked periodically at the discretion of the national government or relevant national policy council

---

[7] On the causes and consequences of participatory governance in Latin America see Avritzer (2009), Cameron et al. (2012), Goldfrank (2011), Levalle et al. (2005, 2006, 2016), Mayka (2019b), McNulty (2011), Selee and Peruzzotti (2009), Wampler (2007), Wampler and McNulty (2011).

to elicit input from grassroots civil society activists about top policy problems and priorities in that policy sector (Mayka 2019b). Between 2003 and 2010, fifty-nine national public policy conferences were held, bringing together approximately seven million people – roughly 5 percent of Brazilian adults – to formulate policy proposals (Pogrebinschi and Samuels 2014: 321).

The restructuring of state policymaking bodies around participatory-governance principles created new institutional channels for government bureaucrats to build alliances with civic activists. Through these participatory spaces, civic activists began to meet with government bureaucrats several times a year to set policy priorities, develop proposals to address these priorities, and monitor their implementation (Mayka 2019b). As a result of their participation in these spaces, an expansive array of activists gained unprecedented access to state officials: not only regular face-to-face meeting time, but also the names and phone numbers of bureaucrats to contact with political concerns, or for clarification about new policy decisions or issues. By the same token, participatory governance committees also provided a channel for bureaucrats to call on activist leaders for advice and technical assistance in developing new policies, and even to engage activists in helping them draft national policy legislation and guidelines. As I preview in the final section of this chapter and then elaborate in Chapter 5, participatory governance institutions also provided channels for bureaucrats to use in mobilizing civic activists as political allies in support of their policy goals. As I will show in Chapter 6, the introduction of participatory governance as a structure for policymaking also provided local grassroots groups with new incentives to build lasting national advocacy coalitions.

TRANSITION TO NEOLIBERALISM

Paradoxically, neoliberal reforms produced the resources to sustain state-sponsored activism. As most scholars emphasize, neoliberal reforms undercut the corporatist system of state–society relations through the privatization of state-owned enterprises and the deregulation of industries, which limited the state's capacity to provide resources and subsidies for labor unions in return for their political support (Collier and Handlin 2009: 52–3). It is for this reason that many assume the neoliberal state no longer helps working-class groups to overcome collective action problems.[8] As I show next, however, just as neoliberal reforms undercut traditional government resources for unions, they also gave rise to sources of government funding for new and more diverse types of civic organizations.

In the 1990s, as part of the second wave of market reforms in the developing world, national governments outsourced the management of public service programs to nongovernmental organizations – often with encouragement by

---

[8] See, for example, Arce and Bellinger (2007), Kurtz (2004), Oxhorn and Ducatenzeiler (1998), Oxhorn (2006), Roberts (2005), Shadlen (2002).

international lending agencies. Across the region, governments ceded a significant degree of responsibility for social-service provision to non-state actors, using them to "fill gaps" in social service provision, provide "social safety nets" during times of economic liberalization or hardship, and to "streamline" the public service sector. This practice was seen as a neoliberal solution to the negative impacts of earlier market-oriented governance reforms in the social-service sector. Providing nonprofit associations with grants to manage health and development programs was viewed as a cost-effective means to assist the poorest groups of citizens who were unable to gain access to social services through market mechanisms. Thus, national executives and international lenders alike looked to civic organizations to solve the twin problems of inefficiency and weak bureaucratic capacity – one that went hand-in-hand with their ultimate goal of shrinking the state.

An overlooked effect of this method for shrinking the state was that it dramatically increased state subsidies for civic organizations across a range of policy sectors. Through this process of outsourcing public service provision, government grants were available for a dizzying array of civil society organizations, such as environmental groups, feminist groups, community health groups, and cultural organizations, to name but a few. As a result of this new global emphasis on "project funding" for civil society, the number of not-for-profit nongovernmental organizations (NGOs) across the developing world grew exponentially, with one study estimating over one million organizations in India alone (McGann and Johnstone 2006). Brazil is an exemplar of this phenomenon, where in the 1990s state actors institutionalized the practice of funding grassroots organizations to manage health and development projects across a wide array of policy areas.

While others have described this trend, most have emphasized the potential for project funding to coopt and fragment grassroots organizations. As many have shown, civil-society organizations that rely on donor funding are often hindered from engaging in long-term strategic planning by the short duration of most grants (Cooley and Ron 2002; Watkins, Swidler, and Hannan 2012). Others have argued that most contemporary nonprofit organizations – with small, inflexible operational budgets and a lean, often-volunteer staff – have few if any resources to divert toward supporting collaboration with other associations (Phillips 1991; Weir 1999). It has also been shown that competition for donor funding can produce tensions and rivalries within civil society networks (McCarthy and Zald 1977; Kriesi 1996). As Thayer (2010) argues, the boom in global funding for civil society in the developing world has exacerbated these divisions, especially between professionalized NGOs and grassroots membership organizations. Cooperation between NGOs and grassroots groups is thus fraught with tension, especially when it comes to determining unified policy stances and to selecting representatives to speak on behalf of the movement in government policy spaces.

Overlooked by existing approaches, however, another outcome of this model of outsourcing government service provision is that it provided state actors with the resources to support civic organization and mobilization around new policy issues. National bureaucrats now controlled new pockets of earmarked funding for supporting civil-society organizations to develop service projects. As I describe in Chapters 6 and 7, government bureaucrats who relied on outside mobilization to support their policy projects could loosely interpret the meaning of project funding – using such money to support political advocacy projects, and to help sustain national social-movement coalitions.

TRANSFORMING BRAZIL'S NATIONAL AIDS PROGRAM
INTO AN ISLAND OF EXCELLENCE

Between 1992 and 1994, Brazil's AIDS program metamorphosed from an underfunded area of the national healthcare bureaucracy to the "rich cousin of healthcare," characterized by capable bureaucrats and a strong, collaborative relationship between the national government and civil society organizations. The development of a strong national AIDS bureaucracy in Brazil has been attributed to a variety of factors. Certainly, social mobilization and public pressure played a role (Parker 1997; Raizer 1997). Other contingent factors were likely at play as well, such as personal support for investment in AIDS among high-ranking political officials (Nunn 2009: 56–60; Solano 2000: 83–4).[9] More striking, however, were the factors that did not affect the development of Brazil's national AIDS program. Leftist partisan politics almost certainly did not play a role. In fact, three different presidents led the two-year transformation of the program, ranging from a right-wing populist who was ultimately impeached to a former economic minister from the center-left. Nor did economic prosperity contribute to Brazil's decision to increase investment in a national AIDS program. To the contrary, the transformation was initiated during a period of economic and political crisis.

The transformation of Brazil's national AIDS program was even more surprising given that it was initiated during the waning days of what was otherwise a disastrous presidential administration led by the populist candidate Fernando Collor de Mello. Collor had been accused of widespread corruption across many sectors of government, including within the health sector. During his first two years in office, a variety of social and economic programs had suffered. The national AIDS program – even though it had never been a national priority (Solano 2000: 76) – was not immune. Resources had disappeared, international cooperation had deteriorated, and HIV prevention campaigns had ground to a halt (Parker 2003: 150–52). Collor's health minister – a conservative politician by the name of Alceni Guerra – even publicly stated that he was unconcerned about the AIDS epidemic (Solano 2000: 82). But in

[9] For more analyses of the development of Brazil's national AIDS policies in English, see Flynn (2015), Gauri and Lieberman (2006), Nunn (2009), Parker (2003). For analyses in Portuguese see Galvão (2000), Teixeira (1997).

early-1992, as a last-ditch attempt to increase his legitimacy, Collor replaced his minister of health (who had been a key suspect in the corruption scandals) with Adib Jatene, a renowned heart surgeon and an admired former health secretary for the state of São Paulo. Adib Jatene took it upon himself to bring back Lair Guerra to coordinate the national AIDS program. As Brazil's first national AIDS program director in the 1980s, Guerra had gradually begun to consolidate and institutionalize the national AIDS program until 1990, when Collor's first health minister ousted her. Following her replacement, nearly the entire technical team of the program had resigned in protest (Parker 2003: 150). When Jatene brought her back to the helm of the national AIDS program, she took up the project to rebuild national AIDS policy in Brazil with renewed vigor – together with the health minister, and with the support of the president.

Like most reformist bureaucrats in Brazil, Guerra faced the obstacle of patronage-oriented politicians in her effort to build a capable national AIDS program. Brazilian bureaucracy is often referred to as a bastion of clientelism, incompetence, and corruption. This image is in part a result of the large percentage of patronage-based appointments within the state. According to Schneider (1991), the president of Brazil is able to personally appoint over fifty thousand bureaucrats – in contrast to countries like the United States, where the president appoints a few thousand, or Japan, where the prime minister appoints only a few dozen (Schneider 1991: 6). Because of the highly politicized nature of bureaucratic appointments, the majority of personnel within state agencies are replaced with each change of administration. As a result, Brazilian bureaucrats have little time to become familiar with their jobs before leaving for another sector of the state; in turn, most state agencies are left with poorly trained personnel (Schneider 1991: 6). At the same time, resources for state agencies are highly unstable and subject to money laundering. Every year, Congress must approve bureaucratic budgets, and legislators regularly use this approval process to shift resources destined for state agencies toward their pet projects. In addition, funding for state agencies tends to disappear between the planning phase and the implementation phases of the policy process. Patronage politics has thus stymied state development through Brazil's modern political history.

While various presidents throughout modern history from Getúlio Vargas in the 1930s until now have set out to develop the Brazilian state, generations of political reformers have faced overpowering opposition by the powerful provincial oligarchs who benefit from the system of pork-barrel politics (Schneider 1991). As a result of such political constraints, no presidential administration has succeeded in fundamentally modernizing the system of bureaucracy – not even the military regime of the mid-twentieth century (Schneider 1991; Abrucio, Loureiro, and Pacheco 2010).

Traditionally, Brazilian presidents have sought to overcome such political and economic obstacles to building state capacity in what they deem to be priority policy sectors through a strategy that has been called "parallel administration" or, alternatively, "bureaucratic insulation" (Geddes 1990: 225–9;

Nunes 1997). Rather than reforming existing bureaucracies, which could garner opposition by the many interests that benefited from the system of political patronage, presidents would create new state programs outside the traditional structure of Brazilian bureaucracy and surround them with special rules and protections to insulate them from partisan politics – funding them by finding autonomous sources of revenue and depositing the funds directly into their bank accounts, without including them in the federal budget (Geddes 1990: 227). These agencies were consequently accountable only to the executive – not to the legislature – and, thus, managed to avoid meddling by politicians with their budgets and with their personnel recruitments (Geddes 1990: 228). This tradition of institutional layering imbued the Brazilian state with a split personality: corrupt and inefficient in some domains, while progressive and effective in others. High-performing state agencies in Brazil (such as the Foreign Service and the national development bank) are known as "pockets of efficiency" or "islands of excellence," because they have capable, hard-working bureaucrats, and relatively stable, transparent budgets but exist within a broader environment of patronage-based politics (Evans 1979; Geddes 1990).

Guerra used an updated version of the bureaucratic insulation strategy to build the national AIDS program: engaging international organizations as buffers to protect the program from patronage politics (Rich and Gómez 2012: 5–7). First, Guerra – together with the support of the Minister of Health, the Minister of the Economy, and the president – acquired a World Bank loan in 1994, for US$140 million, as a way to secure an autonomous revenue stream for the national AIDS program (World Bank 2004).[10] Second, Guerra contracted United Nations organizations to manage the national AIDS program – first with UNDP and later with UNESCO – using what is called a technical cooperation agreement (World Bank 1998). Through this agreement, UNESCO determined all the rules governing personnel recruitment, salaries, and budget disbursement for the national AIDS program, while Brazilian bureaucrats determined all the substantive aspects of AIDS policy (Stern 2005). This international assistance played a key role in transforming Brazil's national AIDS program from a relatively weak sector of the bureaucracy into a model sector of the Brazilian state.

At the most basic level, the financial capacity of the national AIDS program increased dramatically as a result of this international assistance. Whereas the national AIDS budget in 1991 had been a meager US$2.9 million, in 1995 the budget ballooned to US$160 million (Parker 2003: 154–55). Moreover, because it was the World Bank that provided the AIDS program's revenue and not Congress, its funding was not included in the national budget and did not

---

[10] Brazil had cooperated with several other international organizations during its first push to develop a national AIDS program beginning in 1988, including with the Pan-American Health Organization (PAHO) and the World Health Organization (WHO). However, the magnitude of this early international cooperation paled in comparison to Brazil's later cooperation with the World Bank.

require congressional approval. Consequently, the national AIDS program was protected from political interference by national legislators, and it was spared from cutbacks during the economic crises of the 1990s. This insulation from interference by politicians also strengthened the national AIDS program's policy-making autonomy, by allowing bureaucrats the freedom to use their budgets to develop controversial HIV prevention programs such as needle exchanges.

But even more important than the financial impact was the administrative impact of international assistance. By outsourcing the management of the national AIDS program to UNESCO, bureaucrats in the program could oper-ate much more efficiently than they could have if they were forced to confront the complex bureaucratic machine that has historically limited the Brazilian state's policymaking effectiveness (Câmara and Lima 2000: 59, Stern 2005). Comparing procedures for budgetary procurement represents this administra-tive difference. In most of Brazil's state agencies, complex procurement pro-cedures introduce long time lags between when a spending decision is made and when the funds are actually distributed. UNESCO, with its streamlined procurement requirements, dramatically reduced this lag time. According to one informant who was a career bureaucrat, the purchase of a new AIDS med-ication could take twelve months to be approved under Brazil's standard gov-ernment procedures, whereas under UNESCO's management, approving the purchase of a new medication took somewhere on the order of twelve days.

International assistance also allowed Guerra to recruit policy experts and activists to run the national AIDS program. Whereas most state employees in Brazil are subject to a rigorous public-sector exam and chosen on the basis of their scores, UNESCO rules freed the national AIDS program director to recruit and hire individuals with specialized expertise such as lawyers, epide-miologists, and anthropologists, who may not have been selected through a standardized procedure – or may not have been willing to invest the time and energy required to study for the more than four-hour exam. UNESCO also offered higher salaries than the standardized public-sector wage, providing a financial incentive to lure some of these highly qualified individuals into mak-ing the sacrifice of moving to the remote desert outpost that is Brazil's capital city (Nunn 2009; Stern 2005). As of 2011, all but nineteen of the 219 national AIDS program bureaucrats were hired as "consultants" through contracts with United Nations organizations (Arnquist, Ellner, and Weintraub 2011).

Through the technical cooperation with UNESCO, the National AIDS Program was thus populated by a cadre of expert specialists who were ded-icated to improving AIDS policy. Prior to 1994, AIDS policy experts worked primarily in the private sector, in public-health schools, or in state-level and municipal health secretariats. By the mid-1990s, however, dozens of activists, doctors, and scientists had flocked to Brasília to work for the new National AIDS Program. According to one account, more than half the bureaucrats employed by the national AIDS program in 2011 had worked previously in AIDS NGOs – including the vice-director (Arnquist, Ellner, and Weintraub

2011). In contrast to the popular image of the Brazilian bureaucrat as either corrupt or uninterested, Brazil's national AIDS program was suddenly populated by dedicated workers who had uprooted their comfortable lives in Brazil's more cosmopolitan centers for the purpose of building a path-breaking national AIDS program.

To a certain extent, these advances in the national AIDS programs trickled down to the state level. As Silvia Ramos, the former AIDS activist from Rio, recollected:

AIDS programs also began to grow within state-level health secretariats. And by contrast, the program for variola had had a single bureaucrat working in it for the last fifty years. The program for pneumonia was four guys with a typewriter, for the last two hundred years. These other programs didn't have anyone; they had nothing. But the AIDS program already had a computer, it had new bureaucrats, it had people working under contract.[11]

Suddenly state-level AIDS programs were better equipped and better staffed than other long-standing programs in the public health sector, creating some tension and competition among bureaucrats from different programs within the public health sector. However, as I detail in Chapter 5, the autonomy and capacity of subnational AIDS programs varied significantly across states.

The transformation of Brazil's National AIDS Program into a well-funded, politically autonomous, and administratively efficient national bureaucracy translated into striking policy advances. Free condoms were made widely available in public facilities and distributed in abundance during events such as Brazil's famous Carnival. Needle exchange programs were developed that offered clean syringes to tens of thousands of injection drug users (Sekles, *Population Reference Bureau*, 2001). While the effect of Brazil's AIDS policy model on the national incidence of HIV has not been rigorously assessed,[12] assessment of HIV/AIDS services compare quite favorably to the overall quality of national healthcare services in Brazil.[13] AIDS policy thus emerged as Brazil's flagship social-sector program, touted by politicians as an example of great post-transition strides in social sector development. In contrast to Brazil's beleaguered healthcare system, the national AIDS program was known popularly as "the healthcare system gone right."

[11] Interview with Silvia Ramos, founding member and first director of the Brazilian Interdisciplinary Association for AIDS (*ABIA*), September 3, 2008.

[12] The inability to assess the impact of policy on HIV outcomes is an important yet global problem, which is one of the reasons why the global AIDS community is still copying national policy models from countries that seem to have had success in reducing their incidence of the virus in the somewhat blind hope that the policies are indeed the causal factors. However, the causal impact of national policy models versus other epidemiological factors in reducing AIDS incidence has already come into question in several renowned success cases, such as Uganda.

[13] See, for example, Flynn (2008), Gauri and Lieberman (2006), Nunn (2009), Parker (2009), Stern (2005a), World Bank (2005).

IMAGE 4.1. *The national STD/AIDS department office building*

In addition to its policy implications, the redesign of Brazil's AIDS Program laid the foundation for state-sponsored activism to emerge as a new national model of civic organization and mobilization. In contrast to many older state agencies, the new national AIDS program was run by bureaucrats who were dedicated to policy reform and who enjoyed enough autonomy to develop their own strategies for achieving these policy goals. As I describe below, the national AIDS program also incorporated institutionalized mechanisms for cooperation between bureaucrats and civic organizations. Thus, when Brazil's AIDS-sector bureaucrats encountered obstacles to directly achieving their policy goals, they could easily call on allies within civil society to support them from outside the state.

Participatory Governance Institutions

Guerra offered civil society organizations institutionalized mechanisms for participating in the policy process by basing policymaking procedures on the principles of participatory governance. While the first national-level AIDS commission (*CNAIDS*) bringing together state and society had been created in 1986, as an ad hoc response to the public health emergency, the number of participatory governance institutions within the national AIDS bureaucracy expanded dramatically after 1994. (See Figure 4.1.) By 1998, participatory governance institutions had

IMAGE 4.2. *National HIV prevention campaigns*

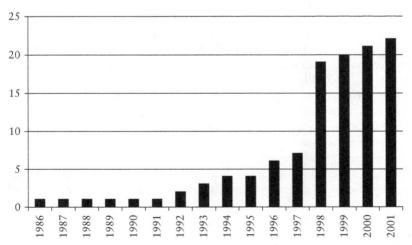

FIGURE 4.1. *Number of national government councils or commissions with seats allotted for AIDS activists (1986–2001)*

been created to oversee almost every area of AIDS policy, from the highest-level challenges to the most minor of issues. At the highest level of policy, for example, CNAIDS debated national AIDS policy priorities and the national AIDS budget (Spink 2003). The Commission for Engagement with Social Movements (CAMS) was developed to discuss the role of different social movements in Brazil's national AIDS policy. Other participatory AIDS policy institutions included the Vaccine Commission and the Commission for Inter-sectoral Monitoring of STD/AIDS policy. At the same time, a changing array of informal "working groups" structured state–society collaboration over specific AIDS policy concerns; these include the Committee on Therapeutic Consensus, the Committee on Pharmaceutical Assistance, the Committee for Adherence to Medical Regimens, the Committee on Epidemiology, the Committee for Ethics in Research, the Committee on Men who have Sex with Men, and the Committee on Lesbians.

In addition, Guerra built a new sector of the federal bureaucracy that was dedicated solely to developing the relationship between the national AIDS program and civil society groups. Created in 1993, the Sector for Engagement with NGOs (later renamed the Unit for Engagement with Civil Society and Human Rights, or CSHR unit for short) was one of the seven core units of the federal AIDS bureaucracy, with twelve employees and commanding a large percentage of the national budget for HIV prevention.[14] Their main programmatic objective was to monitor and support the activities of civic AIDS groups across Brazil.

While these new institutions were designed initially according to a technocratic logic, they also laid the foundation for future political collaboration between bureaucrats and activists. Suddenly, AIDS activists had the names and phone numbers of bureaucrats to contact with political concerns, or for clarification about new policy decisions or issues. In this way, the new lines of communication with national bureaucrats helped activists to influence national AIDS policy through back channels. Participatory governance committees also made it easy for bureaucrats to call on activist leaders for advice and technical assistance in developing new policy frameworks. National AIDS bureaucrats were encouraged by this ease of communication with civic groups to engage activists in drafting national AIDS policy legislation and guidelines. At the same time, participatory governance committees helped civic AIDS organizations to serve as government watchdogs. By providing a regular forum for civic groups and government bureaucrats to interact, participatory policymaking bodies allowed bureaucrats and citizens to rapidly exchange information about on-the-ground problems they detected or about government misbehavior, and to develop problem-solving strategies together. Participatory governance institutions in Brazil's AIDS sector, thus, provided the structure for future political alliances.

---

[14] Personal communication with Rubens Duda, bureaucrat in the Unit for Engagement with Civil Society and Human Rights, July 26, 2010.

OUTSOURCING PUBLIC-SERVICE DELIVERY TO NGOS

Guerra also instituted the practice of outsourcing HIV prevention projects to civic organizations. The development of competitive grants for civic AIDS groups was not in its original intent designed to support civic advocacy. Rather, it was broadly viewed as a neoliberal strategy for developing HIV programs by outsourcing the administration of prevention projects to non-state, nonprofit organizations. But by providing government funding for hundreds of new civic associations to invest themselves in the fight against AIDS, national AIDS bureaucrats introduced a significant new flow of funding to support grassroots political organization and mobilization around AIDS policy.

The budget for funding civic AIDS groups was at first provided by the World Bank, framed as an apolitical, technocratic strategy for "outsourcing HIV prevention services to nonprofit organizations" (World Bank 2004: 7). Using a logic that centered on the "competitive advantage" of civic organizations in reaching marginalized communities,[15] the World Bank loan delegated responsibility to "non-governmental organizations and civil society organizations (NGOs/CSOs) ... for carrying out projects covering a range of activities, including: prevention, human rights, care and treatment" (World Bank 2004: 5). Correspondingly, ten percent of Brazil's national HIV prevention budget was earmarked for civil society projects, which amounted to a total of US$25.5 million in funding for civic AIDS groups between 1994 and 2001 (World Bank 2004: 53).[16] Given that the Brazilian government had never before instituted the practice of contracting civil society groups to implement social-service projects, this constituted a dramatic jump in the amount of money available for civil society organizations in Brazil.

This practice also institutionalized the flow of state resources to civil society groups in Brazil's AIDS policy sector. While no budgetary data are available for the years prior to 1994, it is widely acknowledged that federal funding for civil society was essentially non-existent in these years, and what little money was distributed was based largely on personal connections between elite activists and government insiders (Nunn 2009: 55). By contrast, over 500 civil society projects were funded between the years 1994 and 1998 (World Bank 1998). In an even more striking contrast to pre-1994 numbers, Brazil's national AIDS program funded an astounding 2,884 civil society projects between the years 1999 and 2003, with an average of 577 projects per year. (See Figure 4.2.)

At the same time, the massive influx of resources for civil society projects dramatically increased the number of civil society organizations working on AIDS in Brazil after 1994. Whereas several dozen nongovernmental organizations in Brazil worked on AIDS in the late 1980s (Galvão 2000: 60–84), 508 AIDS associations were officially registered with the National AIDS Program

---

[15] Interviews with three anonymous World Bank officials, November 14, 2006, November 14, 2006, January 7, 2007.
[16] See also Boyd and Garrison, 1999.

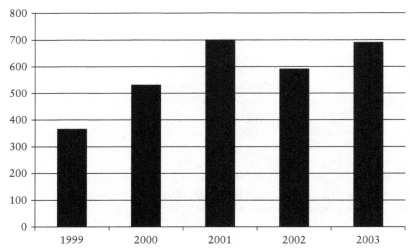

FIGURE 4.2. *Number of federally-funded civic AIDS projects per year (1999–2003)*

by 2002 (Ministério da Saúde 2003). This growth in the number of AIDS associations was most dramatic in Brazil's underdeveloped regions (the North, Northeast, and Center west), due to the National AIDS Program's particular focus on mobilizing civic associations in underserved areas. In the late 1980s, AIDS associations had been almost entirely concentrated in the four industrialized states of São Paulo, Rio de Janeiro, Porto Alegre, and Bahia. By 2002, however, AIDS associations existed in all twenty-six states of Brazil – including in the North and Northeast, Brazil's two most impoverished regions, which are covered largely by jungle and desert, rank lowest nationally on levels of education and income, and have been dominated politically until recently by land barons. (See Figure 4.3.)

Federal funding for NGOs also increased the number of AIDS associations within already-established centers of civic AIDS mobilization, such as the Southeastern states of Rio de Janeiro and São Paulo. In 2009, in those two states alone, I personally counted 231 officially registered "AIDS associations," an additional 100 community-based organizations belonging to an AIDS prevention network, and approximately 1,000 associations distributing government-provided condoms.

While the World Bank was the source of funding for nongovernmental groups, Brazilian bureaucrats determined how the money was distributed. According to Teixeira, who was a key participant in Brazil's negotiations with the World Bank over civil-society participation:

For us, we wanted [to fund] civil-society [groups] with a community base, not tied to governments, not-for-profit, and who shared our vision of public health. [By contrast],

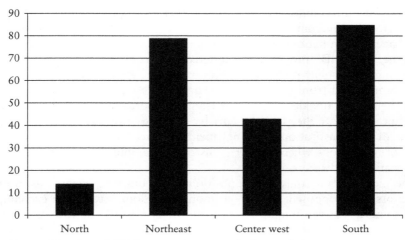

FIGURE 4.3. *Number of AIDS associations outside the southwest, 2002*

the Bank, as a neoliberal institution, worked a lot more with large institutions [that were] professionalized, most of them [with strong ties to] the American government... [When] the Global Fund and the American delegation [from the World Bank], refer to civil society, they're talking about pharmaceutical companies, health provider companies, medical technology companies. It's a totally different political vision [from ours].

So some of the consultants from the World Bank pressured us to focus our engagement with civil society on those kinds of groups, and they wanted us to pick them a priori as our policy partners. And we imposed a different format on the [loan] agreement ... we imposed a public selection process instead.[17]

Numerous accounts corroborate his claim that Brazil's new bureaucrats designed the system of providing project funding for NGOs. What's more, several civic activists themselves participated as consultants in designing the World Bank loan, playing an especially central role in areas related to funding for civil society.[18] As I describe next, bureaucrats in Brazil's national AIDS program opened space for political activism among federally funded civil-society groups by shaping the rules that determined how funding for civil society would be distributed.

THE EMERGENCE OF STATE-SPONSORED ACTIVISM: THE TREATMENT ACCESS CAMPAIGN

By the late 1990s, a nascent political alliance between bureaucrats and civic advocacy groups was already emerging as bureaucrats in the national AIDS

---

[17] Interview with Paulo Teixeira, Director of the National AIDS Program 2000–2003, November 26, 2008.
[18] Source: multiple informant interviews.

program began to confront opposition to their program-building goals from other actors in government. In a state composed of multiple branches and dozens of agencies, in national and subnational levels of government, bureaucrats in the national AIDS program encountered numerous and varied obstacles to advancing their policy preferences from within the state, both from the legislative branch and from other executive agencies. As these bureaucrats developed their program, designing increasingly elaborate national AIDS policy guidelines, the more they found themselves in a situation that Abers and Keck (2013: 6) call "institutional entanglement" – forced to confront a complex array of institutions where power is distributed among many heterogeneous organizations and actors.

The most blatant source of opposition was from religiously conservative legislators, who opposed policies promoting condom use, needle exchanges, or in some cases even human-rights protections for HIV positive Brazilians. One example of such opposition in Congress was a legislative bill from 1999 that proposed to quarantine "aidetic" prisoners in special jail cells.[19] But AIDS-sector bureaucrats also faced more subtle opposition to their goals – especially in promoting AIDS treatment access, which involved relatively large and long-term investments of government money. Bureaucrats in Brazil's AIDS policy sector confronted these various sources of opposition to their policy goals by mobilizing civil society groups, with whom they had already developed close and cooperative relations, as political allies.

One of the most important areas of political cooperation during this time period was around access to anti-retroviral medications (ARVs). In 1996, following a long series of legal appeals by AIDS activists, President of the Senate José Sarney introduced a bill guaranteeing all Brazilian citizens access to AIDS treatment. (See Nunn 2009: 87–91.) Known as Sarney's law (*a Lei de Sarney*), this piece of legislation stands as one of the major turning points in the development of Brazil's national AIDS program. The law also provided new challenges for federal bureaucrats, as they scrambled to figure out how to administer and finance this policy.

Bureaucrats in Brazil's national AIDS program looked to civic advocacy groups for crucial support in confronting the challenges engendered by Sarney's Law. In 1997, for example, bureaucrats used the support of civic activists to help them overcome opposition from the health minister to increasing the national budget for ARVs. After access to ARVs was guaranteed by law, more Brazilians began to get tested for HIV. With the increase in demand for ARVs, the congressionally approved national budget for ARV medications that year was inadequate to keep stocks from going empty. Health minister Fernando Albuquerque, however, was opposed to increasing national spending on ARV medication, commenting that "it was unjust that the government was obligated

---

[19] This proposed law was registered as PL 289/1999. For the complete text, see www.camara.gov .br/proposicoesWeb/fichadetramitacao?idProposicao=15260 (last accessed February 11, 2018).

to spend $428 million reals on a disease that only affects 55,000 people" (cited in Nunn 2009: 99). In response, national AIDS bureaucrats and civic activists coordinated on public pressure campaigns. The national AIDS program director, Pedro Chequer, took to the media himself to publicly lobby Congress and the health minister for increased funding (Nunn 2009: 98). AIDS activists complemented the national program director's advocacy by taking to the streets. According to Nunn (2009), "NGOs such as Pela VIDDA and ABIA, and others nationwide threatened to flood the courts if the health Ministry cut drug expenditure. NGOs protested in the streets for a week, followed the Health Minister to each of his speaking events, protesting loudly each time Albuquerque spoke" (Nunn 2009: 99). These NGO lobby and protest campaigns were not only coordinated with the national AIDS program staff but also financed by the national AIDS program. As Chequer described to me at interview, he actively subsidized their advocacy campaign by funding their research on ARVs, and by feeding them insider information.[20]

National bureaucrats also used the support of civic activists to overcome opposition from the United States to lowering Brazil's purchasing price of ARVs on the international market. Like most other middle-income countries, Brazil had by the late-1990s conformed to global standards for recognizing pharmaceutical patents (Shadlen 2017: 110–38). Because ARVs were new inventions, most were still patented, making them particularly expensive. By 2000, Brazil needed to significantly reduce its purchasing cost of ARVs so that it could continue supplying the drugs to the growing number of Brazilians who had tested positive for HIV (Flynn 2015: 95–119). To accomplish this goal, Brazil needed to either negotiate significant price reductions from pharmaceutical companies or find a way around patent regulations and produce its own low-cost generic drugs (Flynn 2015: 124–45; Shadlen 2017: 193–223). Brazil's national health minister, José Serra, who had been appointed to replace the former minister and was strongly in favor of AIDS treatment access, pursued both of these potential solutions – and made this strategy public at a press conference in 2000 (Nunn, 123). However, the United States, strongly encouraged by the pharmaceutical industry lobby, responded to this declaration by threatening Brazil with trade sanctions. This led Brazil's national AIDS program into a prolonged battle with the United States and the multinational pharmaceutical industry, which played out in multiple international arenas between 2000 and 2001 (Flynn 2015: 95–119). Despite their work, Brazil lacked the political and economic clout to win this conflict by direct negotiation with pharmaceutical companies, or through the World Trade Organization.

Consequently, the health minister and the national AIDS program director pursued victory over the United States through an international public opinion campaign, using the support of both international and domestic advocacy

---

[20] Interview with Pedro Chequer, Director of the National AIDS Program 1996–2000, December 16, 2008.

groups. According to Marco Viana, the health ministry's own international diplomat:

Our idea was that the Health Ministry, working with Itamaraty [Brazil's Foreign Affairs Ministry], was going to win over international public opinion. Our strategy was *not* to defeat the US government; the balance of power was not in our favor. The only way to win is to change the American public's opinion, and the opinion of the world. So that was our strategy, at the WHO, at the Human Rights Commission, at the WTO, with other NGOs, with the New York Times and other countries, to convince the American public to support us." (cited in Nunn 2009: 125)

Because Brazil was weaker economically than the United States, the weight of international public opinion was key to its success in reducing the cost of ARVs to an affordable level.

In pursuing this international public opinion campaign, the national AIDS program director relied on the support of Brazil's AIDS activists. Not only did he mobilize grassroots AIDS groups in Brazil to rally the support of the global AIDS movement in favor of the Brazilian government, but he also mobilized them to rabble rouse during international negotiations and call the attention of the press. According to Paulo Teixeira (the architect of São Paulo's AIDS program, who by 2000 had taken over as the national program director):

One thing we did [in our campaign] was to ask for the support of the big international NGOs like Doctors Without Borders, Oxfam, Amnesty ... a lot of them. Evidently, national and international NGOs are always a little hesitant, or careful, supporting government campaigns. That's the nature of NGOs. So when we launched our own campaign, we mobilized domestic NGOs at the same time as we mobilized international NGOs, asking the Brazilian NGOs to testify that our campaign wasn't being driven by a suspect set of interests or being driven by electoral interests.

A second [thing we did] was to include Brazilian NGOs in all of our international delegations, in all of the Brazilian delegations we sent to international conferences. [The impact of this strategy] was very striking, for example, in July of 2001 (during the meeting of the UN Commission on Human Rights, when Brazil attempted to pass a resolution calling for access to essential medicines). NGOs were part of the Brazilian delegation, and they were extremely active in the assembly. So after that event, [funding NGOs to attend international conferences] became a regular practice too.[21]

In other words, the support of Brazil's AIDS advocacy organizations – who could vouch for the Brazilian government's good intentions, thus throwing the weight of international public opinion behind Brazil – was key.

From a global policy perspective, the importance of Brazil's Treatment Access Campaign cannot be overstated. With Sarney's Law in 1996, Brazil

---

[21] Interview with Paulo Teixeira.

became the first country to guarantee access to ARVs for its citizens and to make access to treatment a centerpiece of its national AIDS policy. In focusing on expanding access to AIDS treatment, Brazil stood against the international policy consensus of the time that purchasing anti-retroviral drugs was an inefficient use of limited funds for AIDS programs. By holding fast to its promise of providing universal access to AIDS treatment in the face of opposition by transnational corporations, and showing a significant national reduction in HIV prevalence as a result, Brazil paved the way for a new global AIDS policy consensus to emerge in the 2000s.

Brazil was thus transformed from a maverick into a global AIDS model. Rather than criticizing Brazil for wasting funds, the global AIDS policy community began instead to praise Brazil's treatment program as a key component of its success on HIV prevention. This new view on Brazil's national AIDS policy is exemplified by the following excerpt of a 2005 World Bank evaluation:

Brazil has invested heavily on prevention and treatment of HIV/AIDS and STIs, providing condoms to highly vulnerable groups, and antiretroviral treatment to all identified patients that qualify for it, free of charge. As a result, Brazil has been able to contain the epidemic below 1% of adult population; and has halved the number of AIDS-related deaths. While early estimates indicated that Brazil would have 1.2 million people living with HIV/AIDS in 2000, the country has now about 600,000 people infected; 364,000 HIV/AIDS cases were notified since 1980, of which 253,000 are presently followed by the Program; 158,000 people are on treatment with anti-retroviral drugs, ensuring a survival of 58 months, comparable to survival for AIDS in OECD countries. Consequently, AIDS mortality has decreased 50% with 90,000 deaths prevented; morbidity decreased 70% and hospitalizations 80%. (World Bank 2005b)

Internationally, thirty-one countries adopted Brazil's prevention and treatment guidelines between the years 2001 and 2003 (Jones, Chicago Tribune, June 8, 2003). The foreign press published articles with headlines such as "Brazil Becomes Developing World Model for HIV/AIDS Treatment, Prevention Strategy" (Kaiser Health News Network June 10, 2003) "What can the world learn from Brazil's experience of dealing with AIDS?" (The Economist, July 28, 2005). In 2003, the World Health Organization (WHO) appointed Paulo Teixeira to design its global AIDS strategy.

From the perspective of state–society relations, Brazil's treatment access campaign is also an important example of how new institutions in the AIDS policy sector facilitated the development of a political collaboration between bureaucrats and civic advocacy groups. However, providing anti-retroviral drugs is only one dimension of the complex set of policy challenges that national bureaucrats faced in advancing their national goals for AIDS treatment and prevention. As Chapter 5 will show, the decentralization of AIDS policy administration in the mid-2000s introduced a new policy challenge

for national AIDS bureaucrats – to ensure that governors and mayors implemented their national AIDS policies. During this period, it became important
to national bureaucrats to connect to local civic advocacy groups in the
more far-flung regions of Brazil – groups who could monitor and pressure
the mayors and governors who cared little about investing their funds and
human resources in building AIDS programs.

5

Expanding the Movement from Above

Between 1998 and 2010, the AIDS movement gradually ballooned from a few dozen civic advocacy groups to more than a thousand associations. Unlike the first wave of the AIDS movement among cosmopolitans, the movement's expansion occurred largely in less-developed regions; with the movement's new grassroots leaders hailing from a diverse range of socioeconomic backgrounds. By 2010, the AIDS movement reflected the face of Brazil, cutting across class, race, gender and regional divides. Also unlike the first wave of the movement, which mobilized in the context of a public health emergency, the AIDS movement expanded just as the AIDS crisis was ending in Brazil – after the central government had built a globally pioneering national AIDS program and committed to providing all HIV-positive Brazilians with antiretroviral drug therapy. This unexpected trajectory – the expansion of civic activism into increasingly poor and isolated communities just as the government was meeting the movement's demands – cannot be explained by the grievances, resources, or political opportunities that drove the initial mobilization of the movement.

How, then, can we explain the growth of Brazil's AIDS movement? Civic mobilization depends in part on grassroots leaders who have resources and opportunities, as well as the skills and motivation to make their voices heard. The poor and isolated are often lacking in both resources and opportunities, suggesting that industrialized, urban areas with a large middle class are most likely to have a strong and active civil society. Brazil's landscape, with its rural majority and long history of political and economic oppression, is often seen as exceptionally inhospitable for civil-society development. How did these new grassroots leaders acquire the resources and the opportunities to take on AIDS advocacy?

I argue in this chapter that the expansion of the movement depended in part on the actions of federal bureaucrats in the national AIDS program, who helped to mobilize grassroots organizations in new regions as AIDS policy advocates by providing them with resources and opportunities to access the state. These bureaucrats provided resources to new groups by expanding funding for HIV/AIDS-related projects across Brazil. This project funding led vast numbers of new civic organizations in all twenty-six states to start working on AIDS. Bureaucrats in the national AIDS program provided these new grassroots groups with opportunities to access the state through invitations to participate in government policymaking circles. By opening space for grassroots groups to participate in AIDS policy discussions inside government, bureaucrats granted new organizations with a significant and previously unheard-of opportunity to influence AIDS policy from the inside.

Bureaucrats in the national AIDS program were motivated to expand independent civic organization and mobilization to help them confront a new threat to their goals: AIDS policy decentralization. In the 1990s, national governments across Latin America devolved responsibility for managing social-sector programs to state and municipal governments – part of the second wave of market reforms in the region, and promoted by international development experts as a way to increase government transparency and accountability. Yet at the same time, decentralization reduced the amount of control that reform-minded national bureaucrats had to ensure that the new policies they designed were actually implemented. Whereas pre-established civic groups could help national bureaucrats in the AIDS policy sector confront opposition at the national level of government, they were often unable to help federal bureaucrats face challenges at lower levels of government – as such challenges were most prevalent in states without an already strong and active civil society mobilized around AIDS policy. National AIDS Program bureaucrats thus attempted to ensure the successful implementation of their policies by mobilizing the new population of civic AIDS organizations to monitor the actions of local politicians in politically corrupt or socially conservative states and pressure them to conform to national policy guidelines. AIDS bureaucrats launched this top–down mobilizing campaign through two key mechanisms: providing *resources* for civil society that centered on political advocacy, and providing *opportunities* for new civic AIDS organizations to become active in AIDS policymaking institutions as well as in the judicial and legislative arenas.

MORE MONEY, MORE PROBLEMS

[W]e are facing the following paradox: on the one hand, there is access to antiretroviral treatment, falling mortality rates, and a decrease in hospitalizations; but on the other hand, it is hard to get a [hospital] bed, a laboratory exam, and medication for opportunistic infections.

Raxach 2005

The federal bureaucrats who were hired into the national AIDS program in the mid-1990s during the period of institutional transformation continued to confront challenges to advancing their AIDS policy goals in the late-1990s and early-2000s despite their relative abundance of resources and despite their relative autonomy of action. The three core policy challenges of the 1980s – treatment and care for the sick, HIV prevention, and combating stigma and discrimination – had not disappeared but, rather, had become more complex. In the early 2000s, the decentralization of AIDS policy posed a new challenge – to ensure adequate implementation of national policy guidelines at the state and local levels. The strong challenges faced by these committed federal bureaucrats are surprising given that the design of the national AIDS program was regarded by many as the best in the world due to its heavy financial investment in combating AIDS, its promise of universal access to anti-retroviral medicines (ARVs), and its collaborative relationship with civic advocacy groups. Yet, as Abers and Keck (2013) note, institutional design alone is not sufficient in a complex environment for bureaucrats to influence how others behave.

Treatment and Care

From the 1980s to the 2000s, the challenge of providing treatment and care for AIDS patients had increased enormously in complexity. This new complexity resulted in large part from the discovery of ARVs and, subsequently, the national political promise to provide free access to all Brazilians. As a consequence of these medical and political advances, a central AIDS policy question became how to acquire, pay for, and distribute each ARV drug. This challenge was constantly evolving as resistance built to existing medications and as new drugs were developed as a result – requiring Brazil's national AIDS treatment guidelines to be frequently rewritten.

Another complicating factor in the challenge to provide adequate treatment for AIDS, closely related to the first, was the constant discovery of new medical ailments resulting from HIV, as well as from the drugs used to treat it. Since HIV is a virus that infects the immune system, it dramatically increases the likelihood that an individual will suffer from what are called "opportunistic infections," which take advantage of the body's weakened ability to protect itself. Tuberculosis is the most prominent among opportunistic infections and is now the number one cause of death among AIDS patients. But the number of opportunistic infections that threaten AIDS patients extends far beyond TB, ranging from Hepatitis C to viral infections that lead to blindness. In addition, the ARV drugs developed to combat HIV each carry their own side effects, from ailments such as excess fat deposits in the face and stomach, to life-threatening problems such as cancer, heart disease, and the increased likelihood of stroke.

Due to the fact that these medical ailments affect a population that is broader than AIDS patients, treatment for them tended to be financed and administered by other health-sector bureaucracies, which possessed neither the financial endowment nor administrative capacity of the national AIDS program (World Bank 2010). According to the president of the Network of People Living with HIV/AIDS in the state of Rio de Janeiro:

The Ministry of Health spends an absurd quantity of resources to treat HIV/AIDS, to buy anti-retroviral [drugs] ... but it doesn't spend a single cent to treat opportunistic infections. It's that old story: the body's covered but the ass is hanging out.[1]

As a result, Brazil provided citizens with poor access to treatment for the co-infections and collateral effects that went along with HIV. This lies in contrast to Brazilians' comparatively strong access to antiretroviral treatment – for combating the direct effects of HIV – which set Brazil apart as a global model for AIDS treatment (World Bank 2010).

During this time period, many of the old AIDS policy challenges persisted. Strikingly, while medical knowledge about how the virus was transmitted and could be treated had advanced dramatically since the 1980s, providing adequate clinical and hospital care for AIDS patients continued to be a major challenge in the 2000s. Echoing the quote in Chapter 2 by the founding member of *ABIA* who reminisced about coming to the aid of desperate individuals turned away by hospitals, in 2005 a newer member of *ABIA* lodged the following complaint:

Every day more people are getting in touch with ABIA looking for help getting medical attention, or simply [for help] figuring out what the fastest way to get their HIV test results would be. (Raxach 2005)

One of the principal problems with patient care that continued to plague AIDS officials and activists was late diagnosis, which in the 2000s was still a major cause of AIDS-related deaths. In 2008, a study commissioned by the Ministry of Health found that 44 percent of AIDS patients had begun their treatment later than recommended, and that 67 percent of these had failed to start treatment until their CD4 cell count had fallen to less than 200 (Barbieri 2008: 18). Delays of up to several months in processing CD4 and viral load tests, which are necessary to prescribe drug therapy for HIV, similarly prevented Brazilians from accessing AIDS care (Valor Econômico 2006).

Hospital beds for AIDS patients were also still in short supply through the 2000s, as were trained doctors. In one of the main AIDS clinics in the city of Rio de Janeiro, for example, there were only three infectious disease specialists in 2010 to attend to 1,500 AIDS patients (Baldioti 2010). Finally, AIDS clinics themselves were also in short supply. According to a 2007 study conducted by the state health secretariat of São Paulo, the municipalities with centers

---

[1] Interview with Willian Amaral, President of *RNP+* Rio de Janeiro and President of the AIDS NGO Forum of Rio de Janeiro, August 6, 2008.

for AIDS testing and counseling (CTCs) covered only 49 percent of Brazil's population and 69 percent of AIDS cases; and among these CTCs, 30 percent lacked the basic infrastructure necessary to provide adequate clinical services (Barbieri and Ferrari 2007).

HIV Prevention

As HIV spread nationally over the course of the 1990s, from a few urban epicenters into a range of underdeveloped areas, national AIDS bureaucrats also faced increasingly complex barriers to the development and implementation of effective HIV prevention campaigns. Whereas AIDS had spread initially in Brazil among circles of gay men who were relatively well-off, by the 1990s, infections began to shift to much poorer subpopulations – and more broadly, to women and children (World Bank 1998: 1). Geographically, the virus was spreading from the wealthy zones of the Southeast into the poorer states of the Northeast and beyond (World Bank 1998: 1).

The economic marginalization and diffuseness of the communities that were affected by AIDS beginning in the mid-1990s posed new challenges to developing and disseminating effective HIV prevention messages (Biehl 2007). Gay men in 1980s Brazil had been wary of government messages, due to the state-sanctioned discrimination they had suffered during the military regime. But they were easy to reach by civic AIDS activists, many of whom were themselves members of the gay community. In the 1990s, however, the number of subpopulations affected by AIDS had ballooned, and the list of "high risk" groups grew to include not only intravenous (IV) drug users and sex workers, but also miners, truck drivers, indigenous groups, women, and the poor (World Bank 1998: Annex).[2] Gay men lacked cultural inroads into these new communities. Moreover, these subpopulations were often dispersed and fragmented. Whereas HIV prevention messages in the gay community could be disseminated efficiently, often through word-of-mouth, disseminating HIV prevention messages among miners, truck drivers, and other groups required new strategies that were tailored to the cultural and social codes of each different subpopulation. National AIDS Program officials, thus, faced the new challenge of reaching a wide swath of communities that existed at the margins of society and the economy.

The problem of reaching economically marginalized subpopulations was exacerbated by the stronger presence of religious institutions within poor communities. Brazil is both highly religious and religiously diverse, with Catholic, Evangelical and Afro-Brazilian religions blending to form a wide array of belief systems that vary regionally. Each of these religious traditions posed different

---

[2] Use of the term "risk group" is now seen as stigmatizing because it insinuates that people (rather than particular behaviors) are risky. "Risky behavior" is the term currently accepted by the global health community.

potential obstacles to HIV prevention. Some considered AIDS to be a punishment from God for immoral behavior; others opposed the use of condoms; and still others proposed that AIDS could be cured through prayer alone. Developing HIV prevention messages that resonated within a diverse set of religious communities required new strategies (Oliveira 2006; Souza 2008b). It also required building relationships of cooperation with organizations that tended to differ greatly in their values, culture, and philosophies from the leftist activists – many of whom were gay – who were in charge of AIDS policy development.

Combating Stigma and Discrimination

Stigma and discrimination also continued to present challenges to national AIDS bureaucrats. Gender and sexuality-based discrimination and violence was still common, especially against LGBT people and sex workers. Such discrimination was seen as a key contributor to HIV, because it led these populations to hide their behavior – complicating government efforts to encourage HIV prevention. Despite national policies to protect people with HIV/AIDS, direct AIDS-based discrimination and stigma also persisted in the 2000s, especially at the local level. In some cases, enforcement of anti-discrimination policies was weak. In other cases, political leaders in socially conservative states were actually proposing discriminatory policies and legislation. A 2009 legislative proposal in the state of Rio de Janeiro, for example, would have required the health secretariat to publish the names and information of all residents with HIV (O Globo 2009b). In poor and rural communities outside the reaches of state institutions, egregious human rights violations still occurred. In 2008, for example, drug traffickers in the state of Rio were escorting *favela* residents to AIDS clinics, forcing them to take rapid-result HIV tests, and expelling those with positive results from their communities (O Globo 2008).

Policy Implementation in a Decentralized System

In addition to the persistence of old policy challenges, the decentralization of authority over AIDS policy to state and municipal governments posed a new challenge to federal bureaucrats. Fiscal and administrative decentralization was a common trend in the 1990s, part of the second wave of market reforms in Latin America. Promoted as a strategy to improve government transparency, accountability, and adaptability to local needs, decentralization was embraced by international lenders and domestic policymakers alike. However, as many have since shown, decentralization did not uniformly improve subnational governance but, rather, heightened the difference between local policy leaders and local policy laggards (Falleti 2010; Grindle 2007; Souza 1998). While decentralization fostered local-level policy innovation, it also gave politicians greater leeway to use resources for advancing partisan or personal goals, rather than for improving social policy (Eaton 2006; Fox 1994; Tulchin and Selee 2004). Moreover, given the long history of centralized governance in Latin America, the sudden devolution of authority over social sector programs revealed a profusion of weak local-level institutions that lacked the capacity to cope with the increase in their responsibilities (Abers and Keck 2013; Grindle 2007). The challenges posed by decentralized governance in the AIDS policy sector reflected these general challenges. Although bureaucrats in the national AIDS program initially embraced the move to decentralize policy authority, they quickly discovered wide variation both in bureaucratic capacity and in the political will to invest in AIDS treatment and prevention programs.

The Context of Decentralized Governance in Brazil

Brazil is often referred to as an extreme case of decentralization because of the high level of autonomy that subnational governments have, as well as the unusually strong degree of state and municipal authority over social service provision. The 1988 constitution advanced decentralization even further by granting both state and municipal governments the ability to create taxes, while supplementing these taxes with inter-governmental fiscal transfers (Souza 1997) – the outcome, in part, of a broad push against the centralization of the authoritarian regime. Municipalities in particular emerged as important political actors through this process: not only were they recognized officially as independent political units for the first time, but the central government provided more revenue to municipalities than to states and gave them responsibility as the principle providers of health, education, and transportation (Arretche 2002; Fenwick 2009). Within this context, national bureaucrats in Brazil possessed particularly weak tools for ensuring adequate health policy implementation.

While the new era of decentralization in Brazil produced significant cases of subnational policy innovation (Abers 2000; Avritzer 2009; Wampler and Avritzer 2004), it also posed strong challenges for democratic governance (Abrucio 1998; Fenwick 2009; Samuels and Abrucio 2000; Souza 1997). Subnational resource constraints, in combination with increased discretion over spending decisions, incentivized governors and mayors to target their budgets toward the most politically popular social programs instead of those with the greatest need (Arretche 2002). Democratic accountability was weak at the state level because state legislatures had little control over governors, and also because citizens were largely unaware of states' policy responsibilities (Abrucio 1998; Souza 1997; Samuels and Abrucio 2000: 61). Local service provision was also inefficient, because governors and mayors lacked political incentives to coordinate their public service programs (Fenwick 2009: 108–9). Moreover, the 1988 constitution's failure to clearly define subnational policy and expenditure responsibilities, which often overlapped among the national, state, and municipal levels of government (especially in the area of healthcare), contributed to widespread redundancies in administrative infrastructure (Arretche 2002). In the area of public health, the outcome of these elements of subnational autonomy was that corruption and foot-dragging were quite common at the state and local levels (World Bank 2007).

Decentralizing HIV/AIDS Policy

The decision to decentralize AIDS policy authority was pushed forward by both Brazilian AIDS bureaucrats and the World Bank, in agreement on the goal. For World Bank representatives, decentralization was one of the guiding principles of their "good governance" agenda, and the Bank had been involved in pushing forward decentralization of the public health system in several Latin America countries (Kaufman and Nelson 2004). Brazilian policymakers were committed to the tenets of decentralized governance over healthcare as enshrined in the 1988 constitution – the outcome, in part, of a specific lobbying effort by public health activists during the Constitutional convention of 1988, who held up decentralized governance as a way to democratize the state and as a way to circumvent entrenched elite interests at the national level. Officials in the national AIDS program, thus, viewed decentralization as a key strategy for democratizing the AIDS policymaking process (Parker 2003).

Federal AIDS bureaucrats also considered decentralization to be a practical necessity for them to be able to expand AIDS programs into new regions and states (Valor Econômico 2006). As AIDS penetrated new areas, national-level bureaucrats – based in the remote capital of Brasilia – found themselves unable to make effective policy decisions for the increasingly diverse set of community needs.[3] Moreover, national bureaucrats sought to institutionalize the flow of federal funding to states and municipalities for AIDS program implementation,[4] given that seventy subnational bureaucracies had already been implementing AIDS programs since 1994, and one hundred seventy seven since 1998 – although without the autonomy to determine the distribution of AIDS funding in their own jurisdictions (Barboza 2006).

Finally, federal bureaucrats viewed decentralization as important for ensuring the sustainability of national AIDS policies and services. Since the Brazilian government had already decentralized the broader public health system without the involvement of international lenders (Arretche 2002), decentralizing AIDS policy authority was seen as important for bringing the AIDS program

---

[3] Informant interviews with Pedro Chequer, Coordinator of the national AIDS program 1996–2000, November 26, 2008; Paulo Teixeira, Coordinator of the national AIDS program 1992–1993, 2000–2003, December 12, 2008 (with follow up on May 5, 2009); Alexandre Grangeiro, Coordinator of the national AIDS program 2003–2004 and Adjunct Coordinator 2001–2003, December 16, 2008.

[4] Informant interviews with Pedro Chequer, November 26, 2008; Paulo Teixeira, December 12, 2008 (with follow up on May 5, 2009); Alexandre Grangeiro, December 16, 2008.

into administrative alignment with the broader public health system.[5] Prior to the 2000s, the AIDS bureaucracy had developed in isolation from Brazil's public health bureaucracy, with its own management and service infrastructure, governed by independent administrative staff at every level from the national program all the way down to local bureaucracies and AIDS clinics. During the initial development of Brazil's national AIDS program, this division was important in light of extreme organizational problems with Brazil's healthcare system, which had led it to rank in the year 2000 a dismal 125th out of 191 countries globally – and 28th out of 33 countries regionally – in health system performance.[6] However, the lack of coordination between AIDS programs and public health programs also resulted in a redundancy of government investments and in various inefficiencies of operation. These problems were exacerbated over time, as AIDS care technologies advanced and became more complex (World Bank 2010).[7]

For all these reasons, the decentralization of authority over AIDS programs was broadly viewed among federal bureaucrats as an inevitable stage of national policy development.[8] Even activists, who were particularly concerned about its effects on AIDS program implementation, agreed on the general need to decentralize AIDS policy. In the words of one informant:

Since one of the guiding principles of the [national health system, known by the acronym SUS] is decentralization, AIDS couldn't work against the system. AIDS had to follow the principles of SUS as well.[9]

Decentralization was, thus, pursued without any major opposition.

Beginning with a series of pilot programs in the early 2000s, AIDS policy management was officially decentralized to the state and municipal levels in 2004, along with a significant portion of the national AIDS budget. Specific responsibilities for administering AIDS programs were divided between states and municipalities, with municipalities carrying most of the implementation responsibility and states the monitoring and coordinating responsibilities. The national AIDS program remained responsible primarily for determining national priorities and guidelines, for coordinating across states and regions,

---

[5] Informant interviews with Pedro Chequer, Coordinator of the national AIDS program 1996–2000, November 26, 2008; Paulo Teixeira, Coordinator of the national AIDS program 1992–1993, 2000–2003, December 12, 2008 (with follow up on May 5, 2009); Alexandre Grangeiro, Coordinator of the national AIDS program 2003–2004 and Adjunct Coordinator 2001–2003, December 16, 2008.

[6] World Health Organization 2000, cited in The World Bank. Governance in Brazil's Unified Health System (SUS): Raising the Quality of Public Spending and Resource Management (Report No. 36601-BR, February 15, 2007).

[7] See also the interview with Alexandre Grangeiro, December 16, 2008.

[8] Informant interviews with Pedro Chequer, November 26, 2008; Paulo Teixeira, December 12, 2008 (with follow up on May 5, 2009); Alexandre Grangeiro, December 16, 2008.

[9] Informant interview with José Marcos de Oliveira, November 22, 2008.

and for monitoring state and municipal implementation of national guidelines (Portaria N° 2.313, 19 de dezembro de 2002).

Decentralization on Paper versus in Practice

The design of the decentralized AIDS policy system – called by its authors the "policy of incentives" (*política de incentivos*) – was explicitly intended to over-come gaps in local political accountability and bureaucratic capacity that have plagued public programs in Brazil through its modern history, including its decentralized public health system.[10] Because the decentralization of AIDS pol-icy was instigated by federal bureaucrats themselves, rather than by politicians looking for easy ways to cut government spending, it was designed specifically to strengthen capacity among federal bureaucrats to face policy challenges at the national level. Rather than downsizing the national AIDS program as an outcome of AIDS policy decentralization, those in charge instead redefined the role of the federal AIDS bureaucracy to focus on the dual mission of oversight and national policy development. Throughout the decentralization process, the national AIDS program retained its staff and its comfortable budget; and what it lost in control over resources was matched by a decrease in the administra-tive burden for federal bureaucrats.[11]

The system was also designed to maximize the capacity of federal bureau-crats to monitor AIDS policy implementation at the state and local levels. For example, as a condition for receiving federal transfers, the national program required each state and municipality to develop its own, detailed annual AIDS policy goals (*Planos de Acções e Metas*).[12] In theory, this stipulation promoted effective subnational planning by allowing local authorities flexibility in setting their AIDS program goals – accounting for vast regional differences in bureau-cratic capacity and in population needs. At the same time, this stipulation served a political purpose, providing national bureaucrats with an irrefutable baseline to use when evaluating and holding subnational politicians account-able for their AIDS program development.[13] Another way federal bureaucrats designed the system to strengthen their oversight over subnational authori-ties was by depositing federal AIDS funding transfers into special accounts, separate from other public health accounts and accessible via the internet by the national bureaucrats who were in charge of monitoring AIDS fund-ing. National bureaucrats checked the flow of money out of these accounts daily.[14] The national AIDS program also incentivized subnational governments

---

[10] On the challenges of public health reform, see Arretche (2002).

[11] Multiple informant interviews.

[12] For a detailed elaboration of this requirement, see "Orientações sobre o sistema de monitora-mento da política de incentivo no âmbito do programa nacional de DST/HIV/AIDS." Brasília: Ministry of Health. 2006.

[13] Interview with Alexandre Grangeiro, December 16, 2008.

[14] Interview with bureaucrat in the planning division of the national AIDS program.

to meet their own targets by offering states up to US$100,000 and cities up to US$50,000 for fulfilling their goals (World Bank 2010).

But despite the elaborate "policy of incentives" that guided the design of their system for decentralized governance on paper, in practice, federal AIDS bureaucrats faced strong challenges to regulating subnational AIDS policy implementation. The most glaring challenge they faced was the lack of political will among many governors and mayors to invest in AIDS programs. In the state of Goiás in 2009, for example, the state-level health secretariat had spent only 57 percent of its federal transfers earmarked for AIDS services since 2003. Not a single *real* of federal AIDS transfer money had been withdrawn from its bank account for thirty-two months (unpublished government document). Snapshots from a study of Brazil's AIDS policy decentralization, commissioned for the Global Health Delivery project at Harvard University, further highlight such problems:

By December 2009, the city of Rio de Janeiro had achieved only 53% of its PAM targets and was 53 months behind on spending its federal AIDS money. Millions of federal funds intended for AIDS programs and NGOs sat paralyzed in a bank account.

Harm reduction programs for IDUs in Rio de Janeiro also suffered under the decentralization policy. The city's needle exchange programs had worked well for about 10 years, but the decentralization policy was described as "the beginning of the end" for them. In addition to the bureaucratic problems of managing the new funding flows, Rio de Janeiro political leaders did not support needle exchange programs.

Brazil's southernmost state, Rio Grande do Sul, and its capital city, Porto Alegre, were among the country's richest and most developed regions. In 2009 they also had the highest rate of new AIDS cases in the country. Porto Alegre's incidence rate was four times the rate in the city of São Paulo. Throughout the 1990s the southern state's AIDS programs and CSOs were considered among the best in the country, particularly for IDU harm reduction. But, as of December 2009 Rio Grande do Sul and Porto Alegre each had implemented only 70% of their PAM targets and were 23 months behind in spending their federal AIDS funding. The state's top AIDS coordinator position had been vacant for six months, and millions of federal AIDS funds went unspent (Arnquist, Ellner, and Weintraub 2011: 14–15).

Although national AIDS bureaucrats could use their monitoring mechanisms to dissuade politicians from misappropriating federal funding for AIDS, they were unable to force politicians to actually spend the transfers they received. Nor could they convince politicians to use the funds that were earmarked for supporting civil society organizations.

Federal bureaucrats simultaneously faced the challenge of overcoming weak state capacity among local health secretariats. Regardless of political will, many states and municipalities lacked the infrastructure – and sometimes even the personnel – to adequately implement national AIDS policy guidelines. According to the same Harvard study:

Aside from the difficult politics, some states and cities lacked organized health accounts and sufficient employees with accounting experience to execute funding transfers.

Additionally, Brazil's complicated budgeting laws made contracting with NGOs an enormous bureaucratic hurdle for many states. Each government budget required approval by the corresponding legislative body, meaning that altering a budget midway through a fiscal year was time consuming, if not impossible. Other laws limited how much a budget could increase from year to year and what percent could be spent on human resources. A health policy professor said, "There is so much red tape and conditions on spending money that were designed to battle the history of corruption, but what it creates is a very difficult system that hampers managers' ability to do their jobs." (Arnquist, Ellner, and Weintraub 2011).

A combination of burdensome rules and perverse incentives had rendered state and local healthcare bureaucracies incapable of compiling even basic budgetary information, such as on their own spending behavior.[15] This lack of capacity to collect data complicated federal bureaucrats' struggle to overcome weak political will. Information, the basic foundation for national bureaucrats to regulate behavior, was missing at the subnational level.

Both national authorities and published documents attributed the failure of subnational authorities to spend federal AIDS funding to a combination of weak bureaucratic capacity and an absence of political will to invest in AIDS (World Bank 2010). According to one national bureaucrat, Gilvane, expanding on the challenge posed by subnational politicians:

Despite [national] resource limitations, the Brazilian government has invested in STD/AIDS policies. But we can't forget that authority is decentralized, where states and municipalities have their own responsibilities. And unfortunately, not all of them comply with their responsibilities. So it's not enough to have the Ministry of Health transferring [sufficient] resources [to states and municipalities]. Frequently, those resources simply sit in their accounts because there is no political will [to move them].[16]

Joel, another bureaucrat, shared a similar viewpoint on decentralization. As he described:

There are some [local] public health officials who don't manage to implement AIDS policies, for N number of reasons ... You can see some of this on our internal website. [Here he shows me the current balance of special municipal bank accounts set up to receive federal AIDS transfers. He points to the municipality of Rio de Janeiro, which has been receiving transfers for 56 months – four years – without having spent any of it on AIDS services.]

---

[15] For more detail on the challenges of weak state capacity in the public health system, see the World Bank report "Governance in Brazil's Unified Health System (SUS): Raising the Quality of Public Spending and Resource Management" (Report No. 36601-BR, February 15, 2007).

[16] Interview with Gilvane Casimiro, bureaucrat in the Unit for Engagement with Civil Society and Human Rights, March 16, 2010.

It's difficult to propose a solution to the balance sitting in the accounts of some municipalities, because the different structures of the public health system – the federal, state, and municipal spheres – are autonomous, independent. Which is to say that one doesn't control the other. There's no hierarchy.[17]

According to the director of the national AIDS program:

It's not money that we need now. We need a new vision. We need to alter the state-level and municipal agenda so that we can plan better. To encourage and strengthen this type of structure is a long-term process. It will not happen during my lifetime, but it gets at the soul of the Brazilian government.[18]

In spite of their efforts to innovate an institutional design for decentralized policy management that included mechanisms for monitoring subnational activity, bureaucrats in the national AIDS program were unable to ensure state and municipal compliance with national AIDS policy guidelines.

Low subnational investment in AIDS program infrastructure translated into serious state and municipal policy problems that threatened Brazil's reputation as a global AIDS leader. Empty stocks of ARVs not only threatened the individual health of AIDS patients but also threatened to foster drug-resistant strains of the virus in Brazil (Estado de São Paulo April 28, 2010b). Delays of up to several months in processing CD4 and viral load tests, which are necessary to prescribe drug therapy for those infected with HIV, similarly prevented citizens from accessing AIDS care (Valor Econômico 2006). In fact, weak investment in AIDS policy at the subnational levels underlay nearly all the AIDS policy challenges.

Federal bureaucrats in Brazil thus confronted the challenge of ensuring subnational implementation of national policies and programs in the face of strong local autonomy and weak incentives for local investment. In the area of fiscal policy, President Fernando Cardoso (1994–2002) had confronted such challenges by reining a degree of fiscal autonomy back in from local politicians, using political tools such as the president's unusually strong powers of executive decree authority to implement the Real stabilization program in 1998 and the Law of Fiscal Responsibility in 2000 (Eaton and Dickovick 2004). In social policy sectors, however, the recentralization of authority over administrative and spending decisions was not an option (Fenwick 2009; Tendler 1997). Bureaucrats in the national AIDS program were thus forced to seek alternative means of influencing subnational policy outcomes.

---

[17] Interview with Joel Nunes, bureaucrat in the Strategic Planning Unity (ASPLAN), March 19, 2010.

[18] Mariângela Galvão Simão, Director, National Department of STD, AIDS, and Hepatitis, cited in Arnquist et al. (2011).

LOOKING OUTSIDE THE STATE FOR SUPPORT

Without effective oversight mechanisms, national AIDS bureaucrats looked outside the state for methods of ensuring that governors and mayors correctly implemented national policy guidelines. Nongovernmental associations stood out as a logical source of support for regulating subnational political behavior due to the close, collaborative relationships that had formed between AIDS bureaucrats and activists during the initial development of the federal AIDS bureaucracy, and due to the federal budget for subsidizing AIDS NGOs that had been included in the World Bank's loan package. In the words of a bureaucrat who worked in the national AIDS program's Unit for Engagement with Civil Society and Human Rights, "What this unit sees is that where civil society is well organized, like the state of São Paulo, everything happens efficiently, and the public administrators that aren't efficient don't stay in office. That doesn't happen where civil society isn't well organized" (Arnquist, Ellner, and Weintraub 2011: 16).

Therefore, federal bureaucrats interested in progressive policy reform aimed to mobilize new AIDS service organizations around Brazil as policy watchdogs by providing them with the resources and the opportunities to engage in the political arena. This effort to cultivate NGOs as political allies for AIDS policy development has been a relatively overt strategy of the federal AIDS bureaucracy, alluded to by AIDS bureaucrats not only in private conversations, but also in the public arena. In a recorded speech in 2007, the director of Brazil's national AIDS bureaucracy from 1996–2000 and 2004–2006 observed: "We need to create conditions to sustain the [overall AIDS policy development] that we [have] experienced. If we don't have a solid social movement, established at the local level, it is going to be very difficult to achieve this."[19] At the same event, a bureaucrat in São Paulo state's AIDS bureaucracy noted: "From inside the state machine, you often cannot, do not manage to, or are not in a position to propose things. This is why it is fundamental for society to be together with us pressuring [government]."[20]

Resources for Political Advocacy

One strategy federal bureaucrats used to mobilize AIDS policy allies within civil society was to target federal funding to civil society projects. While national bureaucrats distributed some of this funding to established AIDS groups to support their ongoing work, they also used this project funding to encourage

---

[19] Pedro Chequer, Director of Brazil's federal AIDS program 1996–2000, 2004–2008. Quoted from a public address at the seminar "Societal Control and AIDS in the State of São Paulo," March 2007.

[20] Artur Kalichman, Adjunct Director of the State STD/AIDS Program, São Paulo. Quoted from a public address at the seminar "Societal Control and AIDS in the State of São Paulo," March 2007.

grassroots groups working with new communities, and in new regions of Brazil, to incorporate AIDS into their mission. AIDS-sector bureaucrats particularly favored civil-society groups in more rural regions of Brazil, where HIV-based discrimination was stronger and where the AIDS movement tended to be weaker. They also favored LGBT groups and sex-worker organizations for project funding. According to a study by Murray (2015), Brazil's first two sex-workers advocacy groups used National AIDS program funding to launch their initial projects (Murray 2015: 62). Later, the leaders of these two organizations used National AIDS program funding to travel across Brazil, planting the seeds for others to organize new sex workers groups (Murray 2015: 63). Ultimately, sex-worker organizations constituted 52 of the first 181 NGOs funded between 1993 and 1997 (Rossi 1998, cited in Murray 2015). Similarly, nearly all of Brazil's first LBGT advocacy organizations received national AIDS program funding. According to the recollections of a prominent LGBT activist from São Paulo, his organization took on its first AIDS prevention project in 2001, after a bureaucrat in the national AIDS program called to see whether he would like to apply for project funding.[21]

Federal bureaucrats were able to employ this strategy by retaining a significant amount of control over how to distribute earmarked money for civil society projects despite the formal decentralization of AIDS policy management. In dividing AIDS policy responsibilities across levels of government in the system of decentralization, federal bureaucrats strategically maintained responsibility for "supporting civil society networks" (Portaria N° 2.313, 19 de dezembro de 2002). This meant that federal bureaucrats continued to distribute nearly half of the earmarked funding for civil society groups, or R$10 million (US$5.9 million) (unpublished government document). The national AIDS program also set aside additional pockets of money each year for civil society support, summing to a total of R$25 million (US$11.5 million) in direct federal funding for local AIDS associations in 2006 (unpublished government document) – again, despite the ostensible decentralization of fiscal and administrative authority over AIDS policy. While these were relatively small amounts of funding, they were able to fund a large number of civic AIDS organizations. For example, Brazil's national AIDS program funded 2,884 civil society projects between the years 1999 and 2003, with an average of 577 projects per year.

By 2002, however, AIDS associations existed in all twenty-six states of Brazil – including in the North and Northeast, Brazil's two most impoverished regions, which are covered largely by jungle and desert, rank lowest nationally on levels of education and income, and have been dominated politically until recently by land barons.

Moreover, the federal AIDS bureaucracy allocated a significant portion of this funding for civil society to support projects that centered on political

---

[21] Interview with Lula Ramires, Coordinator of Corsa and a founding organizer of the São Paulo pride parade, December 13, 2008.

Federal direct support for civil society orgs.	(2006 Dollars)	(% Total)
Political advocacy and events	1,421,250	13%
Advocacy projects	82,957	
Legal aid projects	566,091	
Strengthening civil society networks	59,340	
Gay pride parades	363,182	
Other events	349,675	
Discretionary funding	2,701,230	24%
Funding for service projects	500,675	5%
Funding for work with specific communities	87,650	1%
The Afro-attitude project	612,766	
Children and adolescents	26,374	
Funding for research	6,320,028	55%
Innovation and technology	103,078	
General research	6,216,950	
Total	11,481,100	100%

FIGURE 5.1. *Federal direct spending on civil society groups in 2006*

advocacy.[22] (See Figure 5.1) Whereas 5 percent of the budget for civil society was earmarked for service projects, 13 percent – more than twice that amount – was set aside for what was explicitly called political advocacy projects. Informant interviews further revealed that much of the money listed as "discretionary funding" (a further 24 percent of the total budget) was often used to support political advocacy. In total, then, we might estimate that 37 percent of the national AIDS program budget for civil society projects was in fact used to support political advocacy. This political use of project funding for nongovernmental AIDS groups is unexpected given that the World Bank provided the vast majority of funding for nongovernmental AIDS projects. As described in Chapter 4, the World Bank initially promoted the idea of earmarked funding for civic AIDS associations by using a technocratic logic that highlights the relative "expertise" of nongovernmental groups in reaching "marginalized populations." However, the World Bank left near total discretion to Brazilian bureaucrats to determine the allocation of funding for AIDS associations. Federal bureaucrats, driven by the strategic need to cultivate political support for AIDS policy development outside the state, began to use the

---

[22] Information on project funding for recent years is available at www.aids.gov.br (last accessed on April 26, 2018).

earmarked funding to support political advocacy and activist training projects in the 2000s.

Federal project funding was used to encourage and support a broad array of political activities. For example, the national bureaucracy used "legal aid" project funding[23] to encourage AIDS associations to use the courts to denounce human rights abuses. As I described in Chapter 3, the courts were a critical arena for pushing forward AIDS policy development in Brazil. In the 2000s, the courts became an important arena for policy enforcement. Because national bureaucrats lacked the power to effectively regulate the policies they designed, the courts gained prominence as a channel for public prosecutors and activists to hold government actors to account for policy implementation (McAllister 2008). Yet, despite the strong legal basis for social rights litigation in Brazil, access to the court system varied strongly across states and was weak among the lower classes (Hoffman and Bentes 2008: 111). State-level prosecutors (*Ministérios Públicos*) were often overburdened, underpaid, and under political pressure not to play too active a role in bringing cases against the state (Hoffman and Bentes: 129). Pro bono and other alternative judicial services for the poor were scarce – especially in the more rural regions of Brazil (Hoffman and Bentes: 112).

Although AIDS-based discrimination occurred across the country, it was particularly acute in the Northeast and other regions beyond the urbanized Southeast where the movement was strongest. As described to me by a bureaucrat named Noemia:

In all of Brazil there's still discrimination, human rights violations. But we can see that, for example, in the Northeast region, the prejudice is worse. In other regions I think it's more veiled. For example, in the Southeast people have access to everything, but prejudice exists, so it's more veiled. In the Northeast it's not; people there will discriminate straight to your face, get it?

Compounding the problem of greater discrimination in the Northeast was the weaker access to the justice system for citizens of the Northeast – and especially for poorer citizens.

National AIDS bureaucrats, looking for ways to strengthen AIDS policy regulation in laggard states, created a fund in the early 2000s to help civic AIDS groups file claims through the courts on behalf of people with HIV. According to one federal bureaucrat:

If you don't have action on the part of states that respond to the magnitude of discrimination, of prejudice, of social exclusion that exists – or even recognizing these as factors that exacerbate the epidemic – you have to offer alternatives, right? If states don't offer support, you have to ... offer alternatives ... [So] the [National AIDS Program] launched this legal-aid grant, which offers financial support for a

---

[23] In Portuguese: Assessoria Jurídica em Direitos Humanos e DST/HIV/AIDS.

nongovernmental organization to develop a basic infrastructure [to prosecute human rights violations] with a professional in the legal area, a lawyer, who can attend people who are victims of AIDS-related discrimination and aren't able to get help in the formally established spaces.[24]

Funded groups were required to register human rights violations against citizens in their area, collect and file complaints, and conduct legal education courses to train community leaders in human rights promotion. In other words, national AIDS bureaucrats were funding civic organizations to enter into judicial action against other state agencies – thus forcing them to comply with national AIDS policy guidelines.

This new source of financial support for legal advocacy campaigns was used to help a wide swath of AIDS associations across Brazil gain access to the courts. In 2007, for example, the National AIDS Program funded thirty-seven local legal-aid groups, across all five regions of Brazil, with the largest number of funded groups in the Northeast, a region notorious for human rights violations and gender-related violence.[25] Qualitative interviews and observational research corroborate government data. For example, Ernandes, the activist from the state of Pará, described the following sources of support for efforts to enter into litigation:

We have, for example, that institution I told you about: GAPA Pará.[26] They have a project called Dignity and Rights. Dignity and Rights is a group of lawyers who help, together with the federal government, with the demands of people living [with HIV/ AIDS] and of the [AIDS] movement.[27]

Similarly, an activist from the Northeastern state of Bahia, in a city six hours by bus from the state capital, offered:

When there are [problems] with medicines or prejudice against people who live with AIDS, or with questions related to social security, we enter into the justice system. We used to have a project supported by the national department of AIDS, which paid for a lawyer to support our judicial actions.[28]

As I describe in Chapter 7, judicial action was a core strategy used by AIDS activists in the 2000s for making policy demands on the state.

---

[24] Interview with Barbara Barbosa, federal AIDS bureaucrat, Sector for Engagement with Civil Society and Human Rights, March 17, 2010.

[25] Source: unpublished government document

[26] GAPA Pará is an acronym for, in English, The Group for the Support and Prevention of AIDS: Pará branch.

[27] Interview with Ernandes Marques da Costa, Coordinator of the AIDS NGO Forum of the state of Pará, April 29, 2011 (via Skype).

[28] Interview with Fábio Ribeiro, Member of the NGO Forum of the state of Salvador da Bahia, representing the organization *GLICH* (Grupo Liberdade Igualdade Cidadania Homosexual), April 29, 2011, via Facebook chat.

More common than funding specific forms of advocacy, national AIDS bureaucrats used project funding to help sustain and expand political mobilization on a more general level – leaving it to activists to independently determine their own strategies and campaigns. The reason bureaucrats favored more generic forms of support for civic mobilization likely had to do with the dangers of overstepping legal and territorial boundaries. Funding specific advocacy campaigns – particularly those against other state agencies – would have put national AIDS bureaucrats at the risk of sanction from other actors inside the state, either from independent auditing agencies or from the actors who were threatened by their advocacy campaigns. At the same time, activists' power to influence AIDS policy depended on the public's perception they were acting autonomously, representing societal interests in their campaigns.

One example of national AIDS bureaucrats providing generic support for sustaining political mobilization was a line of project funding they opened in 2009 for training new AIDS activists, called "the formation of young leaders in STD/AIDS." According to a bureaucrat who was involved in designing the project:

This is a pretty innovative initiative, which provides basic training for young people living with HIV/AIDS for more effective political involvement. Young people with HIV/AIDS aren't necessarily involved in activism. And they aren't necessarily familiar with all the details of public administration works, or how the public service network works.

This is a training. It's not exactly an internship because it doesn't have an employment aspect. It has nothing to do with professional qualification. It's a political training, promoting technical and political knowledge. That's why this project is different from an internship.[29]

In other words, national bureaucrats used this funding to train young people living with HIV/AIDS across the country as AIDS advocates – to help spread advocacy skills among leaders in new regions, and to help sustain political mobilization around AIDS as established leaders aged out of activism.

As described by Barbara, the project essentially served as an internship in advocacy. One young leader from each state was selected for the program each year, and the training involved a three-phase paid internship that lasted eleven months: First, participants spent four months in their state-level governmental AIDS programs, attending policy meetings and learning about how bureaucracy functions. They then spent four months in AIDS clinics and laboratories, to learn about the AIDS services that were (or should be) offered and about how the AIDS service provision system works. They capped off their training by spending three months participating in community mobilization, interning

---

[29] Interview with Barbara Barbosa, bureaucrat in the Civil Society and Human Rights unit of the national AIDS program, March 17, 2010.

in a local civil-society organization to learn about the scope and process of AIDS activism in their home state.

Another line of funding called "project networks" was designed, in the words of the bureaucrat in charge, to "mobilize civil society to organize around 'societal control.'" This project paid established AIDS advocacy organizations to train newer civil-society organizations in how to participate more effectively in political spaces. According to Rubens Duda, the bureaucrat I interviewed:

[The leaders who participate in the project] get trained in how to participate in health councils, in NGO forums, in all the different institutions that exist. So the objective of the project, in truth, is for [the leaders of civil-society organizations] to strengthen their skills in this respect, to provide funding so that they can be trained, build their capacity to participate in those spaces.[30]

In this project, the national AIDS program identified four priority "political spaces" they sought to encourage civic AIDS organizations to participate in: state and regional AIDS NGO umbrella networks (known as "NGO forums"), health policy councils, municipal AIDS policy councils (called "AIDS commissions"), or congressional AIDS caucuses (government document).[31]

These examples constitute just a few of various lines of project funding the national AIDS program used to support social-movement mobilization – projects that changed from year to year. Broadly, by using federal funding that was set aside for civil-society projects to encourage and support political advocacy, national bureaucrats were explicitly mobilizing local civic groups as political advocates – and, consequently, strengthening outside pressure on state and local-level politicians to improve AIDS policy management.

Opportunities for Participation in Policy Discussions

Federal AIDS bureaucrats also used non-financial mechanisms to mobilize policy advocates among civil society. Institutionally, the national AIDS program began using the Sector for Engagement with Civil Society to expand its relationships with grassroots leaders at the local level. In doing so, it changed its name to the Civil Society and Human Rights Unit (CSHR). According to Arnquist, Ellner, and Weintraub, "Since it no longer oversaw all NGO contracts, the National Department's human rights and civil society unit concentrated its efforts in places struggling most under decentralization. These tended to be areas where civil society advocacy was weak and encountering government resistance" (2011: 16). Eduardo Barbosa, the former director of the CSHR described his mission in similar terms,

---

[30] Informant interview with Rubens Duda, bureaucrat in the Civil Society and Human Rights unit of the national AIDS program, March 18, 2010.

[31] See also Biancarelli 2012.

telling me that his main job was to "maintain an independent and coherent civil society response to AIDS; provide civil society information so that they have the tools to do advocacy; and strengthen local AIDS movements so they can have local political influence, monitoring government and promoting progressive AIDS policies."[32] In other words, the key objective among bureaucrats in the CSHR unit of the national AIDS program became to mobilize nongovernmental AIDS interest groups to support their AIDS policy goals.

One way they pursued this objective was by offering these new grassroots AIDS organizations access to policymaking circles. Federal bureaucrats in the CSHR unit pursued this strategy in part by engaging civil society participation in committees for participatory governance. As I described in Chapter 4, Brazil had given civil society groups an official seat at the table in policy debates by constitutionally mandating that social policy priorities be set not by government officials, but by participatory councils that allotted equal numbers of seats to representatives of government, service providers, and civil society organizations. The explicit goal of these councils was to broaden the representation of interests in policy design across social classes. In the area of AIDS policy, federal bureaucrats began in the early 2000s to use national participatory councils for strategic political purposes as well: to maintain a regular flow of communication and foster trust between federal bureaucrats and local civil society groups, which bureaucrats utilized to gather information from nongovernmental associations about local AIDS policy challenges. Using Brazil's participatory governance model of policymaking, federal bureaucrats created additional councils, committees, and working groups to bring government policymakers and activists together to discuss AIDS policy, and designated certain numbers of seats on them for activists from each region of Brazil.

For example, during the pilot stage of AIDS policy decentralization in 2003, the federal AIDS bureaucracy created a new participatory policy group called the National Commission of Engagement with Social Movements (CASM).[33] Multiple sources of evidence suggest that a main impetus behind the council's creation in 2003 was to strengthen collaboration with civil society groups in response to the challenges that decentralization posed to sustaining Brazil's AIDS policy success. For example, Article II of the CASM bylaws describes one of the council's principal objectives as "promoting the technical, ethical, financial, and political sustainability of [Brazil's national AIDS policies] in the context of a decentralized national health system."[34] Moreover, a review of

---

[32] Interview with Eduardo Barbosa, Adjunct Director of Brazil's National AIDS Program and former director of the Civil Society Unit, November 18, 2008.

[33] In Portuguese, called the Comissão de Articulação com Movimentos Sociais (CAMS).

[34] Internal bylaws Article ii, found within the text of CASM meeting minutes from March 25, 2004. Meetings minutes available at www.aids.gov.br/pt-br/gestores/comissoes-e-comites/comissao-de-articulacao-com-os-movimentos-sociais-cams (last accessed on April 26, 2018).

the minutes (from 2004 through 2009) shows that problems directly related to AIDS policy decentralization were discussed in nineteen out of twenty-one recorded CASM meetings. In these meetings, civil society representatives frequently raised concerns about government misbehavior in their states or regions, and government representatives often raised discussion about ways to foster more organized civil society involvement in monitoring and controlling government behavior. In other words, CASM served as an important tool to monitor decentralized AIDS policy administration by institutionalizing information sharing and collaboration between national bureaucrats and local civil society groups. Moreover, CASM was only one of many participatory AIDS councils that structured collaboration between the state and civil society groups at the national level.

Bureaucrats also used the structure of participatory governance meetings and AIDS policy events to pass information to activists about budgets, incipient policy challenges, and the like (multiple informant interviews). According to an informant who was once second-in-command of the national AIDS program:

Those [participatory spaces] serve to help civil society get the information they need to hold government accountable. Once civil society gets information from government, *then* civil society can take action. The result [of getting information from government] could be more effective demand-making in policy spaces; it could be criticizing government through the media; it could be participation in working groups ... whatever interventions they believe to be best.[35]

In other words, bureaucrats valued these participatory policymaking spaces because they allowed bureaucrats and citizens to rapidly exchange information about on-the-ground problems they detected or about government misbehavior, and even to develop problem-solving strategies together.

Federal AIDS bureaucrats also cultivated civil society allies through meetings and events that took place outside the purview of participatory policymaking institutions. On the one hand, the bureaucrats in the national AIDS program flew local civil society leaders to the national capital of Brasília for an endless array of additional conferences, workshops, training sessions, and rallies. And on the other hand, AIDS bureaucrats themselves traveled regularly to all twenty-six states in Brazil to attend events that involved local civil society groups. According to the Harvard study,

Chequer [the former national AIDS program director] believed the National Department staff should spend even more time outside Brasília to strengthen NGOs in rural areas. 'In Brazil, the NGOs are good about talking to the press about the national problems, but they aren't organized enough to put pressure on the local government,' Chequer

---

[35] See note 32.

said. 'More and more there is a need to have NGOs get organized and learn the political process. Locally, there is not enough social pressure in terms of implementing activities and using the money correctly.' (Arnquist, Ellner, and Weintraub 2011: 16)

These events often served multiple purposes. On the surface, they addressed specific national AIDS policy challenges. In addition, these events and meetings deepened collaborative relationships between bureaucrats and nongovernmental leaders (and among civil society leaders) through the experience of collective problem solving and through extended periods of intense interaction. According to a former director of the CSHR unit, Barbosa, reflecting the opinions expressed to me by all of his colleagues:

[Participating in local events] is fundamental. I try to accept almost all event invitations ... because there I get a sense of what is going on, whether it be about a patient that is not being attended well or about the relationship between government and local civil society. There, I get that signal of how the local government is viewing the actions of civil society, how civil society relates to government ... and I believe that those spaces also end up strengthening ties when you are present. You establish channels of confidence, so you end up getting information – [and] you end up acting as an advocate and a mediator for some [difficult local] situations.[36]

These events also constituted opportunities for civil society leaders to share detailed information about local policy failures with national bureaucrats – helping national AIDS bureaucrats determine where, when, and how to intervene in the policy process.

Federal bureaucrats used these personal relationships with civic AIDS leaders to mobilize them as state and local political advocates. For example, federal AIDS bureaucrats played a key role in encouraging civic associations to participate in the legislative arena of politics. Prior to the mid-2000s, civic AIDS activists had broadly viewed the legislature as a den of corruption and inefficiency. Moreover, because AIDS associations had direct contact with the National Program – whose budget was decided outside of Congress – they had no immediate need to build ties with members of parliament. AIDS bureaucrats, however, had by the late-1990s perceived a crucial need to build legislative support for the advancement of AIDS policy. Working inside government to design and promote AIDS policies, they witnessed directly the general lack of interest within Congress in dealing with AIDS and its negative consequences. In particular, the lack of congressional support to bring AIDS policy proposals to a vote had meant that few legislative proposals promoted by the National AIDS Program had yet become law. By 2003, there were approximately seventy AIDS-related legislative proposals languishing in

---

[36] Interview with Eduardo Barbosa, November 18, 2008, Adjunct Director of Brazil's National AIDS Program and former director of the Civil Society Unit, November 18, 2008.

Congress, in need of support to bring them to a vote.[37] Because AIDS policy management had been centralized until the mid-2000s, the lack of AIDS awareness of interest among members of congress was even more acute at the subnational level.[38]

Unable to rally broad legislative support for AIDS programs on their own, federal bureaucrats looked to civil society groups around the country to convince their individual senators and representatives to join the AIDS caucus. Instead of providing financial resources to civic AIDS groups as they had done to mobilize grassroots legal advocacy campaigns, federal bureaucrats promoted legislative lobbying by encouraging civic associations to take up the effort on their own. To convince civic AIDS groups to organize congressional lobbies, federal bureaucrats traveled personally to every state – conducting awareness campaigns and instructional programs about the legislature with state-level activist leaders, and providing advice and technical support to civil society groups once they agreed to take on a congressional caucus project.[39] According to the bureaucrat currently responsible for congressional caucus development:

At the local level, we don't have that ... we aren't so much of a presence there. So it is important that civil society strengthens those ties with the legislative power. At the local level, we incentivize civil society to build a direct channel of communication with the legislative power. And we sit back as a rearguard – for when they need, when they ask, when they have a question, when there is some event that's important for us to go to, for when they need orientation ... We give every kind of support; but we try to avoid being too [much at the head of the effort] because then it would turn back into a relationship between us here in Brasília and the people inside the [subnational] state, and not civil society working with those inside the state, you see? So that is our strategy: try as hard as possible for [civil society] to identify [congressional allies], for *them* to go in pursuit. We give all the support possible, but so that it is a relationship developed by them.[40]

Underlying this practical logic, a more explicitly political reason may also have driven federal bureaucrats to encourage civil society to lead congressional caucuses efforts at the subnational level. Since local political lobbying clearly lies outside the purview of the federal bureaucracy, a state attempt to build congressional constituencies around AIDS runs the risk of a political backlash. By deploying civil society groups to lead the effort, federal bureaucrats could

[37] *Dossier Frente Parlementar: 2001–2007.* An unpublished history of the National AIDS Caucus, written by bureaucrats in the National AIDS Program (December 2007.)

[38] Interviews with Rubens Duda, March 18, 2010, Roberto Pereira, August 25, 2008.

[39] Interviews with Rubens Duda, Noemia Lima, Barbara Barbosa, March 17–19, 2011. Information corroborated in the *Dossier Frente Parlamentar 2001–2007.*

[40] Interview with Noemia Lima, bureaucrat in the National AIDS Program, Sector for Engagement with Civil Society and Human Rights, March 19, 2011.

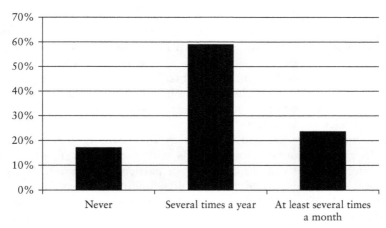

FIGURE 5.2. *Frequency of contact between civic AIDS associations and federal bureaucrats*

lobby for progressive AIDS legislation without seeming to overstep their juris-dictional boundary.

Results from the Brazilian survey of AIDS NGOs, which I conducted in the states of São Paulo and Rio de Janeiro between February and May 2010, support these federal bureaucrats' claims about the frequency of their contact with civil society leaders. (See Figure 5.2.) Eighty-three percent of the directors of local AIDS groups reported some form of personal contact with a federal AIDS bureaucrat at least a few times a year, and an impressive 24 percent of respondents reported personal contact with a national bureaucrat several times a month or more, despite the fact that AIDS policy authority was con-centrated among state and municipal officials. In qualitative interviews, civil society informants from five states reported their relationships with national AIDS bureaucrats to be excellent; and most leaders who began working with AIDS before 2005 claimed that their relationship with federal bureaucrats had not weakened post-decentralization.

CONCLUSION

This chapter identified a new strategy utilized by national AIDS bureaucrats to face the challenge of what Abers and Keck (2013) call institutional entan-glement – the distribution of power among a large and diverse group of inde-pendent institutions and individuals. For bureaucrats operating in such an environment to accomplish their policy objectives, they need to put pressure on all of these organizations and actors to get them to move in the direction they want. As bureaucrats in Brazil's national AIDS program succeeded in develop-ing an increasingly elaborate national policy framework, the sustainability of their success depended more and more on the cooperation of actors outside their control. When AIDS policy was decentralized in the early 2000s, federal AIDS officials found themselves particularly limited in their capacity to control the behavior of subnational politicians. To ensure the implementation of their national policies, activist bureaucrats in Brazil's national AIDS program sought to develop new allies outside the state: mobilizing civil society groups across Brazil to monitor the actions of local politicians and pressure them to conform to national policy guidelines.

Federal bureaucrats pursued this strategy by providing grassroots organizations in new communities and regions with a combination of resources and opportunities that would facilitate their participation in the AIDS policy process. Resources centered on giving project funding – money for grassroots groups to run AIDS service projects – to grassroots groups in new communities. Although project funding typically involved meager amounts of money, it helped small grassroots organizations – who often suffered a precarious existence – to keep their doors open. Project funding also brought awareness about AIDS as an issue to new groups. As a result of these funds, the number of civic AIDS organizations in Brazil ballooned from a few dozen organizations in the late 1980s to over a thousand organizations in 2003. National bureaucrats also offered these new grassroots AIDS organizations access to policymaking circles. By opening space for grassroots groups to participate in AIDS policy discussions inside government, bureaucrats were providing new organizations with an opportunity to influence AIDS policy.

Yet, as I show in Chapter 6, resources and political opportunities were, on their own, insufficient to mobilize new grassroots groups as political advocates. Whereas the AIDS associations that had organized in the 1980s had always focused on advocacy, the associations that had organized around AIDS in response to inducements by state actors tended to be relatively apolitical with respect to AIDS, prioritizing service provision over making policy demands on government. In contrast to Brazil's older AIDS advocacy groups, these newer organizations had neither the capacity nor the incentives to invest themselves in political advocacy. Typically, they were small-scale operations, with minimal budgets and only a few staff members. Most of their time was dedicated to essential administrative tasks such as managing their service provision projects, preparing reports for funders, and applying for new sources of funding. These new AIDS NGOs also tended to work on multiple issues at once, and had often organized initially to confront some other key social issue. In other words, they had neither the time nor the motivation to dedicate themselves to learning about AIDS policymaking or about political advocacy.

But, as I elaborate in the following chapter, bureaucrats also provided less visible but crucial indirect forms of support to expand the AIDS movement into new regions of Brazil, by supporting established AIDS advocacy groups in their efforts to mobilize these new grassroots AIDS associations into political advocates. They did this by providing funds for established advocacy organizations to expand and institutionalize a national coalition of AIDS NGOs. They also provided additional funds to established organizations to train the leaders of new grassroots groups in political advocacy. This horizontal/bottom–up effort to expand the AIDS movement was both incentivized and shaped by government bureaucrats. It also, in turn, had an independent effect on the movement.

6

Expanding the Movement from Below

Political opportunities and material resources are necessary for a civic association to be able to participate effectively in the political arena, but the way opportunities and material resources affect political participation depends on an organization's skills and motivation. While participatory governance institutions open a new point of access to the state for civic groups, a civic association must possess political skills to be capable of pursuing its goals by participating through this channel. While material resources help civic organizations to be effective in the political arena, an association must have a compelling reason to be willing to invest some of its resources in participating in the political process. It is largely because of this gap between opportunities and material resources on the one hand, and skills and motivation on the other, that the vast amounts of global financial and technical support for NGOs across the developing world has largely failed to mobilize new civil society constituencies (Watkins, Swidler, and Hannan 2012).

The immediate effect of government efforts to expand grassroots AIDS advocacy reflects this broad challenge. The direct forms of support I described in Chapter 5 had, on their own, only a limited effect in mobilizing new grassroots groups to join the political arm of the movement. Whereas the AIDS associations that had organized from the bottom up in the 1980s were focused on political advocacy, the associations that had organized around AIDS in response to inducements by state actors tended to be relatively apolitical with respect to AIDS, prioritizing service provision over making claims on government. How, then, do civil society organizations acquire the skills and the motivation to participate in the political arena?

In this chapter, I show that Brazil's new service-providing AIDS organizations acquired the skills and the motivation to participate effectively in politics not directly from federal bureaucrats but, rather, from the experienced civic advocacy organizations that had mobilized around AIDS in the 1980s. This chapter, thus, focuses on the contribution of bottom–up forces to the political mobilization of new advocacy organizations – examining both why and how Brazil's experienced activist organizations incorporated newer service-providing groups into the fold of the political AIDS movement. Specifically, experienced AIDS activist groups mobilized Brazil's new service-providing organizations as political advocates because of institutional opportunities for these groups to influence policy. In the context of a participatory governance model of policy-making, an influx of politically ineffective and uninterested civic AIDS groups threatened to obstruct the goals of the national AIDS movement through their participation in policy development discussions. Brazil's experienced AIDS advocacy organizations responded to this threat by providing the diverse array of new civic AIDS organizations in Brazil with the motivation and the political skills to effectively promote the movement's broad policy agenda through these new channels of access to the state.

Brazil's experienced AIDS activist organizations pursued this grassroots-mobilizing campaign by building what I call a federative coalition of AIDS advocacy organizations and engaging new service-providing groups to partici-pate in it. This national grassroots alliance played a key role in mobilizing new civic groups as effective political actors by facilitating the flow of information, resources, and values across organizations. The multi-layered, hierarchical nature of the coalition also provided a mechanism for delegating authority upward from the local level to the national level, helping the movement to develop a coherent national political agenda, as well as a skilled and authori-tative set of national movement leaders.

By the same token, this grassroots coalition did not emerge autonomously. AIDS associations, like most nonprofit associations around the world, lacked the resources to support a strong structure for inter-organizational collabora-tion. Rather, it was progressive bureaucrats in the federal AIDS bureaucracy who, in pursuit of streamlining and strengthening their collaboration with civil society organizations, financed the development of Brazil's AIDS advocacy coalition from a loose social movement network into an institutionalized civil society alliance.

THE CHALLENGE OF MOBILIZING NEW
GROUPS AS POLITICAL ADVOCATES

As I showed in Chapter 5, the massive influx of government funding for AIDS associations had led to a boom in the number of service-providing organiza-tions working on AIDS. However, this funding did not immediately expand political mobilization around AIDS policy. Whereas the AIDS associations that had organized from the bottom up in the 1980s were focused on political advocacy, the associations that had organized around AIDS in response to the influx of federal funding tended to be relatively apolitical with respect to AIDS, prioritizing service provision over making claims on the state. In part, this was because the two new types of civic associations that had engaged in HIV prevention in response to top–down inducements possessed neither the resources nor the political opportunities to influence AIDS policy development or implementation.

First, federal funding for civic AIDS projects had given rise to a large number of "poor" organizations that were dependent on a single donor, often the state (Galvão 2000: 93). Whereas the small group of organizations that had mobilized in the 1980s continued to rely primarily on international foundations for support, by 2003 the overall degree of reliance on state funding was quite high among AIDS associations. (See Figures 6.1–6.3.) The leaders of these AIDS associations tended to come from poorer socioeconomic backgrounds and had little political experience.

Second, federal funding for AIDS projects had also encouraged the directors of civic organizations that were focused primarily on other issues to take on HIV prevention as a way of expanding or diversifying their sources of income. As one informant from the state of Rio explained:

What happened is that we needed to get project resources, and [simultaneously], in the community [we worked with] there began to emerge a demand for work with sexuality in the two units for adolescents.

And so one fine day in the middle of that story there was a competition for consultants to develop an [HIV education] project. And my team … they had various ideas … everyone in my team knew about [the project competition] and was talking about it. We were between projects, and so we needed to do something … [we were] in a moment without money coming in. And so everyone said: Let's apply for the consultancy … And I took one look at [the announcement] and said: 'I'm not going to [do that].' But they bothered me so much about it.

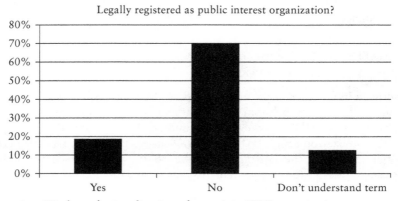

FIGURE 6.1. *Weak professionalization of new civic AIDS organizations*

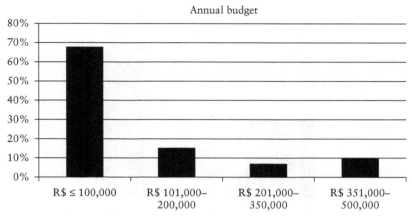

FIGURE 6.2. *Relatively small budgets of civic AIDS groups*

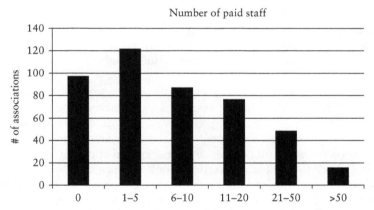

FIGURE 6.3. *Large number of associations with little or no paid staff*

I was the last one to apply, and I handed in the application fifteen minutes after the deadline, but I was the only one to be chosen. I went.[1]

While Kátia is now a major AIDS movement activist, she first engaged her civic association in HIV prevention work out of pure financial expediency. These new "AIDS associations" included core members of other social movements, such as the Afro-Brazilian movement and the feminist movement. Thus, in response to the expansion of federal funding for nongovernmental groups,

---

[1] Interview with Kátia Edmundo, Executive Coordinator of *CEDAPS* (Center for the Promotion of Health), September 6, 2008.

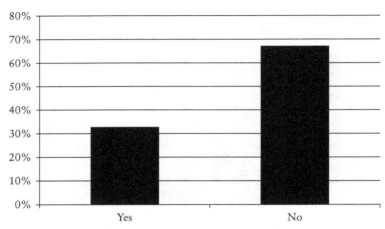

FIGURE 6.4. *Percent of AIDS associations dedicated exclusively to the issue of AIDS*

the population of associations working on AIDS issues in Brazil also grew to include a large number of groups that merely *incorporated* AIDS into their agendas, sometimes as one among many issues (Galvão 2000: 101–3). (See Figure 6.4.)

These new AIDS associations possessed fewer resources and opportunities to participate in the AIDS policy arena than the earlier generation of AIDS associations in Brazil. Organizing effective political campaigns requires a significant amount of time and energy; so does managing short-term service-provision projects, preparing reports for funders, and applying for new sources of funding. Since these new associations took on their first AIDS projects in response to the incentive of (and often the desperate need for) organizational funding, they had been focusing their scarce human resources on completing their service projects and renewing their contracts. At the same time, political demand-making requires the capacity to assign blame for policy failures, which also requires resources – in the form of a staff member with the training and the dedicated time to gaining an understanding of the complicated technical and medical aspects of AIDS policy in Brazil. These new AIDS associations, which were dedicated to multiple issues at once and were often primarily focused on other key social issues, lacked the time and resources to gain such in-depth knowledge about the mechanics of AIDS policy development and implementation. As I described in Chapter 5, national bureaucrats recognized this challenge and responded by developing projects to train newer associations in political advocacy. Yet, on its own, project funding for political advocacy had only a limited effect.

As I show below, established AIDS advocacy groups provided this new generation of civic AIDS organizations with both the incentives and the skills to participate in political advocacy by engaging them in a national AIDS advocacy coalition. What, then, motivated these established AIDS advocacy organizations, already successful in their own efforts, to invest themselves in mobilizing new members of the movement?

THE HIDDEN THREAT OF PARTICIPATORY GOVERNANCE

Brazil's experienced AIDS advocacy organizations were motivated to mobilize the new array of service-providing associations as political advocates because of the participatory governance structure of the Brazilian state. It was not project funding itself that posed a threat to established AIDS advocacy organizations. In a context of unregulated access to the state, such as under the pluralist model, Brazil's AIDS activist groups could have ignored these newer NGOs altogether. With their strong social and political capital, they could easily have crowded out these relatively unskilled groups from the political arena. However, the participatory governance structure of policymaking in Brazil provided a level of political relevance to these new civic AIDS organizations that they would not have achieved on their own; by opening space for insider access to the state, collaborative policymaking bodies provided opportunities for political influence to civic organizations that lacked advocacy skills, or even political goals. This opening of access to inside influence over policy decisions by politically unskilled and uninterested "civil society representatives" threatened to reverse the past political and policy achievements of Brazil's established AIDS advocacy organizations. AIDS activist groups responded to this threat by mobilizing the new generation of civic AIDS organizations as political allies.

This threat occurred at both the subnational and the national levels of government. At the subnational level, the principal problem was that spaces were set aside on local-level policymaking committees for nongovernmental organizations even in states without an AIDS movement presence. By allocating spaces in local AIDS policy arenas for civil-society groups in regions without an organized AIDS movement, the state gave a political voice to grassroots leaders who lacked the motivation and skills to engage in AIDS policy debates on their own initiative. This incorporation of unskilled, apolitical civic organizations as AIDS movement representatives on government policymaking bodies threatened to enable conservative government officials to make policies that conflicted with the core human rights principles of the AIDS movement – helping them to legitimize their policy proposals by claiming that the AIDS movement was represented in their policy decisions.

The participatory governance model of policymaking also posed a challenge for the AIDS movement at the federal level. Because spaces for civil-society representatives within national-level AIDS policy bodies were distributed evenly by region, inexperienced leaders of new AIDS service organizations from underdeveloped regions were brought into national AIDS policy debates.

Bringing these unskilled civic groups into national political discussions diminished the coherence of the AIDS movement's representation within national policymaking bodies – which, in turn, threatened to weaken the AIDS movement's ability to influence national policy development through inside channels. Diminishing the coherence of the AIDS movement within national policy arenas also threatened to weaken the national political reputation of AIDS activist groups as highly skilled, rational, and politically stable actors. Thus unable to crowd new civic AIDS groups out of the political arena, the older generation of AIDS activist organizations in Brazil chose instead to mobilize them as political allies: providing them with advocacy skills and encouraging them to adopt the established groups' broad political vision of AIDS policy.

BUILDING A NATIONAL COALITION

The way that Brazil's experienced AIDS activist groups mobilized the newer generation of civic organizations as effective political advocates was by developing an institutionalized and hierarchical national AIDS advocacy coalition – what I call a federative coalition – and engaging new civic organizations to participate in it. The institutionalized, hierarchical nature of coordination among AIDS associations in Brazil is striking because, like most twenty-first-century social movement activists, they tend to reject authoritative leadership on principle. Moreover, at first glance, Brazil's AIDS movement seems to embody network-based activism. In my research, nearly all the activists I interviewed emphasized the central importance of social movement networks to the past and future success of the movement. In practice, a dizzying array of activist networks contribute in various ways to the AIDS movement, from the National Network of People Living with HIV/AIDS (RNP+) and the Network for Action on AIDS, International Policy and Development (UMUL), to entities such as The Brazilian Network for the Integration of Peoples (REBRIP), dedicated in part to intellectual property rights, and *Comunicaids*, a network dedicated to the politics of communication about the AIDS epidemic in Brazil. Yet, while the national coalition of AIDS advocacy organizations was not a formal entity, without even a label or name to describe it, in practice the national coalition of AIDS NGOs flouted the principles of informality and consensual decision-making in its core features.

The national coalition of AIDS NGOs was hierarchical in that it was organized according to a three-tiered pyramid structure, delegating authority upward from the state level to the national level. The basic units in the coalition were the AIDS NGO forums, which were located in state capitals and were composed of the individual NGOs working with AIDS in each state. The forums were aggregated into regional NGO conventions called ERONGs (*Encontros Regionais de ONGs*), held once every other year, which coordinated state-level priorities and elected delegates to the national convention. The supreme body of the movement was the semi-annual national NGO convention called the ENONG (*Encontro Nacional de ONGs*), consisting of 350

IMAGE 6.1. *Voting at the 2007 ENONG*

voting delegates and an additional 120 observers (ENONG 2009, unpublished data).[2] The national convention created the AIDS movement's political platform and elected movement representatives to participate on national and international policy committees (ENONG 2007, unpublished data). During the long periods between conventions, the highest authority was a body called ANAIDS (*Articulação Nacional de Luta Contra a AIDS*), which was the functional equivalent of a national secretariat. This national secretariat was composed of forty NGOs, which were elected by the different constituencies that comprise the national convention in a system that attempts to ensure diversity of representation.

ANAIDS was the effective seat of power within the movement. It was, in essence, a committee composed of the movement's most powerful leaders. One representative from each of the twenty-seven state NGO forums sat on the committee. Joining them were all of the movement representatives who had been elected by the national convention to national and international AIDS policy commissions and working groups, and representatives from each of the three national networks of people living with HIV/AIDS (ANAIDS 2011).

---

[2] The number of voting delegates is determined by the organizing committee and, thus, varies somewhat from year to year.

Meeting several times a year, ANAIDS was vested with the authority to implement the AIDS movement's agenda that was set by the national convention. ANAIDS was also responsible for setting new agendas in response to political developments. At the same time, the members of ANAIDS spoke to the government and to the public on behalf of the movement.[3] They also supervised the activities of the movement's forums, networks, and individual NGOs.

The national coalition of AIDS NGOs was, moreover, a relatively stable and permanent structure, based on explicit bylaws and statutes. At the federal level, ANAIDS was a permanent and elected body, guided by established rules and procedures. At the state level, AIDS NGO forums were permanent entities with their own statutes or bylaws, some of which had their own headquarters and budgets and were formally registered with the state.[4] For example, Brazil's Catholic AIDS service organization, the *Pastoral da AIDS*, requested membership in the movement's state-level forums with the following formal proposal, approved by vote during the 2007 ENONG and incorporated into the final resolution:

We solicit the State AIDS Forums to recognize the *Pastoral da AIDS* as a space for political coordination in the Fight against AIDS, considering that all our local associations are covered under our registration as a national nonprofit organization, and that the *Pastoral da AIDS* is present and active in all the states of the Federation. We propose that the Forums recognize the work of the *Pastoral da Aids* and open space for it to become an affiliated organization according to [the forums'] statutory rules.[5]

This proposal is significant because it reflects both a general recognition of NGO Forums as the official local-level expressions of the AIDS movement and deference to the established rules and procedures for engaging with the movement.

Despite these characteristics, the coalition was not a traditional federation either. Unlike many traditional federations, it was forged from the bottom up among a diverse group of advocacy organizations. Activist leaders from São Paulo and Rio developed the idea to spread NGO forums across Brazil because they recognized that collaboration with state officials would be more effective if the AIDS movement in other states were organized as well. They implemented this plan at first by traveling to states where local NGOs had expressed interest in organizing themselves into AIDS forums, leading training sessions about how to develop the structure of a forum. Leaders spread the idea to the remaining states of Brazil, where grassroots AIDS leaders had not yet shown

---

[3] See, for example, *Agência AIDS* 2013. "Articulação Nacional de Luta Contra a AIDS manifesta seu desagravo contra à 'Moção de Repúdio' encaminhada ao Conselho Naional de Saúde."

[4] Interview with Rubens Duda 2011. Forum de ONG AIDS do Estado do Rio de Janeiro. 1997. "Carta de Princípios do Fórum de ONG/AIDS – RJ. Rio de Janeiro." Forum de ONGs/AIDS do Estado de São Paulo 2007. "Estatuto do Fórum das ONG AIDS do Estado de São Paulo." Available at www.forumaidssp.org.br/site/modules/news/article.php?storyid=5 (last accessed on October 14, 2013).

[5] ENONG (2007, unpublished data: Article 29).

interest in the idea of coordinating among themselves, during national AIDS conferences and meetings – where they explained to local leaders the importance of AIDS forums for increasing their own political influence. Later, activist leaders from the Southeast developed the regional-level layer of the federative coalition – the ERONGs – in response to similar challenges and in the same way as they had expanded the model of state-level AIDS NGO forums – by pitching the idea to activists across Brazil. Ultimately, the national movement approved the proposal by vote.

Another difference from traditional federations is that Brazil's coalition of AIDS NGOs accommodated diverse forms of organization among its individual member groups. Networks of individuals participated as members of Brazil's national AIDS movement coalition alongside professionalized NGOs. The National Network of People Living with HIV/AIDS (RNP+) and its two offshoots for HIV positive women and for teenagers (*Cidadãs Posithivas* and RNJP+), were even permanent members of the coalition's national executive committee (ANAIDS 2011, unpublished data). Moreover, some of the organizations that belonged to the coalition were organized into their own national networks, such as the national network of Pela Vidda organizations. AIDS associations also autonomously developed informal, "virtual" networks of communication among themselves. FONAIDS, for example, was an email listserve used to share information among organizations. Virtual networks among individual activist leaders also operated under the umbrella of the national coalition, such as Facebook groups. As I will argue below, the federative structure of the national AIDS movement coalition played a key role in facilitating negotiation and collaboration with the state, while simultaneously helping the movement to resist cooptation and maintain its capacity for protest.

SPREADING POLITICAL SKILLS AND
MOTIVATION TO NEW GROUPS

Through the structure of the national AIDS advocacy coalition, Brazil's experienced activist organizations provided a significant portion of the new population of service-providing AIDS organizations with the skills and the motivation to promote AIDS policy advancement in the political arena. The permanent and centralized structure of the AIDS advocacy coalition factored critically into their ability to do this.

The institutionalized nature of the AIDS movement coalition helped experienced activists to cultivate a common set of skills and strategies among movement leaders, through the frequent meetings and conferences that served as the movement's infrastructure. While much of this exchange of skills and expertise occurs spontaneously, during the course of discussions about particular challenges, skill building was also an explicit emphasis of coalition meetings at all levels of the movement. At the state level, forum members frequently organized conferences and seminars about themes related to their specialty (Biancarelli

2012: 21). At regional and national conferences, workshops were offered to train new grassroots leaders as political advocates and as effective organizational leaders. These "capacity building" or "breakout" sessions covered such political topics as how to obtain greater representation in policy arenas, how to promote progressive policies at the local level, and how to confront specific political challenges, in addition to organizational issues such as how to apply effectively for funding, and how to achieve financial sustainability. According to a long-time AIDS activist from the state of São Paulo:

The [NGO] forum has always been a space for learning, a big school of activism and militancy. A space for political capacity building, but also for technical capacity building. The NGO that knew how to access a certain population passed its knowledge to another. The NGOs that had experience with a certain kind of action, that had accumulated knowledge about a certain issue, shared it with everyone.[6]

According to the leader of a community-based group from a poor neighborhood of Rio de Janeiro:

[W]e are learning a lot because the Forum has NGOs that work only with people living with HIV. And we ... we do everything ... Now that [the Forum has] a working group [on AIDS in poor communities] it has gotten even better, because we learn a lot from their experiences ... because they have only one area of work. And seeing that work helps us a lot.[7]

According to a newly minted AIDS activist from the Northeastern state of Bahia, the most important benefit of national meetings and conferences is that it allows him to "multiply what has worked in other states, [using their experiences] as model[s] for us to reproduce."[8]

At the same time, by integrating new civic AIDS groups into a stable and institutionalized activist alliance, the national AIDS advocacy coalition also provided new civic AIDS groups with resources to leverage in making demands on government. Information, for example, was one important resource that civic AIDS groups acquired through their membership in Brazil's AIDS advocacy coalition. According to the leader of another community-based organization from the state of Rio, "The Forum is very important, because through [the Forum] we know what is happening. The information that doesn't get [directly] passed to us, the Forum knows, and the Forum passes [that information] to us institutions."[9]

---

[6] Interview with Mario Scheffer, member and former President of Grupo Pela VIDDA São Paulo, December 11, 2008.

[7] Interview with Márcia Helena de Souza, President and Founder of Centro Comunitária Raiz e Vida, September 25, 2008.

[8] Interview with Fábio Ribeiro, Member of the NGO Forum of the state of Salvador da Bahia, representing the organization *GLICH* (Grupo Liberdade Igualdade Cidadania Homosexual), April 29, 2011, via Facebook chat.

[9] Interview with Tânia, Director of Associação de Mulheres de Edson Passos, September 25, 2008.

IMAGE 6.2. *Soliciting feedback at AIDS movement workshops*

At the regional and national-level meetings of the coalition, information exchange was also important and happened in both formal and informal contexts. For example, important information was often exchanged as activists deliberated formally over the movement's priorities for the upcoming two years, but activists also passed critical information to each other informally, during casual conversations that took place over meals or during other breaks. The extensive array of formal and informal opportunities for information exchange that occurred over the course of these bi-annual, five-day conferences is one reason that older AIDS activists considered the ENONG and ERONGs to be essential elements in their capacity to build a compelling national political agenda.

An important social-capital resource that civic AIDS groups acquired through their participation in the national coalition was powerful political allies, who could support their demand-making efforts or intervene on their behalf. According to an AIDS activist from the state of Pernambuco:

[The Forum] is a space where we strengthen each other collectively, to agitate politically, to act and to pressure government trying to minimize the lacunae that exist ... And it's a political space ... a political space where we also heighten the visibility of [how well the movement is organized] to society. Because in Brazil, all the states have forums ... so that strengthens us a lot. It even helps us get government to listen to us, to take us seriously.[10]

---

[10] Interview with Jair Brandão, member of the NGO Forum of the state of Pernambuco, representing the organization *GESTOS*, November 22, 2008.

Even simply having their local demands included in the movement's national activist agenda gave these newer civic organizations political leverage by bringing them into the national political spotlight.

The institutionalized attributes of the coalition also helped experienced AIDS activist groups to *motivate* the new generation of AIDS associations to participate in politics, both by inculcating them with new political values and by giving them career incentives to invest themselves in political advocacy. The national conferences and meetings that structured the alliance helped activists develop shared political values the same way as it facilitated the development of political skills: by bringing new organizational leaders into extended periods of close contact with experienced activists. The AIDS movement's compelling frame, and the personal stories of leading activists, assisted in this process. In the words of one AIDS advocate, reflecting sentiments that were often expressed to me in my own interviews with activists, "the AIDS movement won me over as a militant when I perceived that it was in the field of a fight for democratization ... it was a movement of reconstructing citizenship" (Roberto Chateaubriand Domingues, cited in Murray 2015: 57). Another important lesson that came from attending national AIDS movement gatherings is that the label "AIDS activist" carried a strong degree of cachet, garnering admiration and respect both in Brazil and around the world.

The structure of the national AIDS advocacy coalition also motivated the leaders of new civic AIDS organizations to invest themselves in political advocacy by providing significant opportunities for career advancement. As grassroots leaders move up the career ladder from state to national AIDS movement representatives, the professional training they received, in tandem with their increasing immersion in professional networks, inculcated them with a shared set of values and norms – in a process that Dimaggio and Powell (1983) label normative isomorphism. By the time activists made it to the top of the movement's leadership hierarchy, they all possessed a significant degree of technical expertise in AIDS policy, strong experience in participating on government committees, and a common understanding of the movement's core mission and values.

The effect of this type of assimilation among activists was particularly dramatic in regions such as the North of Brazil, where there are strong opportunities for career advancement due to the region's small population and disproportionately large representation on many national AIDS councils and committees. The following narrative from an AIDS movement leader in the northern state of Pará represents stories I heard many times during interviews with leaders who had become involved in AIDS advocacy since the 2000s. Describing his process of engagement with the national AIDS movement, he wrote in an email to me:

It was as Coordinator of the AIDS NGO Forum of Pará that I paved my way in the movement. In 2001, when I participated in the ENONG in the [state of] Recife, I was a neophyte. I didn't know anyone, and it was my first incursion into the [AIDS] movement, as I had previously worked with the movement for drug prevention ... But as time passed, I conquered my space. In August of 2008, I [was elected] Representative from the State of Pará to the [National] Commission for Engagement with Social Movements (CAMS); and that was [quite] a learning experience. [Then] in 2009, I was elected Representative for the Northern Region to the National AIDS Commission (CNAIDS) ... [Most recently], due to these [prior] roles, I ended up participating in the elaboration of the three documents Brazil produced for the United Nations UNGASS Special General Assembly Session on AIDS.[11]

In other words, as this AIDS movement activist gained experience and skills, he was promoted over time to increasingly important government policy committees. By the time he reached the point of participating in a major national policy committee, he was already a sophisticated political advocate.

Building a federative coalition was also an important factor in strengthening the movement's leverage over state actors. For example, the federation empowered national activist leaders to credibly claim that their criticisms or policy demands represented the sentiments of the movement's entire national constituent base. According to a movement leader from the state of São Paulo, "One thing is for the movement to have some of its member institutions to criticize the health minister by writing letters or going to the press. Another thing is to have someone criticizing government on behalf of the entire movement. This carries a lot more weight, because of the number of institutions that are behind that official criticism ... [Having a formal national secretariat is] important, because without it you don't have any [credible] way of saying that you represent the national AIDS movement."[12]

Having a centralized leadership structure also helped the AIDS movement resist cooptation by government officials. According to the same informant from São Paulo:

Say the government decides to create a working group to discuss an issue that the movement has been demanding the government address. Instead of coming to the movement to ask who we want the AIDS-movement representatives on the working group to be, the government might instead take someone they already know from [another policy commission] and invite him or her to participate in the working group. But perhaps that particular person doesn't have the technical knowledge or expertise to adequately discuss that issue. What's more, the government might sometimes choose that person precisely because they think he or she won't make waves. But we can [combat this by saying] "no, the movement has ANAIDS. ANAIDS will let you know who's going to represent the movement in your working group."[13]

Because the AIDS movement had its own democratic mechanisms of electing representatives to policy committees, government officials were hindered in their attempts to assert control over the process.

---

[11] Interview with Antonio Ernandes Marques da Costa.
[12] Interview with Claudio Pereira, President of *Grupo de Incentivo à Vida*, São Paulo, May 8, 2014.
[13] Ibid.

In summary, Brazil's established AIDS advocacy groups helped to politically mobilize Brazil's new civic AIDS organizations by building a national coalition with rules and procedures that allowed them to delegate authority to individual members of the AIDS movement who had proven themselves to be capable of effectively representing the interests of the broader coalition. They were motivated to build a federative coalition by the new participatory governance structure of policymaking in Brazil. In contrast to the pluralist model of governance, which provides unregulated access to the state, the participatory governance model concentrates access to the state within formal policymaking committees. Under a pluralist model of governance, the key to avoiding divisive power struggles among ideologically diverse organizations within a social movement coalition is to preserve the autonomy of each alliance member. By contrast, under a participatory governance model, the key to avoiding conflict is to develop rationalized procedures for delegating authority to represent the movement on national policymaking committees. Even though Brazil's AIDS activists tended to reject authoritative leadership on principle, Brazil's new state structure incentivized civic AIDS organizations to develop a centralized structure for demand-making by concentrating access to the policy arena among officially sanctioned organizations.

FEDERAL SUPPORT FOR COALITION-BUILDING

National advocacy coalitions are not, however, built on motivation and dedication alone. Perhaps even more importantly, building a strong national coalition across a geographically dispersed set of organizations requires resources – funding to cover the cost of regular meetings, and time to coordinate events and other common activities. When resources are abundant, organizations are able to use some of their own resources to cooperate with other groups and achieve shared political goals, but when resources are scarce, organizations face a stronger need to ensure their individual organization has the resources to survive (McCarthy and Zald 1977). Most nonprofit organizations – with small operational budgets and a lean, often-volunteer staff – have few if any resources to divert toward supporting collaboration with other associations. This resource mobilization challenge has been highlighted by some academics as a key reason why recent social movements have failed to come together at the national level in anything more than loose networks (Phillips 1991: 768; Weir 1999).

In Brazil's AIDS policy sector, however, state actors mitigated the resource mobilization challenge to civil-society coalition building by providing the resources that sustained the national advocacy alliance. Not only did the national AIDS Program finance all ERONG and ENONG meetings, but it also provided financial or material support for most of the twenty-seven state-level forums. By paying for the space, food, lodging, and transportation to state-level, regional, and national meetings, bureaucrats in Brazil's national AIDS program provided critical assistance in helping NGOs overcome otherwise insurmountable costs to the development of formalized, regularized structures for coordination. In the words of a key informant, "The participation of the national AIDS program was fundamental [in the institutional development of the national advocacy coalition], because without those resources nothing would have happened. It would have remained at the level of good intentions."[14]

At the state level, the national AIDS program supported the month-to-month operation of most NGO forums by subsidizing travel expenses for representatives of member organizations and, in some cases, by paying for other operating expenses such as the rental of forum headquarters. The state provided direct support for the forums that were legally registered, while it provided indirect support for the forums that were informally incorporated by channeling funding or material resources, such as computers, through a "host" association that participated in housing and coordinating monthly meetings.

At the regional and national levels, the national AIDS bureaucracy financed the semi-annual ERONG and ENONG meetings through its "events" budget. Federal travel subsidies were particularly important to the operation of the national coalition, given the relatively high cost of transportation in Brazil, the large geographic area covered by each state (similar to in the western United States), and the relatively low incomes of associational leaders living outside capital cities. The national AIDS bureaucracy had automatically approved funding for all ENONGs since 1993 and for all ERONGs since they first emerged in 2001 (through a contract with the AIDS movement). The 2011 ENONG was financed with approximately R\$1.5 million (about US\$ 1 million in 2011) of federal funding.

Evidence suggests that the national AIDS program provided similar support for activists from adjacent movements to build national civic coalitions. For example, the national AIDS program began subsidizing national LGBT movement *encontros* in 1995, and it was as a result of this funding that participation in these national meetings ballooned from a small handful of organizations to become a large event on the scale of the AIDS movement *encontros* (Facchini 2005; Dehesa 2010). The national AIDS program also subsidized the monthly meetings of statewide LGBT forums, paying for activists' travel and lodging.[15] Moreover, until 2011 the national AIDS program provided project funding for the Brazilian Prostitute Network, a national coalition of thirty-two sex-worker advocacy organizations (Murray 2015: 128).

[14] Interview with Rubens Duda 2011. Forum de ONG AIDS do Estado do Rio de Janiero. 1997. "Carta de Princípios do Fórum de ONG/AIDS – RJ. Rio de Janeiro." Forum de ONGs/AIDS do Estado de São Paulo 2007. "Estatuto do Fórum das ONG AIDS do Estado de São Paulo." Available at www.forumaidssp.org.br/site/modules/news/article.php?storyid=5 (last accessed on October 14, 2013).

[15] Interview with Lula Ramires, Coordinator of Corsa and a founding organizer of the São Paulo pride parade, December 13, 2008.

Motivations of Federal Bureaucrats to Support
a National AIDS Advocacy Coalition

Like Brazil's established AIDS advocacy organizations, federal bureaucrats in the AIDS policy sector were also motivated to support cooperation and coordination among AIDS activists by the participatory governance structure of the Brazilian state. Three problems in particular led them to finance a national structure for grassroots cooperation.

Firstly, federal bureaucrats faced the same incentives to support the development of a nationally organized activist coalition as did the established AIDS advocacy groups in Brazil: to increase the capacity and the motivation of the new generation of civic AIDS organizations to support their policy goals through political advocacy. While federal bureaucrats could encourage the organization of new nongovernmental AIDS organizations by providing them with financial and material resources, and while they could open institutional opportunities for them to influence AIDS policy decisions, they could not themselves ensure that the new generation of civic AIDS organizations would take advantage of these new channels for influencing local AIDS policy, nor that they would be effective political advocates. As I described in Chapter 5, national AIDS bureaucrats had attempted to solve this problem by creating lines of project funding specifically for training civil-society organizations as political advocates. These bureaucrats realized that a national advocacy coalition would amplify the impact of their project-funding efforts.

Secondly, the diverse array of associations claiming to represent the interests of the AIDS movement had led to confusion for federal bureaucrats who were looking to incorporate civil-society representatives into collaborative policy committees. According to one former National AIDS Program director, in the early 2000s even a "simple decision," such as which grassroots leader would represent Brazil in UN Special Assembly on AIDS, led to conflict within the movement. According to the official who directed the National AIDS program in the mid-2000s:

We felt the need to interact with a forum. Or [rather, we felt the need] to interact with the movement, but ... we in government [had] problems achieving this; we [would] go to talk with civil society, and there we [would] have twenty organizations [to choose among]. If they are organized in a forum, it is a lot better for dialogue [between state and society], understand? We see this clearly.[16]

In the words of another federal AIDS official, referencing one particular group from the Amazon:

Before, we had no reference ... no one who was coordinator. Today they have a coordinator, José Raia, from Manaus, Amazonas. Today we can talk directly to him ... He does

---

[16] Interview with Alexandre Grangeiro, Coordinator of the national AIDS program 2003–2004 and Adjunct Coordinator 2001–2003, December 16, 2008; follow-up interview on May 5, 2009.

the channeling of communication ... He leads discussion among member organizations there in Manaus and then comes to us with a decision agreed upon among them. This pertains to any partnership we may propose and to any discussion we take up ... It facilitates the relationship [between us and the movement].[17]

According to them, the presence of clear, singular movement representatives made communication and collaboration with civil society significantly more efficient.

Thirdly, the sudden increase in competing claims to represent the AIDS movement threatened to weaken the political boost that federal bureaucrats had gained through incorporating civil society representations into policy decisions. For AIDS associations to effectively legitimate the agendas of federal AIDS bureaucrats, these associations must have some claim to their own legitimacy as a national movement. When associations come together in a loose, "networked" structure of collaboration, competing agendas may coexist within a movement – detracting from the legitimacy of any single spokesperson. Once the state opens institutional spaces of access for popular associations, the coexistence of competing agendas may lead to prolonged power struggles over participation in government policymaking bodies. Consequently, any policy decision made with the support of one movement representative may simultaneously contain significant factions of dissenters – thus, detracting from any state claims to represent broad societal interests in their policy guidelines.

However, when bureaucrats developed policies in collaboration with activists who clearly represented a broad activist base, these bureaucrats could make strong claims that their policy recommendations were developed in consensus with civil society and thus represented the public interest. In the words of one bureaucrat: "[a scaled-up movement is important] to us, government (referring to the national AIDS program), because it allows civil society to present us with much more organized demands."[18] In the words of another bureaucrat, "representatives [to participatory policymaking bodies] have to be legitimated by organized civil society."[19] This ability to claim that their policy decisions represented the public interest protected bureaucrats from opposition by politicians who may not otherwise have supported their policy goals and strategies. Federal AIDS bureaucrats, thus, discovered they were able to more fully harness the power of the AIDS movement to push forward their objectives if the nongovernmental groups with which they collaborated carried the political weight of all the member AIDS associations. Consequently, federal AIDS bureaucrats financed the efforts of Brazil's established AIDS activist groups to develop an institutionalized national advocacy coalition.

---

[17] Interview with Rubens Duda, bureaucrat in the Unit for Engagement with Civil Society and Human Rights, August 24, 2011.

[18] Interview with Eduardo Barbosa, Adjunct Director of Brazil's National AIDS Program and former director of the Civil Society Unit, November 18, 2008.

[19] Interview with Adele Benzaken, Director of the National Department of IST/AIDS/Hepatitis, August 2, 2017.

By the time I conducted follow-up fieldwork in 2017, federal bureaucrats were unable to imagine dialogue with civil society without a nationally organized movement. For example, when I asked the national AIDS program director in 2017 why the program continued to subsidize a national civic coalition, she said:

The ENONG is where the AIDS movement chooses their representatives to participate in the national AIDS commission (CNAIDS), and it's also where they develop the policy platform they will promote in CNAIDS. If the ENONG didn't exist, how would CNAIDS function? ... How? Like, I myself am going to choose who's going to represent the movement in CNAIDS? No! For the love of God!

According to national AIDS bureaucrats, in other words, the presence of clear, singular movement representatives made communication and collaboration with civil society significantly more efficient and effective. By helping the AIDS movement construct a national coalition, bureaucrats thus strengthened the political leverage they gained through participatory institutions.

This chapter examined how service-providing associations acquire the motivation and the skills to participate in the political arena. In general, the global development community has focused narrowly on shaping government institutions and on funding NGOs as twin strategies to encourage the growth of civil society in the developing world. By contrast, this chapter suggests that access to institutional opportunities and resources are insufficient for a civic association to be able to participate effectively in the political arena. While participatory governance institutions open a new point of access to the state for civic groups, a civic association must possess political skills to be capable of pursuing its goals by participating through this channel. While financial and material resources help civic organizations to be effective in the political arena, an association must have a compelling reason to be willing to invest some of its resources in participating in the political process.

Civic associations in Brazil's AIDS policy sector acquired the skills and the motivation to participate effectively in politics not from federal bureaucrats but, rather, from the experienced civic advocacy organizations that had mobilized around AIDS in the 1980s. In the context of a participatory governance model of policymaking, the influx of politically ineffective civic AIDS groups that had emerged in response to federal funding opportunities threatened to obstruct the goals of the national AIDS movement through their participation in policy development discussions. Brazil's experienced AIDS advocacy organizations responded to this threat by providing the diverse array of new civic AIDS organizations in Brazil with the political skills and the progressive ideologies to effectively promote their broad policy agenda through these new channels of access to the state. Brazil's experienced AIDS activist organizations pursued this grassroots-mobilizing campaign by building a national confederation of AIDS advocacy organizations and engaging the participation of the new civic groups.

7

The Rise of Hybrid Social Movements

By 2010, when I was conducting my fieldwork, Brazil was recognized internationally as a standard-bearer for national AIDS policy development. To be sure, bureaucrats continued to confront serious challenges to cementing that legacy, most of which were related to failures within the broader public health system. But in comparison to most other areas of public health, AIDS policy fared well. Since the 1990s, Brazil's health ministry had continued to guarantee citizens free access to life-saving anti-retroviral drugs – a social benefit not observed even in wealthier countries such as the United States and many in Europe. The national legislature had continued to pass explicit legal protections against discrimination for people living with HIV/AIDS. Brazil's presidents and health ministers together had battled multinational pharmaceutical companies, international lending organizations, and economically powerful countries such as the United States over access to generic drugs – a necessary condition for the government to continue providing free treatment to HIV-infected citizens.

It is widely recognized that politicians and bureaucrats did not achieve this success on their own. National politicians as well as the leaders of major international organizations (including UNAIDS and the World Bank) have praised civic organizations' work on advocacy in the 1980s, and on policy implementation in the 1990s. This perspective, however, overlooks the continued role of AIDS advocacy groups in driving these policy decisions. Behind the scenes, civic associations in the early 2000s continued to be central figures in the negotiation, development, and implementation of nearly every AIDS policy decision at both the national and the subnational levels. On the streets, AIDS organizations protested in key moments. They regularly turned to the media to publicize policy failures and criticize bad government behavior.

For scholars of Latin American social movements, Brazil's AIDS movement is important not only for its political influence, but also because it does not reflect conventional models of civic mobilization in Latin America. First, in stark contrast to the urban workers' movements of the mid-Twentieth Century, Brazil's AIDS movement encompassed a wide range of groups that cut across traditional cleavages such as class, race, gender, religion, and geography. In contrast to the wealthy interest groups that traditionally influence politics, the vast majority of Brazil's AIDS associations operated with limited resources – relying on few donors, small budgets (if any), and mostly-volunteer staffs. The socioeconomic and geographic diversity of organizations that belonged to the AIDS movement was especially remarkable in Brazil, a country renowned for extreme socioeconomic and political inequalities.

Second, Brazil's AIDS movement achieved political influence by combining two strategies that much of the existing literature suggests are mutually opposing: institutional strategies for achieving reform and contentious behavior. On the one hand, the leaders of AIDS associations held official seats in Brazil's most important state-run AIDS policymaking commissions, participated in countless backdoor meetings with government officials, advanced government policy through judicial rulings, and worked to forge strong alliances with local and national politicians. On the other hand, the AIDS movement made frequent use of the media and sometimes took to the streets to criticize government shortcomings. Paradoxically, Brazil's AIDS associations were both politically privileged and combative.

Third, Brazil's AIDS movement used this dual tactic – contentious behavior in addition to collaboration with government – despite deep financial and personal ties to the state. As I show in this chapter, the vast majority of the nearly 1,000 nongovernmental AIDS groups in Brazil relied on some form of governmental financial support for organizational survival. Smaller associations often depended almost entirely on governmental contracts or on material assistance such as electronic equipment, basic supplies, and travel allowances. Even the largest and wealthiest AIDS associations relied on state actors to finance key meetings and conferences. In addition, the personal ties between grassroots AIDS advocates and bureaucrats were extensive. One might expect these friendship bonds to dampen the criticisms leveled against the government, but instead of co-opting these activists into silence, the strong linkages that tied the leaders of Brazil's AIDS movement to state actors encouraged them to shout louder.

AIDS advocacy in Brazil thus represents a form of political organizing and interest representation in Latin America that has been overlooked by traditional scholarship – in which social movements are sustained by their connections to the state, even while they make aggressive demands on the state. Though this model of interest representation exists widely in certain sectors throughout the region, it has received scant attention in scholarly literature. The rest of this chapter will describe, first, the diverse composition of Brazil's AIDS movement in the 2000s and, second, the hybrid strategies used by activists to influence policy.

BRIDGING SOCIAL AND ECONOMIC CLEAVAGES

By 2010, the AIDS movement in Brazil included a melting pot of socially and economically diverse communities that were disparate in style, substance, and experience. From a service-delivery perspective, the wide array of NGOs working on AIDS in the 2000s is perhaps unsurprising. As a large literature on resource mobilization has shown, an expansion of the resource pool – such as the influx of AIDS project funding I described in Chapters 4 and 5 – tends to inspire organizational entrepreneurs to capitalize on such opportunities by expanding their operations.[1] What is more surprising, however, is that the introduction of project funding for AIDS ultimately led not only to a larger number of groups delivering AIDS-related services, but also to a broader range of groups that acted as AIDS policy advocates.

To be sure, many of the experienced and skilled activists from the 1980s and early 1990s continued to be leaders of the movement. Take, for example, a few of my research informants. Veriano, a gay man who spoke four languages fluently, directed a well-funded organization that had conducted research and advocacy on the AIDS epidemic in Brazil since the 1980s, and whose organization helped train AIDS advocates throughout Brazil. Gabriela, a sociologist by training and former prostitute by vocation, ran an advocacy organization that fought for civil rights and STD prevention among sex workers. She also directed the Brazilian Prostitutes' Network, which brought together thirty sex workers' associations across Brazil and included over 20,000 members. Gabriela had been featured in media outlets such as Marie Claire UK, Le Monde, The Miami Herald, and PBS. These were leaders with long experience in the movement.

However, other leaders of the AIDS movement worked for organizations that had joined the movement only in the 2000s. Take, for example, Kátia, a psychologist, who had taken on her first AIDS prevention project in 1996 merely as a way to tap into a new source of funding for her community health association in a poor neighborhood of Rio de Janeiro. By 2010, Kátia had organized the first community-based AIDS prevention network in Brazil, helped to expand the network to eight states, and served as an AIDS advocate on numerous regional, national, and international committees. Maurinho, a gay twenty-year-old from one of Rio's infamously poor *favela* neighborhoods, was inspired by Kátia's organization in 2006 to found an association promoting HIV prevention among LGBT youth and transvestites in his community. At the time of my interview, he was flying around Brazil presenting project ideas to Brazil's most well-established NGOs. Ernandes, from a state in the heart of the Amazon rainforest, initially involved himself in AIDS issues by helping to stem the spread of HIV among injection drug users. Since 2001, Ernandes had participated in leading the AIDS NGO forum in his state and represented his region on Brazil's national AIDS commission. These were part

---

[1] See, for example, the seminal article on resource mobilization by McCarthy and Zald (1977).

of a newer generation of AIDS movement leaders, often from different communities and regions than the earlier generation, but who also participated in AIDS advocacy.

The evidence from my interviews and observations thus suggests that, by 2010, the newer generation of service-providing organizations that had initially taken on AIDS projects in response to financial inducements had since been mobilized as political advocates. Data from the Brazilian Survey of AIDS NGOs, which I conducted in the states of Rio de Janeiro and São Paulo between February and May of 2010, corroborate my findings. As Figure 7.1 shows, by the 2010s nearly all civic AIDS organizations depended on some form of government support; government agencies were the first, third, and fourth most common sources of NGO funding among survey respondents. At the same time, as Figure 7.2 shows, nearly all the NGO directors who responded identified themselves as political activists, and the same percentage reported that they made demands on government at least a few times a year. (See Figure 7.2.)

Survey data also corroborates my observations that, in contrast to the relatively well-educated, middle-class community of AIDS activists that had mobilized in the 1980s, the new generation of AIDS activists in Brazil bridged the class divide. While approximately 30 percent of organizational directors in the survey had a postgraduate degree, another 20 percent had completed only high school or less. Moreover, over 10 percent of them earned less than the minimum wage, with nearly 50 percent earning less than five times the minimum wage (a lower income category in Brazil). Survey data showed that the new

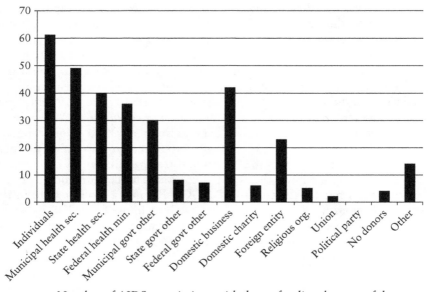

FIGURE 7.1. *Number of AIDS associations with donor funding, by type of donor*

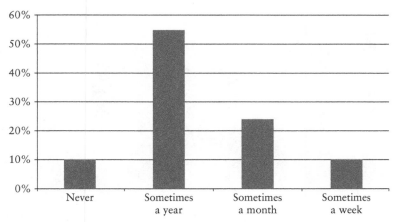

FIGURE 7.2. *Frequency of demand-making on government*

generation of AIDS activists in Brazil also bridged other traditional cleavages in Brazil, such as gender and religion. For example, approximately 10 percent of organizational directors in the survey became involved in political activism initially through the Afro-Brazilian movement, and around another 10 percent became activists initially through the feminist movement. Nearly 40 percent of associations in the survey dedicated themselves to other social issues in addition to AIDS.

The new generation of AIDS advocacy groups in Brazil was also more diverse in terms of their levels of professionalization. In contrast to the relatively wealthy AIDS advocacy organizations that had emerged in the 1980s with support from multiple international agencies, by the 2000s the movement included groups that operated with limited resources – relying on few donors and small budgets. Most AIDS associations in the survey had only between one and five employees; only 40 percent had an institutional website; and only about 20 percent received funding from a foreign donor. At the same time, most AIDS associations in the survey possessed at least a basic organizational infrastructure. Nearly all associations in the survey were legally registered entities; over 90 percent had their own bank account; over 80 percent had an institutional headquarters; and over 75 percent had paid staff. (See Figure 7.3.) Moreover, nearly 90 percent of respondents identified their organizations as NGOs, which are commonly thought of as more professionalized organizations than community-based groups. This suggests that state funding had provided new groups with just enough resources for them to develop a basic institutional structure. (See Figure 7.3.)

In contrast to the more homogeneous community of AIDS movement leaders that had mobilized in the 1980s, these newer AIDS movement leaders represented a wide swath of interests and communities that had historically been

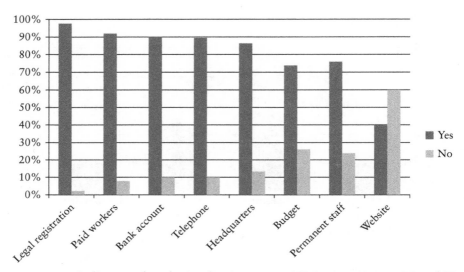

FIGURE 7.3. *Indicators of professionalization among AIDS associations in RJ and SP states*

excluded from the political arena in Brazil. By 2010, the leaders of Brazil's AIDS movement came from the poorer and rural areas of the North and Northeast, as well as from the industrialized regions of the South and Southeast. Within each region, AIDS advocacy groups hailed from both middle-class communities and poor neighborhoods (known as *favelas*). They claimed to represent a number of distinct identities, in addition to people living with HIV/AIDS (PLWHA) including gay, lesbian, and transgendered individuals, prostitutes, injection drug users, the disabled, women, children, and a variety of different races and ethnicities. In contrast to the era of corporatism, when civic organization and mobilization centered on a narrow slice of urban workers, the AIDS movement in the 2000s encompassed a wide range of groups that cut across traditional cleavages such as class, race, gender, religion, and geography.

HYBRID STRATEGIES

Brazil's AIDS activists also stood out from earlier generations of social movements by employing a hybrid set of strategies to achieve the movement's policy objectives. Activists continued to use traditional, public-pressure strategies to influence policy. But activists also worked through a variety of government institutions to influence policy. While public pressure tactics were crucial for the movement's capacity to assert influence in times of crisis or conflict with government, working through government institutions was particularly important to the movement, as a way to influence the design and enforcement of the national laws and policies that govern AIDS programs in Brazil. The hybrid nature of the movement's strategic repertoire presents a stark contrast to earlier generations of protest movements in Brazil and across Latin America.

Institutional Strategies

The way the movement made use of democratic institutions to influence policy was perhaps the most striking contrast between Brazil's AIDS movement of the 2000s and earlier generations of social-movement activism. Earlier generations of activism, operating in a context either of dictatorship or of exclusionary democracy, took place primarily on the streets. By contrast, Brazil's AIDS movement was operating in a context of an open democracy, which incorporated institutional channels for citizens to engage in dialogue with government officials. As I show below, the movement took advantage of all the democratic channels that were newly available to them to influence AIDS policy.

Participatory Governance Institutions

AIDS activists looked first to "participatory governance" institutions to influence government policy. Participation on government policy commissions and committees was the most frequently used strategy that AIDS activists used to make demands on government in the 2000s, according to both survey responses and semi-structured interviews. In the states of Rio de Janeiro and São Paulo, over 60 percent of associational leaders in the sample considered taking part in participatory AIDS policy committees and commissions to be an important strategy for achieving their organization's goals. (See Figure 7.4.) They also

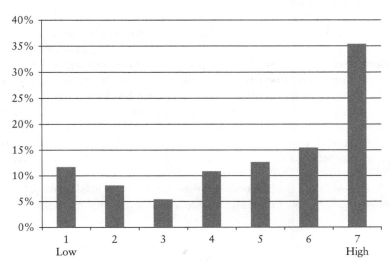

FIGURE 7.4. *"How important for your group is it to serve as a consultant or counselor for a government body?"*

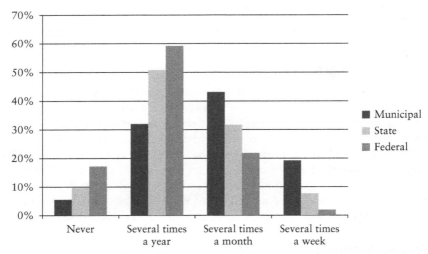

FIGURE 7.5. *Frequency of contact between civic AIDS groups and government bureaucrats*

reported a strikingly large amount of regular contact with AIDS-sector bureaucrats, which further supports the claim that they participated broadly in government policy discussions. (See Figure 7.5.) In this respect, the AIDS movement's strategies corroborate the findings of a growing literature that has suggested participatory governance institutions have become important venues for nonelite groups to exert influence over social and development policies.[2]

The most prominent of the participatory institutions through which AIDS activists sought access to the government policy process was the national health policy council, which, founded in 1991, is the oldest and most established set of modern participatory institutions in Brazil.[3] The movement enjoyed a permanent seat on the council of forty-eight representatives, and through this space, AIDS activists had a formal vote over high-level national health policy decisions. In addition to influencing policy as a voting member of the national health policy council, the movement was able to keep AIDS issues at the forefront of the council's policy agenda through a permanent "working group" within the national health council that was dedicated to policies on AIDS and other STDs.

AIDS activists used health councils at the subnational level as well, but interviewees expressed less enthusiasm to me about state and municipal councils

---

[2] Important examples of such recent scholarship include Abers (2000); Avritzer (2009); Baiocchi (2005); Goldfrank (2011); Mayka (2019b); Wampler (2007).

[3] For more information on the history of Brazil's national health council, see Mayka 2019b. See also http://conselho.saude.gov.br/apresentacao/historia.htm (last accessed April 26, 2018).

than they did about the national health council. When I asked activists to describe the main spaces they used for controlling government (*controle social*), they would often mention health councils, but only after they elaborated a long list of other spaces. Activists tended to be somewhat more enthusiastic about health councils in the states and municipalities where they functioned relatively well. In São Paulo, where Brazil's health councils originated, the president of their AIDS NGO forum provided a relatively long explanation for why the AIDS working group within their state health council was important to the movement's long-term goals, and he could easily name the movement's representatives on the state and local councils.[4] In general, however, activists seemed to view state and local health councils as important for their symbolic value and for supporting the long-term goals of the movement, but of little use for their day-to-day pursuit of political influence.

Yet health councils were not the only, or even the primary, channels that AIDS activists used to access government policymakers. As I showed in Chapters 4 and 5, a wide array of participatory policymaking spaces offered activists a seat at the table in AIDS policy discussions. Some of these spaces were called "commissions": such as the Commission on AIDS and STDs (CNAIDS), the Vaccine Commission, the Commission on Prevention, the Commission for Monitoring AIDS Policy, or even the Commission for Intermediation with Social Movements (CAMS). Other such spaces were called "committees": such as the Committee on Therapeutic Consensus, the Committee on Pharmaceutical Assistance, the Committee for Adherence to Medical Regimens, the Committee on Epidemiology, the Committee for Ethics in Research, the Committee on Men who have Sex with Men, and the Committee on Lesbians. At the same time, a range of *ad hoc* "working groups" brought activists into short-term series of discussions over policy with bureaucrats.

These spaces – commissions, committees, and working groups – are not contemplated by most existing scholarship on participatory governance because they refrain from offering activists a formal vote over policy decisions; rather, activists are included as consultants.[5] In Brazil, these spaces are usually referred to as "consultative" spaces, to distinguish them for "participatory" (or what they sometimes call "deliberative") spaces.

However, the activists I interviewed tended to perceive these spaces as even more central to strategies for accessing government than the technically "participatory" spaces that offered them an official vote. In fact, participatory institutions offered the AIDS movement such a strong degree of informal influence over policy that activists tended to discount the value of wielding a formal vote over policy design. According to José Marcos de Oliveira, who at the time of

---

[4] Interview with Rodrigo Rinheiro, President of the AIDS NGO Forum of the State of São Paulo, November 12, 2008.

[5] In Portuguese, these spaces are known as *espaços consultivos* (consultative spaces), in contrast to *espaços participativos* (participatory spaces).

our interview represented the AIDS movement in Brazil's national health policy council, most AIDS activists tended to prefer working through AIDS-policy commissions and committees than through the national health council. In his words:

> The AIDS movement is very present, effectively participating in consultative spaces, but it's not so present, so active in the [formally designated] deliberative spaces ... Why? Because whereas I'm alone in the National Health Council, in the National AIDS Commission I'm with forty colleagues.
>
> In deliberative spaces you operate in isolation ... why do I say isolation? Because you can't bring thirty people there with you. You only get one organizational representative, get it? So that makes each representative feel theoretically isolated. Because, for example, I represent the AIDS movement in a space that has forty-four other representatives. These guys aren't forty-four representatives from the AIDS movement; they're forty-four representatives from other social movements ... Which is to say that I am in that lion's den trying to convince them of the importance of AIDS policy.[6]

José Marcos clearly regarded the national health policy council as important for AIDS activists to influence the Brazilian health policy agenda. Yet, although health councils were the only type of participatory institutions that gave activists a formal vote over policy design, José Marcos was suggesting AIDS activists preferred the consultative spaces that were specific to AIDS policy – bringing multiple activists into contact with AIDS sector officials – and that through such "consultative" spaces activists wielded real influence. This general preference held true in conversations about state-level policy-making as well.

Participatory governance institutions, broadly defined, were the preferred channel for influencing policy not only by activists in Rio de Janeiro and São Paulo, but also by activists in the more far-flung regions of Brazil. For example, a grassroots leader from the Northeastern state of Pernambuco reflected:

> There are a lot of strategies [that we use]. But before anything you have dialogue. Before we do any of these other things that we do, we call in a state representative for a discussion. I believe that dialogue is indispensable.[7]

Similarly, Ernandes from the state of Pará noted that "the most common political strategies we use are activities on government health councils – both state-level and municipal level."[8] These statements, representative of the sentiments expressed to me by other activists across Brazil, suggest that the newer, more diverse generation of AIDS organizations used this new channel of access

---

[6] Interview with José Marcos de Oliveira, AIDS – Movement delegate to the National Health Council, November 22, 2008.

[7] Interview with Jair Brandão de Moura Filho, staff member of GESTOS, an AIDS NGO in the state of Pernambuco, November 22, 2008.

[8] Interview with Ernandes Marques da Costa, Coordinator of the AIDS NGO Forum of the state of Pará, April 29, 2011 (via Skype).

to the state to influence policy as well as the older, more economically privi-leged, cosmopolitan, and male generation of activists.

AIDS activists used the venue of participatory governance institutions in multiple ways to influence AIDS policy. Certainly, they used these government commissions for their officially intended purpose: to influence the design of AIDS policy proposals. For example, one of the terms that was used repeatedly in my interviews was the word "pact." Government bureaucrats and activists alike explained to me that AIDS policy was not created from above, but was "pacted" with civil society, meaning that AIDS policies were created through deliberation and negotiation with civil society. Others used similarly direct statements, such as the bureaucrat who told me, "Whenever we design policies, we always engage activists."[9] In the states where policy experts ran the AIDS program, such as in São Paulo, government bureaucrats repeatedly emphasized to me that civil society wielded strong influence over AIDS policy formulation through this channel. According to an AIDS-sector bureaucrat from the state of São Paulo:

AIDS policy, here in the state of São Paulo, isn't made vertically. These policies ... they don't come from the state, imposed. They come as a product, which is discussed, pacted; and decisions are taken in the collective. There doesn't exist any imposition; there exists a *construction* of policy.[10]

According to an activist from Rio de Janeiro, reflecting sentiments expressed to me by multiple activists, "Participation on these government committees helps us confront the most challenging AIDS issues ... When we participate in these spaces, we denounce the problems we see, but we also try to bring proposals for how to solve these proposals. "(Interviewer: "So, would you say these spaces give you a channel for directly influencing policy?")" Yes, yes, for direct influence."[11] The policy design stage is a particularly important part of the policymaking process because it is when the broad terms of the policy debate are set. These initial discussions over what new policies should look like tend to determine the scope and boundaries of all subsequent policy discussions.

But in addition, the structure of participatory governance provided AIDS activists with new *informal* opportunities for influence over policy. For exam-ple, activists gained useful contact information through their involvement in participatory spaces. Suddenly, AIDS activists had the names and phone num-bers of bureaucrats whom they could call when they had political concerns

---

[9] Interview with Juliana Givisiez, bureaucrat in the National Department of IST/AIDS/Hepatitis, August 2, 2017.

[10] Interview with Jean, bureaucrat in the AIDS program of the state of São Paulo, November 10, 2008.

[11] Interview with Veriano Terto Jr., Vice-President of the Brazilian Inter-Disciplinary AIDS Association, August 8, 2017.

or for clarification about new policy decisions. In this way, the new lines of communication with national bureaucrats helped activists to influence policy through back channels.

Activists gained informal influence inside the space of official meetings of participatory governance institutions as well. During the regularly scheduled meetings of government AIDS commissions, committees, and working groups that I attended, AIDS activists typically voiced various concerns that had emerged in the past month and sometimes demanded a response. AIDS-sector bureaucrats would often listen to the problems that were raised by civic advocacy groups during these informal discussions and then discuss potential solutions. This dynamic of information sharing and collective problem-solving was a constant in participatory governance meetings, and the issues raised ranged from the mundane to the life-threatening. A particularly illustrative example of how activists wielded informal influence over policy design through participatory governance was given to me by Adele Benzaken, Director of the National AIDS program during a brief period of follow-up fieldwork in 2017. Reflecting on a working-group meeting, Adele recounted:

One of the conversations we had [in the working group for trans populations] was so interesting: trans men and the difficulties they have in going to the gynecologist. Because with a masculine social name, upon entering the gynecologists' office, they aren't able to get an appointment. But they *need* gynecological exams. I had never in my mind imagined that situation![12]

Bureaucrats also used these forums to bring activists' attention to emerging policy problems, which enabled civic organizations to seek solutions to new policy challenges before they developed into more serious problems. These observations support the arguments of scholars such as Avritzer (2009) and Wampler (2007), who claim that local participatory governance institutions have succeeded in expanding direct citizen influence over policy in political contexts where governors and mayors are willing and where civil society is strong and cohesive.

AIDS activists also used participatory institutions in ways that have not been addressed by existing scholarship. Participatory governance committees were just one among several important democratic channels for civic AIDS groups to influence government policy, and their utility as a channel for demand-making was, in important cases, predicated on the simultaneous use of these other channels for influencing policy. In fact, when AIDS activists failed to directly influence policy through participatory institutions, they sometimes used such institutions as venues to organize demand-making campaigns in other political arenas.

---

[12] Interview with Adele Benzaken, Director of the National Department of IST/AIDS/Hepatitis, August 2, 2017.

One context in which activists would complement their participation on government committees with other forms of demand-making was in places where governors or mayors obstructed AIDS policy. As others have noted, the direct impact of participatory governance on policy at lower levels of government depends on the support of the governor or mayor and his or her health secretary, who are often able to ignore policy recommendations (Wampler 2007). In other words, participatory governance institutions have no direct impact when bureaucrats lack the autonomy or the capacity to enact policy. This type of problem was reflected in a conversation I had with an activist from Rio de Janeiro, who had come away rather dejected from a meeting of the state AIDS policy commission. As a bemused Willian complained to me:

Every meeting has been a tidal wave of reports ... report, report, report, and nothing has progressed. Because [it turns out] the health secretary didn't ... wasn't signing [anything handed to him by the commission], because (listing the excuses that had been proffered by the health secretary) he's in the secretary of administration's office, because he's waiting for the secretary of the treasury to approve the resources, because the governor didn't sign the pact, because legal council delayed negotiations with UNESCO, and on and on.

And on top of it, the last two ... the last two meetings of the state commission were horrible, weren't they? It turns out that inside the health secretariat there was a true organized crime ring to rob the state! The health secretariat wasn't there to provide the population with health, with health services, or to prevent illness. No. There was an organized crime ring inside the state health secretariat to rob state resources. And with the support of everyone, including the governor![13]

Willian's recollection of these recent state AIDS commission meetings offers two broader lessons. On the one hand, it highlights the limits of participatory governance in a context of obstructive politicians. And on the other hand, by suggesting that Willian was informed about such corruption inside the meeting of the state AIDS commission, it highlights how participatory governance institutions facilitate information sharing between bureaucrats and civil society – an aspect of participatory governance that has been relatively overlooked by existing studies.

Willian's summary of the corruption with Rio's health secretariat was no exaggeration. At the time of completing this manuscript, the governor of Rio de Janeiro from 2007 to 2014, Sergio Cabral, was in jail on charges of leading an organized crime ring that stole over US$64 million from state coffers. Arrested in that same week of November 2016 was the governor of Rio de Janeiro from 1999 to 2002, Anthony Garotinho, also jailed on corruption charges.

In these cases, AIDS advocacy groups turned to other forms of political persuasion. For example, the same grassroots activist from Pernambuco who

---

[13] Interview with Willian Amaral, President of the Rio de Janeiro state branch of the Network of People Living with HIV/AIDS (RNP+) and representative to the State HIV/AIDS Commission, August 6, 2008.

had earlier stressed the importance of dialogue with AIDS-sector bureaucrats added, "If we fail to resolve the problem with dialogue, we have to turn to those other instruments, those other means, those mechanisms [for getting things done]."[14]

Participatory governance committees served as strategic venues for planning these other types of political campaigns. Often, they served as channels for beleagured AIDS-sector bureaucrats to supply activists with information to help them confront politically appointed health secretaries. For example, the same activist who had complained to me about the inefficacy of monthly AIDS commission meetings also mentioned how at a subsequent meeting the coordinator of the state AIDS program gave the activists at that meeting all the information they needed – statistics on specific AIDS policy failures – to use for their upcoming protest and in talking to the press.

One case of such political organizing occurred in a series of meetings I attended during my fieldwork. In this case, a pressure campaign was organized in response to a health secretary threatening to eliminate the autonomy of AIDS-sector bureaucrats to make their own policy management decisions. Closing the door of the meeting room – located within the building of the state health secretariat – the state's AIDS program director suggested to the AIDS advocates in attendance that they independently address the problem with the governor, using their bargaining power to negotiate a change in policy. A subsequent "extraordinary" meeting of the AIDS policy commission was then arranged to plan the campaign (a meeting I also attended), held this time at a location several hours away from the state health secretariat building but attended by bureaucrats and civic advocates alike – using a government van as transportation. This was a clear example of activists and interested bureaucrats jointly using the venue of participatory governance committees to plan a broader political advocacy campaign. I either witnessed or heard about many examples of participatory governance institutions facilitating this kind of political collaboration during my time in the field, although most cases did not involve such an overt role by government bureaucrats.

Overlooked by existing scholarship on participatory governance, such stories of strategizing by AIDS activists suggest that participatory governance institutions are just one new channel for civic groups to influence policy in Brazil, and that whether civic groups succeed in influencing policy through participatory governance institutions depends in part on their activities in other political arenas. In some cases, the AIDS movement's failure to influence policy through participatory governance committees was followed by a success in other arenas. In other cases, activists were effective in influencing policy through participatory governance committees only because they simultaneously worked through other channels to influence policy. As I show next, civic

---

[14] Interview with Jair Brandão de Moura Filho, November 22, 2008.

AIDS organizations made demands on government not only through the institutional spaces constructed explicitly for them, but also through the courts, the legislature, the media, and the streets.

The Courts

The courts were another favored strategy for influencing AIDS policy development among AIDS activists. As Chapter 2 highlighted, Brazil's AIDS advocacy groups were pioneers in using the courts as strategic venues for advancing AIDS policy (Hoffman and Bentes 2008: 113, 125–6). As I described in Chapter 5, the courts gained broader prominence in the 2000s as strategic venues for enforcing policy. Given the weak regulatory capacity of Brazilian bureaucracy, prosecution was a particularly important tool for ensuring that victims of discrimination were compensated, and that people living with HIV were provided adequate services and treatment. HIV-based discrimination was still common in the 2000s. Such discrimination ran the gamut from subtle forms, such as employees who were "laid off" after their HIV status became known, to explicit, such as drug lords forcing *favela* residents with HIV to move out of their communities. More commonly, private businesses and state agencies shirked their obligations to provide social safety net benefits that were mandated by national AIDS policy – such as free bus passes to facilitate doctor visits, or social security payments to sustain those who could no longer work, or to force public hospitals to refill their stocks of anti-retroviral medications.

Thanks in part to the National AIDS Program funding for legal aid projects that I described in Chapter 5, AIDS activists' use of the judicial system as an AIDS advocacy strategy had expanded by the 2000s to new regions of Brazil, and the number of legal claims filed at the state and municipal levels had increased dramatically. According to one count, over 3,000 health-related cases – mostly AIDS-related – were brought to court in just four state-level tribunals alone (Hoffman and Bentes 2008: 117) According to survey responses, nearly half of AIDS advocacy groups in Rio de Janeiro and São Paulo perceived the courts to be a key channel for making claims on government. (See Figure 7.6.)

Qualitative interviews corroborated the survey evidence that civic AIDS groups in Brazil used litigation as a central political strategy. According to an activist in Rio de Janeiro, "We use the public prosecutor's office to force the state to give us what is rightfully ours."[15] According to an activist in the state of Rio Grande do Sul:

Another strategy we have used a lot, and that has been effective, is partnering with legal aid groups and public prosecutors.[16] [For example], in the municipality of Porto Alegre, the health secretary had a vision of politics and a vision of AIDS that was very different

---

[15] Interview with Willian Amaral, August 6, 2008.
[16] In Portuguese: *promotorias públicas*.

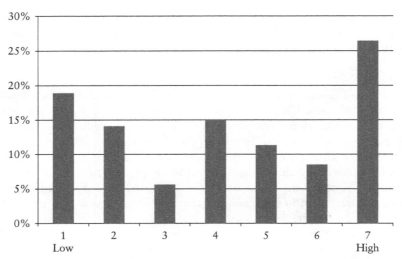

FIGURE 7.6. *"How important for your group is it to enter the legal system through class action suits or other legal means?"*

from the national AIDS policy in Brazil, which is what civil society works with. [He] didn't want to make policies on behalf of the groups we saw as priorities – who were mainly gays, trans, and prostitutes, because in Brazil the epidemic is still very concentrated among gays and transvestites. And [the health secretary] didn't want to make any policies [that benefited them]. Because he thought that gays were freaks of nature, he didn't see the need for policies directed toward gays. So [in Porto Alegre], we succeeded in advancing [AIDS policy] mainly through the prosecutor's office.[17,18]

My observation in the state of Rio de Janeiro was that legal aid groups filed a significant portion of their complaints against government agencies to enforce existing policies such as providing worker benefits.

As I described in Chapter 4, Brazil's social-democratic constitution provided leverage for activists to use in making demands through the courts. As an activist from São Paulo described:

So that's how we manage to make use of the judiciary, guaranteed with the laws of our national health system (*Sistema Único de Saúde*). Article 196 of the Federal Constitution makes it clear that health is an obligation of the state and the right of the citizen ... And from that law there is a subjective law, which is what fits under its responsibilities? It's on the citizen to enter into action in the courts. And the forum does that. That's a form of *controle social* (societal control).

---

[17] In Portuguese: *procuradorias.*
[18] Interview with Marcia Leão, activist from the State of Rio Grande do Sul, April 5, 2011.

[For example,] I need a particular medication that will save my life. And I go to the hospital and they don't have that medication. But the Constitution says the following: "It is your right and an obligation of the state." Damn, but why don't they have that medication? They were supposed to have it, but they don't have money. So fine. Then I go fight in the courts to get it. And I don't win medication by my actions in the executive branch. I win my medication through my actions in the judiciary. The courts give me the medication. It's very interesting how the structure of politics works in this country, isn't it?[19]

In this activist's mind, it was clear how the 1988 constitution changed the playing field for activists to make demands on government, as well as how constitutional reform introduced the courts as a new channel for demand-making.

Interviews further revealed that a wide range of AIDS organizations used the courts, including the newer generation of AIDS groups that had mobilized in the 2000s in response to project funding. According to an activist in the Northern state of Pará, for example, "When a situation isn't resolved via council, or with the bureaucrats in the AIDS sector directly, or with the health secretary through that initial dialogue with the bureaucrats, we go to the public prosecutor's office, and from there we enter into judicial action."[20] Similarly, an activist from the state of Bahia explained that they used the courts "where medications run out or where there is discrimination against people living with AIDS, or with questions related to social security, then we go to the courts."[21] Nearly all of my informants, in all states, cited judicial action as a key recourse when dialogue with bureaucrats failed to produce positive results.

The Legislature

Together, the courts and participatory governance institutions provided two significant new channels for civic advocacy groups to influence AIDS policy across Brazil. But there were also important limitations to the use of the executive and judicial branches. While the judicial branch could advance structural reforms by interpreting the meaning of the social rights guarantees within Brazil's constitutional framework, many judges saw it as the role of the executive and the legislative branches to define the specific way in which policy should be shaped to protect these rights (Hoffman and Bentes 2008: 106). While the executive-branch bureaucracy could develop new policies, these policies were harder to enforce and easier to overturn than policy that had been made through legislation.

In practice, the legislature posed both an opportunity and a threat to the AIDS movement's goals. It provided the opportunity for the movement to consolidate national policy guidelines by translating them into legislation. For example, a Workers' Party senator from the state of Minas Gerais, Serys

---

[19] Interview with José Roberto Pereira ("Betinho"), member of the leadership of the São Paulo state AIDS NGO forum, November 27, 2008.
[20] Interview with Ernandes Marques da Costa, April 29, 2011.
[21] Interview with Fabio Ribeiro, April 29, 2011, via Facebook chat.

Slhessarenko, had proposed in 2005 a law that would criminalize discrimination against people based on their HIV status.[22] If this bill were passed, the human rights protections outlined in Brazil's national AIDS policy guidelines would gain powerful legal backing. By contrast, other proposed legislation threatened to reverse national AIDS policy guidelines – such as the bill floating around Congress that would make it a crime for someone to infect another with HIV.[23] More mundane legislation also threatened the AIDS movement's goals, such as legislation that created obstacles for CSOs to access their earmarked funding.[24] This type of legislative barrier was especially common at the state and municipal levels, where AIDS policy was implemented. AIDS activists viewed congressional lobbying as important both for taking advantage of legislative opportunities and for combatting threats. Thus, in the 2000s they began to strengthen their efforts to influence legislative politics.

Activists used the structure of congressional AIDS caucuses to lobby congress, both at the national level and at the state level. As I described in Chapter 5, the initiative to build congressional AIDS caucuses at the state level was inspired by federal bureaucrats, but led by activists. By 2010, congressional AIDS caucuses had spread to eight states and two municipalities. While the AIDS policy leaders of the industrialized Southeast and South were among the earliest states to inaugurate the congressional caucuses, underdeveloped AIDS policy laggards such as Amazonas and Rio Grande do Norte were also included. Informant interviews revealed initiatives to develop AIDS-related caucuses in the Northeastern state of Bahia and the Northern state of Pará as well.[25] While some of these caucuses focused specifically on AIDS, others addressed both AIDS and tuberculosis, and still others addressed public health in general. All of these caucuses were developed by AIDS movement leadership, and whether to incorporate other public health causes as a central focus of the congressional caucus was the subject of internal debate.

While the ostensible purpose of developing congressional caucuses was to pass new AIDS legislation, informant interviews suggest that AIDS advocacy groups used the caucuses most frequently to help them enforce existing laws and policies. Even with congressional caucuses, advancing AIDS legislation was a belabored process. Members of congress had to balance a large number of competing priorities in determining which legislative proposals to bring to a

---

[22] This law was registered as Lei nº 12.984 de 02/06/2014.

[23] See https://unaids.org.br/2017/05/pl-19815-que-criminaliza-transmissao-hiv-vai-audiencia-publica/, https://nacoesunidas.org/grupo-de-trabalho-critica-projeto-de-lei-que-criminaliza-trans missao-do-hiv/, and http://www.aids.gov.br/es/node/64818 (last accessed February 10, 2018)

[24] For a list of current legislative proposals related to HIV/AIDS, see www.aids.gov.br/pt-br/o-departamento/projetos-de-lei-em-andamento (last accessed February 10, 2018)

[25] In 2010, the states with congressional causes were: Amazonas, Ceará, Minas Gerais, Paraná, Rio de Janeiro, Rio Grande do Norte, Rio Grande do Sul, and São Paulo. The municipalities were Alfenas, in the state of Minas Gerais, and Santos, in the state of São Paulo (unpublished government document).

vote; generally, they favored proposals that appealed more directly to their core voter constituencies. By contrast, sympathetic members of congress could easily help to enforce existing policies or legislation. By summoning politicians or their appointees to a public hearing,[26] legislators could quickly call governors and mayors to account for bad behavior. Thus, at the time of my fieldwork, AIDS activists were looking to the legislature primarily as a means to increase political pressure on governors to comply with existing AIDS policy guidelines.

The activists I interviewed offered many examples of using the legislature as a source of political pressure on governors and mayors. Marcia, an activist from the state of Rio Grande do Sul, provided a particularly illustrative example of how AIDS advocacy groups use the congressional caucus to enforce the implementation of current AIDS policy guidelines. In this case, the state health secretary of Rio Grande do Sul had failed to publish specific vaccine guidelines for people with HIV during the H1N1 "swine" flu epidemic of 2010. Marcia provided the following description of how civic advocacy groups used the congressional AIDS caucus in pressuring the health secretary to correct this AIDS policy failure:

We went to the health council to demand a solution to the [problem], and the state didn't comply with the order. Then we went to the AIDS commission, [and the state still didn't do anything]. Beforehand, we had already sent an official letter [to the health secretary] on behalf of the NGO forum, and nothing. So what did we do then? We arranged a meeting with the coordinator of the congressional AIDS caucus, [asking him to help us]. Immediately, he managed to put a discussion of the vaccine guidelines problem on the agenda of the next general assembly meeting of congress; and from there, congress scheduled a public hearing for eight days later. The state AIDS coordinator, the director of the health department, and the adjunct secretary of health all showed up to this public hearing. Obviously, in front of all those congressional members confronting him, and [with everybody witnessing] civil society telling him that he needed to publish vaccine guidelines, the adjunct health secretary had to comply.

The health secretary left there guaranteeing that the next day, *the next day* – it was four o'clock in the afternoon by the time he left the hearing – vaccine guidelines would be published. And the next day, vaccine guidelines appeared in all the newspapers in circulation in the state ... from *Zero Hora*, the newspaper with the largest circulation here, to *Correio do Povo*, *Jornal do Comercio*, in addition to all the other types of media outlets [like radio, television].[27]

An activist from Rio de Janeiro used similar language to explain to me why congressional caucuses were useful to the movement:

It's because in the state legislature things get tied up ... because the state is a behemoth, like any state in the world, like any government. It's bureaucracy. We'll see in what way [the congressional caucus] can facilitate things: either approving laws, or

---

[26] In Portuguese: *audiência pública*.
[27] Interview with Marcia Leão, activist from the State of Rio Grande do Sul, April 5, 2011.

IMAGE 7.1. *AIDS activists meeting with a member of the national congress*

facilitating certain actions, or making demands ... because, actually, what we can't demand directly ... [For example,] if a state hospital isn't attending patients, members of the congressional caucus can call them in to the legislative assembly to explain themselves ... They (politicians) have the power; we don't have it. We can invite them, but they don't always accept the invitation. But when the invitation comes from a staff member of legislative assembly, they have to appear; they have to give their explanation. [The congressional caucus] also guarantees us a broader visibility; it makes us more legitimate. And that's why we [organized] it.[28]

AIDS advocacy groups thus looked to the legislature as an efficient and effective means to pressure governors, mayors, and their politically appointed health secretaries into complying with national policy guidelines.

As I explained in previous chapters, national AIDS bureaucrats depended on activists' lobbying efforts to support their shared AIDS policy goals, and national AIDS program bureaucrats actively supported their lobbying campaigns. As described in Chapter 5, national bureaucrats themselves mobilized activists to build congressional caucuses at the state and municipal levels. At the national level as well, national AIDS program bureaucrats supported congressional lobbying by subsidizing activists' travel to Brasília. In a conversation with one national bureaucrat about the proposed legislation that would criminalize HIV-based discrimination, Noemia described a recent congressional lobbying effort:

---

[28] Interview with Roberto Pereira, Director of the AIDS NGO Forum of the State of Rio de Janeiro, August 25, 2008.

From the end of the year up until now there was a lot of movement, because the legislative proposal was advancing – so that's when a big wave of civil society mobilization started – mobilizing members of congress to bring this bill to a vote...

Why was it important [for them to lobby]? Because sometimes people in the legislature don't always have a solid understanding of the epidemic – the social factors, or the medical factors involved. So they end up inventing a thousand and one things.

(Interviewer: "So this civil society mobilization was to bring the proposal to a vote?)"
"Yes."

(Interviewer: "and are you involved in supporting...?")

Yes. We supported the travel of some representatives of the national networks of people living with HIV, for them to come to Brasília and visit members of congress to sensitize them on how to vote on the bill."[29]

Noemia was telling me, in other words, that the national AIDS program paid for activists to come to the national capital to lobby the national congress. When I conducted a brief period of follow-up fieldwork in 2017, I had a similar conversation with a national bureaucrat, who somewhat more cryptically told me, "There are AIDS activists who come to Brasília every month. Who do you think pays for their travel?"[30]

Contentious Strategies

By using different strategic venues to achieve their policy objectives, AIDS activists sought to expand their opportunities for success. When activists failed to achieve a government response through one channel, such as participatory governance institutions, they turned to another approach. Often, AIDS activists employed several tactics at once. Sometimes, activists would strategically use contentious tactics (such as street protests or media criticism) to increase their leverage through institutional channels (such as participatory governance committees, the courts, or the legislature).

AIDS activists in the mid-2000s were somewhat less disposed to using combative tactics such as protest than they were in the mid-1980s. In the 1980s, they strongly favored protest as a demand-making strategy and only reluctantly incorporated insider negotiation. In the 2000s, by contrast, activists relied on insider negotiation and tended to incorporate protests only when other strategies failed on their own. This shift in the balance of demand-making tactics is unsurprising given the new institutional channels that activists could use to access the state. Institutional strategies such as lobbying, court appeals, and participation on policymaking committees are relatively efficient and effective means of influencing policy. Protest is a rather costly and unreliable method

[29] Interview with Noemia Lima, bureaucrat in the national AIDS program, Sector for Civil Society and Human Rights, March 19, 2010.
[30] Anonymous interview, bureaucrat in the national AIDS program, August 2, 2017.

of demand-making. They require a significant investment of time and effort to organize; and while they may lead to major policy gains, they may also lead to government repression. For this reason, protest is sometimes thought of as a political strategy of the poor, who have no other available option for effecting change (Piven and Cloward 1979). By the 2000s, a variety of insider strategies for influencing AIDS policy were available to civic activists. As a result, they used combative tactics with less frequency than before.

Despite this, AIDS activists in the mid-2000s continued to use combative tactics to influence government behavior – even if they did so with less eagerness than in the 1980s. Activists sometimes protested over the same issues that led them to engage the courts and the legislature – using street marches to give them additional leverage. Activists also used protest in instances when the courts or the legislature were unavailable. For example, proposed funding cuts for AIDS programs posed a strong threat to the movement's goals, but funding levels for AIDS were not protected by law or by constitutional guarantee. Similarly, when a socially conservative health minister decided not to air an HIV prevention commercial that featured a gay couple, citing technical issues, protest was a more viable strategy than questioning the legality of the decision (*Agência Estado* 2012a). When governors or mayors obstructed AIDS policy progress, which was not infrequent, activists turned to public pressure tactics to force policy reform. On one occasion during my fieldwork, civic activists even organized a protest criticizing the national AIDS program itself despite their close personal and financial ties to these federal bureaucrats.

Protest

In semi-structured interviews, activists revealed numerous and varied examples of using protest to criticize government. While survey responses reflected a somewhat weaker preference among civic AIDS leaders for protest than for other types of political strategies, respondents also reported frequent participation in marches and protests. (See Figures 7.7 and 7.8.) Some of these protests and marches were commemorative, designed to call attention to AIDS in general, or to national policy advances. But others were contentious, designed to force policy reform. Both quantitative and qualitative evidence thus suggests that in crisis situations, AIDS activists were still capable of taking to the street to pressure government.

Like in the 1980s, the protests organized by AIDS advocacy groups were generally small in scale and designed specifically to capture news coverage. Willian, from Rio, provided an illustrative example of protest tactics aimed at a media audience. Recalling a protest that criticized the state government for failing to maintain sufficient stocks of ARVs, he told me:

I took part in a protest on World AIDS Day in the central train station, in which we [used bags of empty vials as props]. It took a long time. Together there were three

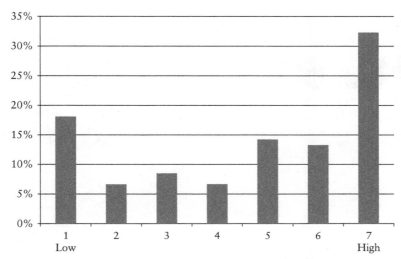

FIGURE 7.7. *"How important to your group is it to organize or participate in public marches or protests?"*

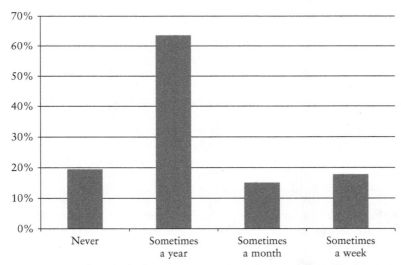

FIGURE 7.8. *"How frequently does your group protest or march with other groups?"*

large trash bags, filled with empty vials. We threw them off the balcony [of the central train station] – that whole mountain of vials. And that gave us a lot of visibility for photographers.[31]

---

[31] Interview with Willian Amaral, Director of the AIDS NGO Forum of the state of Rio de Janeiro, May 1, 2010.

IMAGE 7.2. *2010 Protest in Rio de Janeiro*

According to Marcia, the activist from Rio Grande do Sul:

When we organize political protests, the kind where you blow whistles while circling the building of the [governor or the health secretary], fewer people participate ... For one, we don't call as many people [to these kinds of protests], because otherwise they wouldn't let us in.

For example, we organized a protest in the health secretary's building, with all the governor's cabinet; and it ended up being a protest with forty people. That was the maximum number of people that we were able to fit inside. If you start to enter with a big gang, the building security [will notice, and they] will shut the door and refuse to let you in – because it's a big pain for them to have a protest in their building. And that citizen's right to protest ... that applies to the street, not inside a public building. The governer isn't obligated to let you blow whistles inside his own office, right?[32]

Rather than using disruptive tactics such as street blockages or building occupations, advocacy groups used media-oriented tactics such as provocative signs and clever costumes. Rather than numbering in the hundreds or thousands, AIDS protests generally numbered in the dozens.

In addition to using protests to criticize government, AIDS advocacy groups organized commemorative street marches. Sometimes these marches were organized to provide public support for government policy initiatives. For example, the first AIDS movement march I observed in 2007 was organized to support then-president Lula da Silva's policy decision to allow the health

---

[32] Interview with Maria Leão, an activist from the state of Rio Grande do Sul, April 5, 2011.

minister to buy lower-cost generic versions of the drug efavirenz from India, despite the existing patent on it.[33] Other times they were organized simply to maintain the high public profile of the AIDS movement. According to Ernandes, from the state of Pará:

We have two or three marches that we do during the year, that are planned in advance; they're regular commemorative marches – like the march for World AIDS Day, the march for Health Day.[34]

Even though these commemorative marches often did not include any targeted criticism, they nonetheless served a political purpose. During marches, AIDS activist leaders would publicly comment on the major AIDS-related problems facing Brazil. Publicizing these AIDS policy challenges provided political incentives for politicians to invest in solutions. By publicizing AIDS-related issues, street marches thus went hand-in-hand with more targeted protests to give political leverage to the AIDS movement.

These social-movement marches often furthered the agendas of policy-committed bureaucrats inside government, who faced political obstacles to advancing their objectives. These expressions of satisfaction about the impact of street marches were shared with me not only by federal bureaucrats but also by subnational bureaucrats in states where policy experts were running state and local AIDS programs. According to the bureaucrat in charge of São Paulo's state AIDS program, responding to a question about whether civil society served a political purpose for her:

In a certain way ... if issues are raised, then of course ... (pause) Look, here's [an example of] a civil society demand: [The hospital] Emilio Ribas just built a new wing to perform corrective surgery for lipodystrophy. And of course, the fact that civil society had protested about [the problem of lipodystrophy] on December 1st helped us get the new surgical area built. It helped me in my negotiations with the [health] secretary to get the surgical area built. So when the social movement puts [demands] on the agenda, I think that is very ... it ends up being ... We managed to implement several of the issues raised on the last World AIDS Day [march] during the course of this year.[35]

The fact that AIDS movement protests often served the agendas of government bureaucrats is unsurprising given the state–society alliance I described in the previous chapters.

Yet AIDS activists also protested against state-level health secretariats. While this is perhaps unsurprising given the fraught relations between activists and health secretariats in some states, these protests represent a certain degree of movement autonomy, given that state-level health secretariats controlled over

---

[33] For background information about this decision, see Shadlen 2017: 207–8.
[34] Interview with Ernandes Marques da Costa, April 29, 2011.
[35] Interview with Maria Clara Gianna, Director of the STD/AIDS Reference Center, State of São Paulo, November 10, 2008.

IMAGE 7.3. *2007 Protest in São Paulo*

fifty percent of earmarked project funding for civic AIDS organizations. For example, an activist from the state of Rio Grande do Sul described the following response to a recent decrease in state-level spending on AIDS programs: "We had to return to using social movement intervention: taking to the street, calling the media, using bullhorns, going to the public" (interview with Marcia Leão, activist from the state of Rio Grande do Sul, April 5, 2011). Similarly, the president of Rio de Janeiro's NGO Forum reported having organized three protests in the past year. Media reports from 2010 highlight a series of protests against empty stocks of ARVs; included in these protests were not only the well-established AIDS activist centers of São Paulo and Rio de Janeiro, but also the Northeastern states of Maranhão, Pernambuco, Ceará, and Paraíba (Agência Lusa 2010, *O Estado de São Paulo* 2010b, *Gazeta do Povo* 2010a).

AIDS activists occasionally organized protests against the national AIDS program as well. Paradoxically, given the left-wing political leanings of most individual activists, the AIDS movement protested most often against health ministers appointed by the Workers' Party administrations of Lula da Silva and Dilma Rousseff – an indirect result of their attempts to cultivate evangelicals in congress as political allies. Such protests reached a highpoint under the first Dilma administration, when Health Minister Alexandre Padilha routinely censored HIV prevention campaigns that had been designed originally in collaboration between federal AIDS bureaucrats and social-movement activists (Murray 2015: 104). In 2012, for example, Padilha prevented the distribution of an HIV prevention campaign meant for young gay men during Carnival (Murray 2015: 99). In 2013, Padilha prevented the distribution of an "HIV prevention kit" for adolescents that addressed issues such as homosexuality, drugs, homophobia, and pregnancy (Cartaxo 2018). Also in 2013, Padilha altered HIV prevention materials for International Prostitutes Day that promoted prevention as a part of taking pride in one's work – removing all elements that combatted stigma or promoted citizenship rights for prostitutes (Murray 2015: 100–1). AIDS activists, together with LGBT activists, sex-worker activists, and other social-movement allies, launched aggressive protests and media campaigns to criticize each of these decisions (see, for example, *Agência Estado* 2012a). Ultimately, Health Minister Padilha responded to movement protests and the negative attention it garnered by firing the national AIDS program director, Dirceu Greco. In solidarity, two of his vice-directors, Eduardo Barbosa and Ruy Burgos Filho, also resigned (Cartaxo 2018).

The AIDS movement sometimes even organized protests against the national AIDS program itself – protesting against the very bureaucrats who funded them. In February of 2012, for example, AIDS activists across Brazil launched an "SOS NGOs" campaign, protesting cutbacks in federal funding for civil society projects (*Agência AIDS* 2012b; *Agência Estado* 2012a). After direct appeals to government bureaucrats failed to achieve an increase in funding, the AIDS movement looked to media appeals and street protests to publicly pressure the federal government for reform. That same year they launched a public campaign criticizing the national AIDS program for allowing stocks of anti-retroviral medication to dwindle.

Yet, even in these instances of protest, national bureaucrats continued to support the movement. As the national AIDS program director in 2017, Adele Benzaken, expressed to me during one of my follow-up fieldwork visits:

Our relationship with the AIDS movement is one of respect. When they want … (here she mimics them protesting that stocks of ARVs are low), I have to respect their position. [In protesting,] they're performing their role. That's their role. But when there are things like legislative bills to confront, we work in total synergy. And whenever we design public policy we always call them.[36]

What Adele was expressing to me in this statement – reflecting the views of many other bureaucrats I interviewed – was that even though the preferences of activists and bureaucrats sometimes diverged, in times of crisis they put aside their differences and came together in support of their shared goals. Because bureaucrats and activists shared overarching objectives, the national AIDS program continued to help sustain the movement despite the fact that activists

---

[36] Interview with Adele Benzaken, Director of the National Department of IST/AIDS/Hepatitis, August 2, 2017.

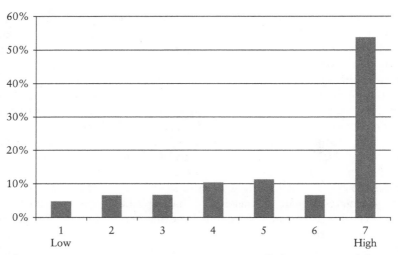

FIGURE 7.9. *"How important is it to your group to call the attention of the press to existing problems?"*

sometimes criticized and put pressure on them. In other words, national AIDS-sector bureaucrats depended on the support of a mobilized AIDS movement to combat threats to their program-building goals from inside government, even if such social-movement mobilization was sometimes a thorn in their sides.

The Media

The AIDS movement also continued to look directly to the media as a strategy for exerting pressure on government actors. In the Brazilian Survey of AIDS NGOs, the majority of associational leaders considered use of the media to be an important strategy for achieving their organization's goals. (See Figure 7.9.) In interviews, activists provided me with many examples, often unprompted, of how they used the media to criticize government. According to an activist from the state of Pernambuco, representing a commonly expressed view of the media, "if we don't manage to get anything out of the council, the media is a strategy [that we use] to give visibility to our demands."[37] Similarly, an AIDS activist from the state of Bahia emphasized, "Every time we have problems and the municipality fails to resolve it or creates impasses, we engage the local media; it is a way to win popular support."[38]

---

[37] Interview with Jair Brandão de Moura Filho, November 22, 2008.
[38] Interview with Fábio Ribeiro, Member of the NGO Forum of the state of Salvador da Bahia, representing the organization *GLICH* (Grupo Liberdade Igualdade Cidadania Homosexual), April 29, 2011, via Facebook chat.

Although AIDS activists continued to rely on close contacts with journalists to garner media attention like they did in the 1980s, by the 2000s their pool of press contacts had broadened significantly to include a diverse range of journalists and media outlets. Moreover, they were based on professional relationships rather than on the personal friendships that had formed the basis of the movement's media ties in the 1980s. According to the founding president of Rio's NGO Forum, Roberto Pereira:

I have the email addresses of a lot of [journalists] who do interviews. For example, there is a journalist from [the newspaper] *O Dia*, Pamela de Oliveira, who has done a lot of reports on AIDS. She even received a prize in 2006 for a series of articles she did in collaboration with the AIDS NGO Forum about people with HIV who were being expelled from *favelas*, and those reports were awarded a prize ... So I have a [good] relationship with press contacts, and we [AIDS associations] pass on these contacts to each other. People even joke: "You talk [to journalists] almost every week – two, three times a week." There is always some sort of [report on AIDS] ... The others [AIDS associations] ... all of them, they have these relationships with the press too.[39]

By the 2000s, the AIDS movement had thus developed extensive ties to the press.

At the same time, the effectiveness of AIDS advocacy groups in garnering media attention was no longer based on the prominence of individual members of the movement, but rather on the general reputation that the AIDS movement had developed as ethical, dependable, and a source of expertise. In the same interview, Pereira also noted:

We also have a certain degree of credibility, which is to say we don't get involved in scandals ... We always have a very ethical position on things. So ... [our reputation] doesn't help us with *everything*, but it helps us a lot. [It means that] people usually listen to us when we denounce something or someone.

The good reputation of Brazil's AIDS NGOs thus helped them capture public attention when criticizing government through the press.

In contrast to Brazil's social movements of prior decades, the AIDS movement of the 2000s used a broad combination of institutional and contentious strategies to influence government policy – a hybrid set of social-movement tactics. At the end of my long conversation with Roberto, we started to talk about how activists were confronting a particular policy challenge in the state of Rio de Janeiro. He summarized the movement's strategy thus:

We first try for a friendly conversation. If that doesn't work, we go to the legislature. If that doesn't work, we make a scandal in front of their door, we call the press, we call everyone.[40]

---

[39] Interview with Roberto Pereira, founding director of the AIDS NGO Forum in the state of Rio de Janeiro, August 25, 2008.
[40] Interview with Roberto Pereira, August 25, 2008.

This was a multi-stage, elaborate plan that combined institutional strategies for policy reform with an implicit threat that they would use more contentious strategies if such "friendly efforts" failed. It was not just the movement's inside access to state institutions that won them this particular policy campaign, but also their ability to credibly threaten protest and negative media coverage.

In turn, the mobilizing power of the AIDS movement helped national bureaucrats advance their own policy goals. AIDS activists' capacity to garner media attention and public support played a key role in helping bureaucrats combat the challenges that constantly threatened to reverse their achievements. The degree to which national bureaucrats depended on civil-society support was brought home to me during a final follow-up visit to Brazil in 2017. This was a time of national political turmoil, after then-president Dilma Rousseff had been impeached on dubious grounds, and the unelected sitting president, Michel Temer, was attempting to reverse many of the social policies and programs that had been introduced by earlier administrations. Expecting to discover that the pioneering AIDS program of the early 2000s had collapsed, what I witnessed instead was a surprisingly well-functioning bureaucracy. Despite serious new challenges and threats, AIDS bureaucrats had maintained both their budgets and their decision-making autonomy. In conversations, these bureaucrats attributed the survival of their agency in part to civic mobilization, and to the positive international reputation that such mobilization had helped them to cultivate. National AIDS-sector bureaucrats, therefore, continued to financially subsidize civic organization and mobilization, and they continued to incorporate AIDS activists into policy discussions. Relations between bureaucrats and activists had in fact improved since the last Dilma administration: they seemed to be in more frequent contact with each other, and AIDS-sector bureaucrats had even created new participatory institutions. What I found, in other words, was the same pattern of mutual support between state and society that I had discovered in my earlier fieldwork.

8

Re-examining State–Society Relations in the Twenty-First Century

The endurance and expansion of Brazil's AIDS movement poses a challenge to the conventional wisdom that Latin American social movements are either coopted or short-lived. Twentieth century labor movements endured because the state supported them, but state actors also coopted them and restricted their behavior. Twenty-first century movements are more autonomous, but assumed to be short-lived – weakly organized and fleeting in the absence of resources for building more stable coalitions. Broadly, scholars and activists accept the idea that civil society faces a fundamental tradeoff between accepting support from the state, in order to help sustain itself over time, or maintaining its independence from the state. Yet Brazil's AIDS movement, one of the most politically influential movements in contemporary Latin America, was neither short-lived nor coopted. Following its initial political success in the mid-1990s, the movement did not disintegrate but instead expanded over the next fifteen years, from a few dozen advocacy groups in a small handful of states to all twenty-six states of Brazil. This expansion depended crucially on financial support from state actors, who subsidized the movement in order to promote their own policy goals. Yet AIDS activists maintained relative political autonomy despite their deep ties to the state, using protest as a strategy for influence even as they also used inside channels of access to government for lobbying and negotiating with policymakers.

The unexpected expansion of independent AIDS activism over time raises a question for social scientists and activists alike: How do some social movements endure without falling prey to cooptation? Social-science that views state–society relations as a zero-sum game, and that subsequently misunderstands social movements' turn to tactics such as protest as an "outsider" strategy, has trouble answering this question. In fact, the trajectory of Brazil's AIDS movement shows that such tactics are often intricately intertwined with the interests of state insiders.

This book developed the concept of state-sponsored activism to help us understand social movements that are both autonomous and enduring. The outcome of state-sponsored activism is a form of political organization and mobilization in which activists make aggressive policy demands, even while relying on the government for financial support. In contrast to traditional perspectives on state–society relations, which suggest that state actors seek to control civil society as a central goal, the concept of state-sponsored activism highlights another goal: to achieve leverage over other actors inside the state. I conceptualize the state as a heterogeneous array of semi-autonomous organizations and individuals, who have different philosophies and goals. In a heterogeneous state, bureaucrats encounter obstacles to advancing their policy preferences not only from actors in society, but also from actors within the state itself. Civil-society groups can offer federal bureaucrats key sources of political leverage to advance their objectives over the opposition of other actors inside government. When bureaucrats seek leverage over other bureaucrats as their dominant objective vis-à-vis civil society, they will support relatively autonomous forms of civic mobilization.

The argument developed in this book has important implications for how we understand the divergent approaches of state actors to civic organization and mobilization at the start of the twenty-first century. Recent scholarship has focused on how state actors ignore or attempt to fragment new popular-sector groups to prevent civil society organizations from interfering with neoliberal reforms. By contrast, this book highlights the way certain sectors of the state harness the power of new civil-society constituencies to serve their own policy reform agendas. In so doing, they facilitate the mobilization of relatively autonomous national advocacy coalitions. Overlooked by most recent literature on state–society relations, this state actor strategy has been adopted side-by-side with more repressive state approaches to civic mobilization. The multiple roles played by state actors in structuring civil society thus helps explain variation in twenty-first century civic organization and mobilization. In this concluding chapter, I further explore the broad theoretical and empirical implications of this finding. To do so, I situate the argument within the context of democratization and neoliberalism, compare this model of state–society relations with other models of state–society relations, explore broader questions related to the role of NGOs in international development, and finally, provide a series of case studies beyond Brazilian AIDS policy to explore the generalizability of the argument.

A NEW PERSPECTIVE ON DEMOCRATIZATION
AND NEOLIBERAL REFORM

The first contribution of the argument is to offer new insight into the impact of the transitions toward neoliberal reforms and democratization on state–society relations in Latin America. In contrast to the view from traditional approaches that highlight the erosion of the incentives and resources that had sustained corporatism, the underpinnings of corporatism did not disappear during the dual transition toward neoliberalism and democracy but rather *shifted* – to different sectors of the state, and to different segments of society.[1]

Many scholars believe that transitions toward neoliberalism and democratization destroyed the underpinnings of the corporatist bargain between state and society (e.g., Chalmers et al. 1997: 545, 555–60; Collier and Handlin 2009b: 48–60).[2] It is often claimed that neoliberal reforms reduced the capacity of state actors to provide resources and subsidies for unions in return for their political support, at the same time as such reforms fragmented societal interests along subnational territorial lines. Democratization eliminated some of the key control mechanisms that upheld government support for state corporatism. In summary, the combination of neoliberal reforms and democratization is widely seen as having undermined the incentives and the capacity for state actors to mobilize and control organized interests in society.

Conventional wisdom, while not entirely wrong, is incomplete. In fact, the combination of neoliberal reforms and democratization offered new incentives and resources for state actors to support civic organization and mobilization, even as they undermined old ones. The neoliberal practice of outsourcing social-service delivery to nongovernmental organizations brought about new financial connections between state and society. Democratization, based on the principles of participatory governance, provided new incentives for civic associations to coordinate nationally among themselves. I suggest, in other words, that the underpinnings of corporatism did not disappear but rather developed into a different set of bargains between state and society – ones that were compatible with a democratic political model and a neoliberal economic model.

The Decline of Old Incentives and Resources

In the corporatist period, the incentives for workers to coordinate nationally were clear cut. From the 1950s to the 1980s, under the state-centric model of economic development, central government technocrats determined the vast majority of industrial policies – including social protections and benefits for workers. National government decisions thus affected the lives of workers from around the country in similar ways, drawing them together through common grievances and policy demands. For the same reason, national government officials were also effective targets for workers who demanded better benefits and protections. Workers from different cities and states, therefore, had a common cause as well as obvious incentives to coordinate national political campaigns.

Scholars point to two processes related to neoliberal reforms that undermined the incentives for working-class citizens to build lasting national coalitions (Collier and Handlin 2009a: 83–4). First, privatization destroyed

[1] And on changes to state-society relations in post-transition Latin America, see Rich et al. (2019).
[2] For a cogent analysis of the fate corporatism in Western Europe, see Schmitter (n/d).

incentives for workers' organizations to coordinate at the national level by shifting control over industrial production from state actors to private firms. When national governments withdrew from controlling industrial production in response to region-wide debt crises, national governments were no longer effective targets for civic advocacy groups to make demands surrounding worker rights and protections. Second, the process of political and adminis-trative decentralization further undermined the incentives for societal groups to build national coalitions around social welfare issues. As decentralized gov-ernance caught on as a global policy trend, national governments across Latin America gave regional and municipal authorities control over key social wel-fare policies (Kaufman and Nelson 2004; Montero and Samuels 2004). With local authorities controlling social-welfare policies and programs, grassroots groups ostensibly had less motivation to invest time and money in building national advocacy coalitions than they had under the centralized political sys-tem of prior decades (Chalmers et al. 1997: 545, 555–60).

Neoliberal reforms also diminished the resources available for national civic coordination. In the corporatist period, state subsidies had ensured a finan-cially stable structure for labor unions to scale up into national coalitions. In Brazil, for example, national labor organization was supported by a trade union tax (*contribuição sindical*), which was collected from all workers regard-less of whether they were union members (Mericle 1977: 314). By law, twenty percent of this tax was earmarked for use by national labor federations and confederations. Union dues, paid by all union members, also provided a steady stream of support for national labor organization. But, in the 1980s and 1990s, the privatization of state-owned enterprises and the deregulation of industries generally limited the capacity of national governments to provide resources and subsidies for unions in return for their political support (Cook 2010; Levitsky 2003; Murillo 2001). As a result, the flow of government funding and subsidies for unions declined precipitously.

Neoliberal reforms also eroded some incentives for central government actors to support civic organization and mobilization. From the perspective of state actors, organized labor no longer constituted a potential political resource for the state to leverage in support of its economic project. Whereas the economic development model of prior decades centered on nationaliz-ing industries, a project that promised real (if limited) gains for the working classes, the neoliberal economic project centered on privatizing industries – a project that cut at the heart of organized labor. While state actors in some cases cultivated business support for neoliberal reforms (Kingstone 1999; Montero 1998, 2002), organized labor was less amenable to supporting the state's broad economic reform policies (Cook 2010; Levitsky 2003; Murillo 2001).[3] At the

---

[3] While labor's reaction to market reforms varied significantly across countries (as discussed by all three authors cited in the text), they were all similarly defensive reactions to a perceived threat – in contrast to the active support for government economic policy during the ISI period.

same time, the perceived power of unions diminished, due in part to the relative decline in formal-sector employment.

Finally, democratization destroyed key control mechanisms that upheld government support for state corporatism. For example, "intervention," outlined in Article 530 of Brazil's labor law, had allowed the corporatist state to seize the headquarters of the unions it deemed to be hostile to government interests and replace elected union officials with government appointees (Mericle 1977: 309). Such practices had served as important levers for state officials to use the corporatist bargain to control labor demands. Democratization, however, rendered such controls illegitimate and illegal. Post-democratization, the corporatist system promised fewer returns for the state. For all these reasons, according to dominant thinking, state actors withdrew in the 1980s and 1990s from engaging organized interests in policy.

The Rise of New Incentives and Resources

Nevertheless, despite the changes in state–society relations that attend neoliberalization and democratization, state actors did not uniformly withdraw. As this book demonstrates, state actors are in fact engaging a wider variety of organized interests in policy than ever before. Overlooked by existing approaches, new incentives and resources for national civic coordination and state–society collaboration emerged at the same time as traditional incentives and resources were on the decline. In Chapter 4, I showed how the incentives and resources for such state–society collaboration arose out of the two processes of democratization and neoliberal reform. Here I tease out the three key conditions related to these processes that lay the foundation for a new type of relationship between state and society: new social questions, new national bureaucracies driven by policy-oriented bureaucrats, and new sources of earmarked funding for civil society. The first two of these conditions worked together to produce the incentives for state support of activism: bureaucrats who shared broad policy goals with activists outside the state, and who were unable to pursue their objectives by acting alone. The third condition produced the resources for such state support: money available for bureaucrats to support civic organization and mobilization.

First, re-democratization brought new social questions to the table as civil society gained space to organize and make their voices heard (Garay 2016; Rossi 2015). As the military regime gradually eased repression and reinstated civil rights, societal groups of many stripes began to organize and make policy demands (Escobar and Alvarez 1992; Eckstein 2001). In turn, the civil-society mobilization that grew out of Brazil's protracted regime transition helped to deepen Brazil's democratic reforms. Of particular importance, civic mobilization put pressure on politicians to allow popular participation in the constitution. One outcome of civil-society participation in constitutional design was that a long list of social rights was enshrined as constitutional guarantees.

Civil-society participation also helped to enshrine participatory governance as a national policymaking model (Avritzer 2009; Goldfrank 2011; Mayka 2019b; Wampler 2007). As a result, new policy demands gained legal backing – forcing elected politicians to respond.

Secondly, national political leaders created new state bureaucracies and recruited policy experts to lead them (Abers and Von Bulow 2011; Abers and Tatagiba 2015). Driven by their policy commitments, these new bureaucrats sought to sustain government investment in their area (Abers and Tatagiba 2015; Rich 2013). Because civic mobilization had either directly or indirectly caused the creation of these bureaucracies, social movements emerged as natural allies for the bureaucrats who worked in them. In contrast to market reforms, which directly opposed the core interests of organized labor, building government social programs was a project that promoted the interests of civic advocacy groups. Because the broad policy agendas of state actors and civic actors aligned, advocacy groups could promote positive agendas in government that sought to shape and enhance existing programs rather than to protest them. Bureaucrats in these state agencies thus had incentives to harness the power of social movements in support of their policy goals.

The third factor, new streams of government funding for civil-society projects, produced the resources for state support of activism: money available for bureaucrats to distribute to civil society. Neoliberal reforms gave rise to new sources of financing for different types of civic organizations even as they undercut traditional government resources for unions. In the 1990s, as part of the second wave of market reforms in Latin America, national governments began outsourcing the management of public service programs to nongovernmental organizations – often with encouragement by international lending agencies. This practice was a neoliberal solution to the negative impacts of earlier market-oriented governance reforms in the social-service sector. Providing nonprofit associations with grants to manage health and development programs was a cost-effective means to assist the poorest groups of citizens who were unable to gain access to social services through market mechanisms. National executives and international lenders alike thus viewed the practice of engaging civic organizations to provide government services as a solution to the twin problems of inefficiency and weak bureaucratic capacity – one that went hand-in-hand with the ultimate neoliberal goal of shrinking the state.

One outcome of this new development strategy was to institutionalize new flows of state funding for civic organizations across a range of policy sectors. Scholars such as Oxhorn (2006) have argued that this type of state funding for civil society mainly serves to coopt and fragment grassroots organizations, providing them with a form of patronage by giving them small amounts of money to sustain themselves. While this outcome is certainly a danger of donor funding, there is another outcome of this new model of outsourcing government service provision that Oxhorn and others overlook: it provided state actors in the twenty-first century with the resources and the capacity to support new types of civic organizations. When it served the purposes of state actors, those resources were used to support civic organization and mobilization. Sometimes, such support even spurred civil-society growth in unintended ways, such as LGBT groups that used funding for AIDS to launch a new gay rights movement (Dehesa 2010; Facchini 2005), or the sex-worker advocacy groups who similarly used AIDS-program funding to help organize a movement to promote rights for prostitutes (Murray 2015).

A NEW MODEL OF STATE–SOCIETY RELATIONS: CIVIC CORPORATISM

A second contribution of the argument – an extension of the first – is to introduce a new model of state–society relations, what I call civic corporatism. By challenging the dominant notion of a central government in retreat, the concept of civic corporatism helps us better understand the fundamental similarities and differences between state–society relations in the contemporary period and the past. Like other forms of corporatism, civic corporatism is a pattern of state–society relations in which actors in the central government actively support national civic organization and mobilization in return for the political leverage over other actors. However, civic corporatism differs in two important ways from traditional variants. First, it involves no overt mechanisms of state control over the leadership or activities of civic organizations. And second, it incorporates a wide variety of societal interests, beyond business and labor, that were excluded from politics throughout most of modern history.

Corporatism and pluralism are the dominant models thought to organize state–society relations in Latin America. Corporatism, the pattern that characterized Brazil in the twentieth century, is a system in which state actors actively structure civil society, subsidizing a small, privileged set of organized interests in society to help them build stable national coalitions and offering them an official seat in social and economic policy discussions in return for a degree of control over their activities. The outcomes of the corporatist bargaining system for civic representation in policy varied significantly by country, depending on the relative strength of the state versus civil society prior to the introduction of corporatism. Where civil society was already strong and cohesive, such as in the Northern European context, the scope of societal interests included in policy was broader – a variant that Schmitter (1974) labels "societal corporatism." Encompassing associations that bargained on behalf of workers and employers constituted umbrella organizations that held together highly coordinated and hierarchically-organized alliances of smaller unions. The civil society representatives who participated in policymaking deliberations, thus, represented a relatively wide range of political and economic interests. Moreover, workers and employers in this context gained meaningful access to the state. However, where civil society was weak or fragmented, such as in Southern Europe and Latin America, what emerged was "state corporatism," in which a much more limited set of societal interests were co-opted into uneven bargaining relationships with the state (Collier and Collier 1991; Schmitter 1974; Stepan 1978; Wiarda 1973).

Under pluralism, the pattern often used to characterize state–society relations at the start of the twenty-first century, state actors adopt a hands-off approach to civil society, leaving organized interests to flourish or flounder on their own. While the concept of pluralism is generally associated with a flourishing array of cross-cutting associations voicing their interests in government, studies of civic engagement in Latin America in the 1990s – a period marked by economic crisis, austerity, and depoliticization – offered a rather negative interpretation of how civic organization and mobilization was affected by this new dynamic. Oxhorn and Ducatenzeiler (1998), for example, labels the state's new approach to civil society "neopluralism," to suggest this new hands-off approach to civic mobilization was not a sign of democratization but rather an active attempt by the state to demobilize and fragment working-class interests. Such approaches decry a decline in the quality and scope of civic mobilization in the 1990s, and declare it a result of the state no longer helping groups in civil society to overcome collective action problems (Arce and Bellinger 2007; Kurtz 2004; Oxhorn and Ducatenzeiler 1998; Roberts 2005; Shadlen 2002).

Similar to traditional varieties of corporatism, civic corporatism involves active intervention by actors in the national state to mobilize and structure civil society. Yet in contrast to state corporatism, the subtype that emerged in Latin America, civic corporatism does not involve active repression of civil society. More broadly contrasting with traditional forms of corporatism, nor does it center a single bargain between the state, business, and organized labor. Rather, civic corporatism involves a *set of discrete bargains* between state and society. These bargains incorporate a wide range of newly salient sectors of policy, thus bringing together new actors in state and society, and resulting in distinct dynamics of mobilization and control.

Similarities to Other Subtypes of Corporatism

Privileged Access to the State

The most readily apparent similarity between civic corporatism and other varieties of corporatism is that state actors offer a subset of civil society privileged access to the state through formal interest representation in the policymaking arena. The infrastructure of civic corporatism in particular bears a striking resemblance to Brazil's corporatist institutions of the prior century – centering on tripartite policy councils that brought together government officials with representatives from employers and from civil society. For example, Schmitter (1971) described the institutional infrastructure for corporatism in twentieth century Brazil as follows:

The key institutional mechanisms for [corporatism] are formal participation in a wide variety of working groups, mixed commissions, ad hoc committees, and consultative councils at the ministerial or inter-ministerial levels, and informal contacts between national confederational presidents and high executive and administrative officials or between associational técnicos and their counterparts in the public bureaucracy. (Schmitter 1971: 325)

Such a description could easily be mistaken for a description of the participatory governance framework of policymaking in twenty-first century Brazil.

A closer look at specific corporatist institutions highlights such similarities. In the twentieth century, state access took the form of tripartite government bodies that brought representatives from labor and business together with government officials. Some of these institutions offered labor and employer representatives an official vote over policy proposals. Brazil's labor courts, for example, were tripartite bodies that gave workers and employers a formal vote in wage-setting, as well as in dealing with worker grievances (Mericle 1977: 311–13). Other corporatist institutions included labor and employer representatives as consultants, offering them a voice in policy deliberations without extending them a formal vote over the resulting policy decisions. Examples of this type of corporatist institution were sectoral commissions, committees, and councils such as Brazil's National Economic Planning Commission, the National Council of Industrial and Commercial Policy, and more specialized groups such as the National Petroleum Council and the Executive Commission for Rubber (Schmitter 1971: 125). Under corporatism, then, officially sanctioned labor groups were offered formal interest representation in the policy process.

Under civic corporatism, similarly, state actors offer a select set of organizations formal representation in government on a wide range of policy committees. As I showed in Chapter 4, the most direct way national bureaucrats engaged the participation of organized interests in AIDS policy was by developing a broad institutional policymaking framework based on the principles of participatory governance (see also Rich 2019). Moreover, whereas literature on participatory governance tends to focus narrowly on the two deliberative institutions that offer citizens a formal vote on policy, participatory councils and conferences, the AIDS policymaking framework included a host of other participatory policymaking spaces as well – including an array of commissions, committees, and working groups. Called "consultative bodies" in Brazil, these types of policymaking institutions incorporated civil-society representatives as advisers – just as did Brazil's corporatist institutions.[4]

State Subsidies for Civic Organization

Also, like traditional variants of corporatism, government in the model of civic corporatism is actively involved in structuring civil society into national coalitions. Under corporatism, state actors also subsidized labor organization – providing resources and making national policies to help unions develop a financially stable structure for scaling up into national coalitions, and in doing

---

[4] Some commissions also offer civil-society representatives a formal vote over policy decisions.

so channel union activity into "nonmilitant endeavors" (Mericle 1977: 314). In Brazil, for example, the two major sources of government support for unions were the trade-union tax (*contribuição sindical*) and union membership dues. The trade-union tax was collected from all workers regardless of whether they were union members and was equal to the salary that workers received for one day of work in the month of March (Mericle 1977). Union dues were only paid by union members, but workers had incentive to pay because they would only be able to access union benefits if they were dues paying members (Mericle 1977). Under corporatism, then, labor interests had a stable source of funding to use in organizing themselves into strong national coalitions.

Under civic corporatism, actors in the central government also offer subsidies to help NGOs structure themselves into hierarchical, centralized coalitions. As I showed in Chapter 6, an important way the national AIDS bureaucracy helped to structure the AIDS movement into a national federation was by financing the movement's national and regional conventions. Federal travel subsidies are important for building an institutionalized national movement coalition because of the relatively high cost of transportation in Brazil, the large geographic area of the country, and the relatively small budgets of most civic organizations. Through such subsidies, state actors help civil-society organizations overcome financial barriers to collective action. On their own, nonprofit civic organizations tend to have small budgets and thus few resources to support national advocacy coalitions. Government subsidies, while not large, provide crucial support for the regional and national meetings and conferences that uphold such coalitions, allowing them to coordinate nationally among themselves and thus provide a broader representation of interests on these committees. Certainly, these dynamics do not resemble the hands-off approach associated with pluralism (or neopluralism), often thought to characterize twenty-first-century governments in Latin America.

But, also like traditional corporatist bargains, state support for civil-society organizations under civic corporatism is double edged. Unlike in a pluralist model, civil society remains dependent on the state under civic corporatism – strengthened as a result of government subsidies and privileged access to policy forums. As I showed in Chapters 5 and 6, smaller nonprofit organizations rely on state grants to stay alive, and even larger NGOs depend on state funding to finance national advocacy coalitions. Moreover, state subsidies for civil-society organizations under civic corporatism are more meager and precarious than they were for unions under the corporatism of the past. Unlike the generous subsidies that allowed labor unions to thrive under corporatism, government funding for civil-society organizations is often barely enough – if enough at all – to cover the basic operating costs of nonprofit organizations. Funding for national coalition-building tends to be more generous but is not guaranteed through legislation. This financial dependence on state actors may contribute to self-imposed constraints on the autonomy of civic action, by moderating the goals and strategies of movement activists and NGO directors who are well aware of their need to maintain government funding for the survival of their organizations. Although the more overt forms of control characterized by state corporatism are not present in the model of civic corporatism, subtler forms of corporatist control persist under the new model.

Differences from Past Varieties of Corporatism

Yet civic corporatism also differs in important ways from traditional subtypes of corporatism. Unlike under traditional corporatism in Brazil, in the model of civic corporatism government actors wield no direct mechanisms of control over the demands and strategies of civic organizations. Moreover, unlike the narrow segment of society that was represented in policy under past forms of corporatism – organized urban labor – a diverse range of interests are privileged under civic corporatism.

Levers of Control

While the corporatist system provided significant resources for national labor organization and mobilization, a fundamental tradeoff to such state support for national civic organization in Latin America was political autonomy, because state actors could use labor's dependence on government largess as a lever of control. In authoritarian political contexts, corporatist states forcibly structured labor organization into a limited set of hierarchical and centralized groups by imposing legal constraints on which groups could organize and on how they could develop as institutions. Brazil's master plan, called the *enquadramento* and specified in the labor law of 1939, involved total top-down restructuring of unions, in which existing unions were forced to disband and reorganize according to the guidelines of the new labor law (Mericle 1977: 307).

This corporatist structure of labor organization was based on three principles. The first was exclusive representation, which meant that only one labor organization was officially recognized for each government-specified jurisdiction. The selected union thus became the official spokesperson for all workers in that jurisdiction, eliminating the opportunity for workers to build competing nonofficial organizations. Radical and more militant union members were thus forced to either fight for leadership positions within the official union or go underground and build clandestine groups and, given the risks involved in building clandestine organizations, most chose to work within the officially recognized union organization. The second principle was functional differentiation, which meant that union jurisdictions covered all workers in "identical, similar, or connected trades." The third principle was geographic fragmentation, which meant that no horizontal relationships linked unions representing workers in other industries in the same geographic area, or with unions representing workers in the same industry in other geographic areas (Mericle 1977: 307). Under corporatism, then, the state sought to structure labor organization with an eye to scaling up unions vertically. The goal was to build a small body of centralized leadership that state actors could manipulate to control rank-and-file workers, and to fragment labor horizontally so that no broad coalition could form that would pose a threat to state power.

State actors also used the policy access and state subsidies they offered to unions as levers of control, even as they strengthened labor organization. Policy access divided the interests of the included sectors of the labor movement from the interests of the excluded sectors of the labor movement. Policy access also coopted labor leadership through the individual perquisites they enjoyed thanks to their special status in government. Subsidies coopted unions and union leadership into quiescence by making them financially dependent on the state for survival. In many cases, state actors in corporatist systems also used more overt levers of control by forcibly structuring labor into more easily controllable forms of organization, such as by banning unions from forming horizontal linkages across industrial sectors. One of the subtler ways the state used such regulations to control civil society was through intentional distortions in representation – giving underrepresentation to urban labor unions with large numbers of workers and overrepresentation to the smaller union with few workers that were easier for the government to control.

In contrast to the era of state corporatism, contemporary civil-society organizations enjoy greater freedom of action. Under civic corporatism there is no legislation like the *enquadramento* that restricts which interests may organize, how CSOs and civil-society coalitions can be structured, or who is allowed to lead such organizations. There is no national legislation explicitly aimed at coopting organized interests through government subsidies only for cooperative organizations. Nor is there a contemporary equivalent to corporatist legislation that allowed the state to "intervene" in uncooperative labor unions.

Certainly, democracy plays a role in protecting civic organizations from state control: democratic institutions restrict state actors from making rules that explicitly violate civil liberties. Yet the relative autonomy that civil-society organizations enjoy under civic corporatism also serves the interests of state actors: civil-society organizations draw their power from their capacity to act unruly, and from their perceived legitimacy as representatives of autonomous societal interests. When government bureaucrats impose overt controls on civil-society groups to prevent them from turning too radical, these groups also lose their power to mobilize pressure in support of bureaucrats' goals.

Who is Incorporated

Perhaps the most striking difference between civic corporatism and historical variants of corporatism is in who gets access to the state. In the past, corporatism centered on urban labor. Factory workers could offer state actors political leverage to support their industrial policy goals with their strong capacity for mass mobilization. At the same time, labor's capacity to organize posed a threat to state actors, who were aware that such mobilization could turn against them. Because they worked together in groups on factory floors, large numbers of urban workers were in daily contact with each other. In this arena, they could exchange ideas and grievances, and potentially develop strategies for coercing government in to adopting new labor policies. Urban labor also possessed a high capacity for disruption, due to their ability to halt manufacturing production.

Under civic corporatism, by contrast, a much wider range of actors participate in the policy arena. Take, for example, the participatory governance institutions that form the infrastructure of the new model. In 2010, the Brazilian government incorporated national participatory institutions into their official policymaking process in fifty-four policy sectors (Mayka 2019a; Mayka and Rich forthcoming). These included areas as diverse as health, education, the environment, women's rights, energy policy, urban policy, crime and punishment, foreign trade, sports, and culture. All of these councils involve joint state–society governance of the policy process by incorporating civil-society representatives and employer representatives in discussions about the design and implementation of policies. Similarly, fifty-nine national public policy conferences took place between 2003 and 2010, which brought together millions of civil society activists to formulate policy proposals on a broad array of issues (Mayka and Rich forthcoming). This wide range of national participatory governance institutions, together with the many instances of government subsidized national civic coordination, suggest that there is no longer a single corporatist bargain but, rather, that civic corporatism encompasses a large and diverse *collection* of bargains. These bargains center on newly salient sectors of policy, thus, bringing together new actors in state and society, and resulting in new dynamics of mobilization and control.

NGOS AND INTERNATIONAL DEVELOPMENT

Relationships between state and society do not develop in an international vacuum, and international and nongovernmental organizations, not just domestic movements, play a vital role in policy making. In this context, state-sponsored activism also speaks to broader debates in good governance and democracy promotion. The international development community has touted civil society participation as fundamental to promoting good governance for two reasons: because they fill gaps in state capacity, and because they mobilize pressure on politicians. Much has been written about the first function of civil society groups; relatively little has been written about this second function.

Bureaucrats often depend on civic groups to implement social welfare or public works projects in poor and otherwise marginalized communities. A trend that goes hand-in-hand with the global trend toward shrinking the state, governments have delegated responsibility for delivering a wide array of key social services to civic organizations. Through government and international contracts, non-profit civic organizations across the developing world are now central players in managing social-sector programs in areas such as education, public health, human rights, and environmental protection.[5] In richer countries, the choice to outsource public-service provision to nongovernmental organizations has been based on a logic of efficiency. In the Global South, however, there is often no state alternative to NGO service provision. Despite vast differences in the social, political, and economic makeup of developing countries, one commonality is the challenge of weak state capacity. Bureaucrats who lack the infrastructure and the resources to provide key public services in all communities often depend critically on societal groups to fill gaps in public goods provision.

Bureaucrats in the developing world may also depend on civil-society groups to help them design effective social policies. Project funding has allowed civic organizations to hire highly educated issue experts, attracting them with salaries and working conditions that far exceed those in the public sector. As a consequence, social-policy expertise in the developing world is often concentrated within civic organizations. Bureaucrats who lack the time and resources to develop a command of a particular issue area have, thus, come to depend on the staff of nongovernmental organizations for guidance in designing national and local policies (Brass 2016: 10–13). In Brazil, NGO expertise can serve as critical support to bureaucrats in the planning phase of social policy design (Abers and Keck 2013).

Yet civic organizations can also strengthen a bureaucracy's capacity to achieve its goals by mobilizing political pressure on politicians. In federal systems, for example, civic groups can help bureaucrats to ensure local compliance with national policies by monitoring policy implementation and publicly denouncing misbehavior (Amengual 2016; Rich 2013). Similarly, civil society can use political pressure to help bureaucrats advance new social-sector policies. Bureaucrats may have a hard time convincing politicians to pass new social-policy legislation that threatens the interests of the economically and politically powerful, or that requires increased government spending. As Evans (1996) suggests, the best way for bureaucrats to circumvent the power of entrenched elites may be to seek allies in civil society (Evans 1996: 1128). Civic groups can mobilize political support for policy reform that threatens powerful interests by organizing public opinion campaigns, and by lobbying the legislature. Certainly, the argument that civil society plays an important political role in promoting good governance is not new. What this book shows, however, is that bureaucrats within the state – and, by implication, in international agencies – can encourage NGOs to play this role through well-targeted financial and technical support.

---

[5] For a rich study of the relationship between international development organizations, local brokers, and citizens in the Global South, see Swidler and Watkins (2017).

COMPARATIVE EVIDENCE OF CIVIC CORPORATISM

Although the pattern of state–society relations I describe is a recent phenomenon in Brazil – a product of democratic transition and neoliberal reform – there is already enough evidence to suggest we are likely to find civic corporatism in policy sectors that meet the three conditions I highlighted: they represent new social questions (brought to the agenda by social-movement mobilization); they are governed by new or reformed bureaucracies (run by committed bureaucrats); and bureaucrats control earmarked resources for civil-society projects. To explore the generalizability of this model beyond AIDS policy, in this section I offer brief case studies of state–society collaboration in the early 2000s across three issue areas: waste picking, urban housing, and environmental protection for traditional communities. Together, these three issue areas represent a cross section of what I call the new social questions in Brazil, spanning traditional political divides such as class, ethnicity, and geography. Despite their apparent differences, bureaucrats in all of these cases sought outside political support from social movements. At the same time, variation across these three cases allows me to assess the importance of resources in facilitating civic corporatism. Whereas the bureaucrats who had ample resources for civil-society projects (in the waste-picking policy sector) subsidized national social-movement organization, bureaucrats who did not have access to ample project funding (the cases of urban housing and environmental protection for indigenous communities) provided less support for civic mobilization. Taken together, these cases demonstrate that civic corporatism may arise across a variety of issue areas, and scholars should take note to look for it.

Waste Picking

Perhaps surprisingly, the clearest parallel to the AIDS policy case is of policies pertaining to waste-picking.[6] Waste-picking is the practice of searching dumpsites for recyclable or reusable resources and exchanging those resources for money. Until the policy reforms of the early 2000s, waste-picking involved individuals picking recyclable materials out of garbage by hand in open-air dumps. This was dangerous work: regular hazards included infections from touching disease-ridden waste, injury from falling on sharp objects, and suffocation from falling unseen into a large waste pile. It was also one of the most stigmatized professions in Brazil – seen as attracting only the most desperate and down-on-their-luck. Yet, as the documentary film *Wasteland* (Walker et al. 2010) so eloquently depicted, the conditions of waste-picking also fostered community-building and civic mobilization: workers laboring together for long hours in a risky environment.

---

[6] For a more thorough analysis of state–society relations in the waste-picking sector, see Brandão 2018.

Though different from AIDS policy in that waste-picking involves a lower-class occupational group, it is similarly one of the new "social questions" that arrived on the national political agenda as a result of civic mobilization in the 1980s and 1990s. Like AIDS policy, multiple presidents responded to such civic mobilization by developing national policies to support waste pickers and by creating new state institutions to administer them. Similarly, outside policy experts were recruited to help run these new institutions and, when they found themselves unable to promote their policy agendas alone, they cultivated social-movement support by providing grassroots leaders with resources and opportunities for civic organization and mobilization.

Unregulated and unsupported by the central government throughout the twentieth century, waste pickers organized a social movement during Brazil's re-democratization in the 1980s and 1990s to demand political inclusion. Like many other movements during Brazil's democratic transition period, waste pickers began at the local level, spreading gradually across Brazil in the 1990s (Pereira and Teixeira 2011: 896–7). By 1999, local waste-picker associations around the country had joined forces to form the National Waste Pickers Movement (MNCR), which used its newfound political space to organize frequent mass protests (Pereira and Teixeira 2011: 897, 905). By 2001, the movement had held a national conference and developed a formal set of demands for government recognition and support of their work, such as: the inclusion of "waste picker" as an official government work category; a national policy to promote waste separation; the eradication of dangerous open dumps; and funding to support waste-picker cooperatives (Pereira and Teixeira 2011: 906). By 2001, in other words, waste-picking had made its way onto the national political agenda.

The governmental response to the issue of waste-picking further parallels that of AIDS in that involved the creation of a new bureaucracy, populated by committed and capable bureaucrats. Like AIDS policy, both presidents of the early 2000s responded to waste pickers' social-movement demands by creating new government policies to support them, and by creating new state agencies to oversee these policies. In 2002, outgoing-president Cardoso formally recognized waste pickers as a group by adding the category "waste picker" to the Brazilian Code of Occupations (Pereira and Teixeira 2011: 906). In 2003, incoming president Lula da Silva created a national government committee to support waste pickers. This new institution emerged with a rather unwieldy name that nonetheless directly signaled its inclusionary goal: The Inter-ministerial Committee for the Social Inclusion of Waste Pickers (abbreviated as CIISC). CIISC brought together policymakers from twenty-four government ministries and agencies to design a policy framework for protecting and supporting waste pickers, with representatives from the national waste-pickers movement participating in nearly all meetings as invited guests (email correspondence with Igor Brandão, November 27, 2017).[7]

---

[7] See also www.planalto.gov.br/ccivil_03/DNN/2003/Dnn9975impressao.htm (last accessed February 13, 2018).

Also similar to AIDS policy, a large number of policy experts and activists entered the state to fill these new government agencies. At the highest level, a politician named Patrus Ananias was tapped by Lula to head the Ministry for Social Development, the key ministry involved in coordinating the committee. Although not an activist himself, Ananias had developed expertise and a strong commitment to supporting waste pickers during his time as mayor of Belo Horizonte, when he innovated the first set of waste-collection policies in Brazil. Upon his appointment as minister, Ananias created a new secretariat that was dedicated in part to forging relationships with civil-society organizations (originally called the Secretariat for Institutional Articulation and Partnerships), and he brought in a waste-management expert to lead it, Heliana Kátia Tavares (Pereira and Teixeira 2011: 906). Tavares, in turn, recruited a variety of experts and activists to fill mid-level positions within this secretariat, just as experts and activists took up new positions within the various other ministries that participated in CIISC. While a large number of career bureaucrats also worked in these new government institutions, they also developed, over time, a strong normative commitment to supporting waste pickers, cultivated by working alongside experts and former activists (conversations with Igor Brandão, August 1, 2017 and November 17, 2017). In sum, the bureaucrats in charge of national waste-picker policy were committed to policy advancement and were experts in their field.

In a further similarity to the AIDS policy case, the bureaucrats who designed Brazil's national waste-picking policies confronted political opposition to their objectives, which rendered them – despite their commitment and their expertise – dependent on social-movement support. For example, a national legislative proposal that the members of CIISC designed in 2007, called the Law of Solid Waste, engendered strong political opposition from business leaders in both the packaging industry and the waste collection industry (correspondence with Igor Brandão via Skype on November 17, 2017 and via email on November 27, 2017). Prior to the proposed law, municipal governments had been responsible for waste disposal, and they had typically contracted private waste-collection businesses to provide collection, transportation, and storage. The proposed legislation would not only create new government recycling programs and contract waste-picker cooperatives as partner organizations, but it would also make the businesses that produced the waste partially responsible for recycling their own products. While municipal governments generally supported the legislation because it saved them significant amounts of money on waste collection, it actually threatened large corporations, because it created for them a significant new financial burden. The legislation threatened waste-collection businesses because it reduced the amount of business they would receive – both by diminishing the overall amount of waste that municipalities needed to collect and by giving away the responsibility for recyclables to waste-picker cooperatives. In response to this threat, industry federations lobbied heavily to block the legislation (conversation with Igor Brandão via Skype, November 17, 2017). Bureaucrats depended on the support of the national waste-pickers movement to counter such industry lobbying with public opinion campaigns, and with the movement's own lobbying efforts. In other words, the bureaucrats who designed national waste-picker policies depended on the political support of an organized social movement to be able to *enact* and *implement* their policies.

Furthermore, similar to what they did in the AIDS issue realm, bureaucrats in CIISC cultivated their political alliance with the national waste pickers movement in part by offering activists resources for civic organization and mobilization (conversation with Igor Brandão via Skype, November 17, 2017). CIISC bureaucrats could offer resources to activists because they controlled earmarked funding for civil-society projects, which was supplied by various state agencies and foundations but distributed by bureaucrats in CIISC. Some such support was justified according to an economic logic compatible with neoliberalism – helping waste-pickers to build "economies of scale" by organizing them into associations and cooperatives. But national bureaucrats distributed some of this project funding for explicitly political goals, such as for providing political advocacy training to promising activists and for "strengthening the national movement" (Pereira and Teixeira 2011: 907). National bureaucrats also used project funding to help waste-picker activists and advocacy groups organize at the national level by supporting local, regional, and national political events – such as state, regional, and national "*encontros*" and "Trash and Citizenship Forums." Although these events were not solely for social-movement activists (they brought together waste-picker activists, experts, and policymakers), in practice they provided a structure for the movement's national leadership to hold their meetings. Just as in the case of AIDS policy, such governmental support for civic organization and mobilization was made fairly explicit. For example, an official federal document from 2009 delineated two categories of funding for waste pickers: the first of which was meant to help them organize into collectives, and the second of which was meant to help waste pickers "achieve a process of national mobilization and debate about government policy to support waste pickers" (Ministério do Trabalho e Emprego 2009: 7).

National bureaucrats also offered activists access to policymaking circles as a strategy for cultivating their alliance with the waste-picker movement. The waste-pickers movement was a regularly invited guest to CIISC, the interministerial committee that guided national policy at the highest level. According to dissertation research by Brandão (2018), these bureaucrats also created a wide variety of other types of participatory policymaking groups to incorporate activists into discussions about policy design and implementation. For example, during the fight to pass the Law of Solid Waste, CIISC created working groups to discuss strategies for supporting the proposed legislation that included both bureaucrats and movement activists. After the legislation was passed, the members of CIISC held various "evaluation seminars" – which included both bureaucrats and activists – to identify implementation challenges and propose solutions. In meetings of these working groups, bureaucrats would sometimes offer activists information to assist them in political pressure campaigns (Brandão and Vilaça n.d., 15). Evidence suggests that CIISC-sponsored events also provided the waste-pickers movement with important access to policymakers. During the annual *encontros* and Forum meetings, for example, activists would elicit policy promises from national bureaucrats and politicians and, in the following year, hold government to account for following through on those promises (Conversation with Igor Brandão via Skype, November 19, 2017).

In summary, waste-picking policy was governed by bureaucrats who shared broad policy goals with activists outside the state, and who were unable to pursue those goals without outside support. As a strategy to cultivate allies in civil society, they channeled resources to advocacy organizations and provided opportunities for activists to participate in policymaking circles.

Urban Housing

State–society relations around urban housing policy similarly echo the AIDS policy case. Throughout the twentieth century and until now, millions of Brazilians live in informal, low-income housing settlements known as favelas. These settlements are typically located on steep hillsides or swampy lowlands – locations rejected by professional developers due to their risky and otherwise undesirable topography. Houses in these settlements are often built by their residents using scavenged materials, and they often lack sewage or water systems. The dangers of living in such environments are numerous, from disease contagion to perishing in one of the frequent mudslides that sweep away hillside communities. Favelas proliferated from the 1940s to the 1970s during the "great migration," as rural workers moved to cities in search of jobs, but found themselves unable to afford the higher cost of housing.

Like the issues of both AIDS and waste picking, urban housing was a new social question – a policy issue that gained political relevance through social mobilization during the 1980s and 1990s. Also similar to the AIDS policy case, Brazilian presidents responded to social-movement demands around urban housing by creating new policies and new state institutions to administer them – and by recruiting outside policy experts to develop them. These new bureaucrats not only shared broad policy goals with social-movement activists, but they also depended on them for political leverage. Unlike the case of AIDS policy, however, housing-policy bureaucrats had fewer resources at their disposal to cultivate civic organization and mobilization. Consequently, state support for the urban housing movement was more limited.

After decades of government neglect, interspersed with periods of authoritarian forced-removal policies, a wide array of pro-poor housing activists mobilized during Brazil's protracted democratic transition to demand dignified housing (*moradia digna*). "Dignified housing," according to them, was the outcome of following two basic development principles: small-scale housing developments, and "self-management" (*autogestão*), meaning that citizens and community associations should play a role in building their own houses (Viana 2017: 46–56). By 1985, these housing activists and other pro-poor urban movements had formed a broad national coalition to centralize their efforts, called the National Urban Reform Movement (NMRU)[8] (Carvalho 2007; Maricato 2000; Serafim 2013: 67).[9] Over the course of the 1980s and into the 1990s, this movement coalition intensified its political demand-making, incorporated institutional tactics such as legislative lobbying into its repertoire while continuing to organize marches and occupations (Serafim 2013: 72, 77–94).[10]

As would be expected in a model of civic corporatism, politicians under multiple presidential administrations responded to these social-movement demands by creating new policies directed at low-income housing, and by building new government agencies to administer these policies. Most prominently, the national constituent assembly inserted social-democratic guidelines for urban policy into Chapter II of the 1988 constitution.[11] After several housing-policy developments over the course of the 1990s, in 2001, the national congress passed a federal law famously known as the Statute of the City, which established specific legal principles to mandate social-democratic urban policies.[12] The governmental response to movement demands gained further momentum under President Lula, who had campaigned in part on a promise of inclusionary urban reforms, and who had engaged various urban movements in helping to write his policy platform (Abers, Serafim, and Tatagiba 2014). Upon inauguration in 2003, President Lula created a new government ministry, called the Ministry of Cities, to promote urban reform policies (Loureiro et al. 2013; Rolnik 2011; Serafim 2013).

In 2008, Lula responded to movement demands by creating a new federal low-income housing program within the Ministry of Cities that was based on the movement's two core principles of dignified housing (Viana 2017: 64–8). This program grew out of a broader urban housing initiative called My House My Life [Minha Casa Minha Vida (MCMV)], which Lula and his chief of staff Dilma Rouseff had initially promoted as a countercyclical economic measure rather than as a pro-poor housing plan. Brazil's housing activists had opposed this program because it was based on contracts with large-scale construction firms (thus violating the movement's core development principles) and they responded with social-movement mobilization – protesting and occupying

---

[8] In Portuguese: Movimento Nacional de Reforma Urbana.

[9] In the 1990s, this movement coalition institutionalized into the National Urban Reform Forum (*Fórum Nacional de Reforma Urbana*, abbreviated as FNRU).

[10] Institutional tactics were emphasized by the more professionalized NGOs in the coalitions, but viewed more skeptically by the popular movements, who were concerned about preserving their autonomy and who tended to favor traditional contentious tactics such as occupations and marches (Serafim 2013: 72, 90–5).

[11] For the entire text of Brazil's constitution in English, see: www.constituteproject.org/search?lang=en&q=Brazil&status=in_force (last accessed April 26, 2018).

[12] This law was registered as number 10.257.

buildings, combined with behind-the-scenes efforts to lobby politicians. According to one activist involved in the campaign, "It was fight, fight fight, and at the end of the year we got a meeting with Luiz Dulci, then Secretary-General of the Presidency, where we told him it would be impossible to build a federal housing program without discussing it first with the movements" (cited in Viana 2017: 67, author's translation). It was as a direct response to this social-movement pressure that Lula created a new, parallel federal housing program that offered subsidized small-scale, "self-managed" housing developments for low-income people – called My House My Life–Entities [Minha Casa Minha Vida–Entidades (MCMV-E)].

As we saw under the national AIDS program during prior administrations, the Lula administration recruited outside experts to help run these new sectors of the state. At the top echelon, Olívio Dutra was named Minister of Cities. While by no means a political outsider, Dutra was one of the earliest promoters of participatory governance and inclusionary urban reform in Brazil during his tenure as mayor of Porto Alegre (Abers 2000). Dutra, in turn, recruited two urban planners with close ties to urban reform movements into top positions within the Ministry of Cities: Ermínia Maricato, an urban planner from the University of São Paulo who was appointed as Deputy Minister; and Raquel Rolnik, an architect and urban planner from the University of São Paulo who was appointed as Secretary of Urban Projects (Viana 2017: 57). To be sure, a significant number of career bureaucrats populated the MCMV-E program as well – especially those who entered after 2005, when the initial period of program creation was completed (email correspondence with Rafael Viana, March 1, 2018). However, the presence of experts with prior policy commitments to low-income housing contributed to a strong work ethos and a shared set of norms surrounding low-income housing. Urban housing policy was, thus, governed by committed and capable bureaucrats, working in new state agencies.

Yet, just as AIDS-sector bureaucrats faced opposition from other actors inside the state, bureaucrats in the MCMV-E program confronted a variety of obstacles to implementing their housing program from state actors outside their specific program and at lower levels of government. In the case of MCMV-E, one of their main challenges was to convince bureaucrats in other programs of the value of their project – even within their own Ministry. Because the MCMV-E program was based on an alternative model of development that enacted small-scale, "self-management" projects rather than the traditional large-scale development projects, MCMV-E bureaucrats faced not only resistance from the large-scale construction firms who benefited from the dominant model but also from bureaucrats who were skeptical of the slower pace of the self-management model, and skeptical in particular of working in partnership with nonprofit civic organizations rather than with for-profit enterprises. According to one MCMV-E bureaucrat, "we spent a lot of energy since the very beginning convincing colleagues in our own ministry that our model was viable" (quoted in Viana 2017: 74, author's translation). Resistance was particularly acute at the subnational level, where state and local bureaucrats were especially wary of interacting with civic organizations and frequently refused to comply with the guidelines of the program (Viana 2017: 118–19).

The two conditions that produce the incentives for civic corporatism were thus present in the urban housing sector, just as they were in the cases of AIDS policy and waste-picking policy: it was a new social question, made salient through social-movement mobilization; and it was linked to a new state agency, administered by policy-driven bureaucrats. MCMV-E bureaucrats, blocked on various fronts from implementing their program, thus pursued outside allies for leverage. Sometimes they called on like-minded federal bureaucrats in other parts of the Ministry of Cities to help them resolve disputes or to find creative workarounds to administrative obstacles (Viana 2017: 125–6). But, like AIDS-sector bureaucrats, MCMV-E bureaucrats also called on organized movements *outside* the state for support. They sought the support of movement activists in part to help them monitor the on-the-ground implementation of the program, and to identify cases of local malfeasance (Viana 2017: 121–2). MCMV-E bureaucrats also sought the support of movement activists for political leverage. By publicly voicing their support, activists helped MCMV-E bureaucrats justify their proposals to state actors outside their program – providing MCMV-E bureaucrats with a foundation for arguing that their policy agenda reflected civil-society demands (Viana 2017: 116). They also depended on activists to "sensitize" – i.e., lobby – other actors in the state to the importance of self-management (email correspondence with Rafael Viana on January 29, 2018).

Preliminary evidence suggests that one strategy MCMV-E bureaucrats adopted to cultivate housing activists as allies was by opening spaces for them to collaborate on policymaking – just as in the cases of AIDS policy and waste-picking policy. Using Brazil's system of participatory governance as an institutional structure, MCMV-E bureaucrats created two main spaces for state actors and activists to get together for regular policy discussions. The first space, called "points of control" (*pontos de controle*), met every two months and focused on day-to-day housing policy challenges. In this space, movement activists directly participated in designing new policies and reforming existing policies (Viana 2017: 122). At the same time, bureaucrats used this space to help them monitor policy implementation by having civic organizations pass them critical information about on-the-ground policy failures (Viana 2017: 122). The second space, called the "table of negotiation" (*a mesa de negociação*), was designed explicitly to promote dialogue between state actors and movement activists, and discussions focused on high-level policy issues such as budgetary questions and program goals (Viana 2017: 120, footnote 77). Together, these two spaces facilitated alliance-building by institutionalizing channels of communication between bureaucrats and activists.[13]

---

[13] Another important channel for housing activists to access the state was the National Council of Cities (Concidades). Created in 2004, the purpose of this council was to guide the development

MCMV-E bureaucrats provided fewer resources to support civic advocacy than in the AIDS and waste-picking policies, because they had less earmarked funding for civil-society projects at their disposal. However, MCMV-E bureaucrats found indirect ways to subsidize the housing movement (email correspondence with Rafael Viana on January 29, 2018). For example, MCMV-E bureaucrats set aside a small percentage of the budget for each housing project for "organizing entities" – civil-society organizations created to coordinate the program. Because these very "organizing entities" were created by the housing movement and thus were social-movement organizations, financial support for these institutions indirectly supported activism. Like in the AIDS and waste-picking cases, MCMV-E bureaucrats also supported civic advocacy by funding events that provided space for activists to gather and coordinate. In fact, MCMV-E bureaucrats regularly faced criticism from the media and from other state agencies that the ulterior motive of their program was to finance social movements linked to the Worker's Party. MCMV-E bureaucrats reported fighting on a daily basis to prove that their program was not partisan, and that the "organizing entities" who received state funding were all highly qualified and professional.

The MCMV-E program was thus governed at the national level by bureaucrats who shared broad policy goals with activists outside the state. These bureaucrats, in a context of democratic and decentralized governance, faced opposition from myriad actors inside the state – including within the broader urban housing bureaucracy. They were, thus, unable to pursue their policy objectives by acting alone. Like in the cases of both AIDS and waste-picking, they responded by cultivating an alliance with social-movement organizations outside the state.

Environmental Protection for Traditional Communities

The case of environmental protection for traditional communities in the Amazon represents a somewhat different path toward the development of civic corporatism. The politics of protecting traditional communities in the Amazon has long involved opposition from powerful interests in business and in the state. The Amazon – the vast rainforest region encompassing over half of Brazil – continues to be seen by many as a land of unclaimed natural riches, a "land without people for people without land" (quoted in Hochstetler and Keck 2007: 142). The Amazon has also served as the lynchpin of Brazil's plans for economic development at various points throughout modern history. In recent decades, national administrations from across the political spectrum have

---

of a national urban development program. Within the council, a working group on housing provided activists with an opportunity to engage in in-depth discussions and debates about the MCMV-E program. Activists used this space frequently to criticize government and to make demands (email correspondence with Rafael Viana, March 3, 2018).

promoted development in the Amazon through large industrial infrastructure projects such as dam-building and road construction. Yet the vision of the Amazon as empty territory is hardly accurate: in addition to the approximately 240 indigenous tribes who call the region home,[14] a variety of other groups such as rubber tappers, fishers, and nut gatherers live off the Amazon's forests, rivers, and savannas. The large-scale infrastructure projects designed to harness the region's resources for economic development threaten the livelihoods of these traditional Amazonian communities, through the forests they destroy and the river-basin communities they flood.

Different from the other cases, which all involve new state institutions, the bureaucrats involved in this particular issue area were part of pre-existing state institutions. Moreover, all the bureaucrats in this case were career bureaucrats – arriving at their positions in government through the standard public service exam rather than through special forms of recruitment. Yet, despite differences with AIDS, waste-picking, and urban housing policy, environmental protection in the Amazon exhibits elements of civic corporatism. Committed bureaucrats, who shared broad policy goals with an organized social movement outside the state, and who were unable to independently achieve their policy goals, drove the state agency involved in environmental protection.

Consistent with the larger pattern of civic corporatism, the effort to protect the Amazon's traditional communities gained force during Brazil's protracted democratic transition. The national constituent assembly was a particularly important moment, during which a broad coalition of environmentalists both outside and inside the state asserted unexpected influence over the process through a combination of sustained protest and lobbying (Hochstetler and Keck 2007: 48–50). Ultimately, they succeeded in inserting an entire chapter on the environment into Brazil's new national constitution.

Although not directly linked to environmental activism, other transformations in the Brazilian state during this period produced a new set of bureaucrats with a mission to defend traditional Amazonian communities from the effects of environmental devastation. In particular, the *Ministério Público* (MP) – Brazil's public prosecution service – was granted new autonomy and a new mandate to defend the environment. Although the MP was traditionally a clientelistic agency that focused narrowly on criminal prosecution, reformist prosecutors from São Paulo took advantage of Brazil's democratic opening to draft a new law giving responsibility to the MP to protect new group rights (Coslovsky and Nigam 2015; Hochstetler and Keck 2007: 46; McAllister 2008: 58–59). At first, this law granted the MP authority to enter civil suits in the public interest specifically related to environmental concerns (Hochstetler and Keck 2007: 46). Later laws granted the MP authority to protect a broader array of group rights and granted the MP even more legal weapons, such as

---

[14] Available at www.survivalinternational.org/tribes/brazilian (last accessed on February 13, 2018).

the "inquerito civil," which allows prosecutors to demand information from the state to use in their investigation (Vilaça 2017: 31–2). Ultimately, the MP gained such a strong degree of independence during this period that it became known popularly as "the fourth branch of the state" (McAllister 2008: 56; Vilaça 2017: 32). According to some, the redevelopment of the MP was "the greatest institutional transformation of Brazil's redemocratization process" (Vilaça 2017: 30).

Although policy experts and activists were not actively recruited to join the new MP as they had been in the case of the national AIDS program, Brazilians with prior commitments to social advocacy and environmental protection found their own way into the MP in the 1990s and 2000s. Because of the MP's reputation as a national defender of societal interests, Brazilians who were dedicated to defending marginalized interests opted to take the public service exam for the purpose of advancing their causes from inside the MP. According to one prosecutor, "it wasn't the MP that chose me. I chose it. I want to defend the traditional population of the Amazon. Where can I do this most effectively? As a lawyer? No. In the MP" (original in Portuguese, quoted in Vilaça 2017: 91). More broadly, the MP as an institution aligned itself in the 1990s with societal interests and came to view itself as a representative of environmental and other societal interests (McAllister 2008: 61).

At the same time, MP bureaucrats faced such strong opposition to their goals from actors in other parts of the state that, despite their relative autonomy, they depended on the support of allies to help them pursue their mission. This was perhaps unsurprising, given that their investigations of the potential societal and environmental impacts of economic development projects threatened to disrupt the agendas of several of the most powerful state agencies in Brazil. All of these various opponents inside the state had their own sources of independent political power to use in hindering the work of MP bureaucrats. For example, although MP bureaucrats had the power to file civil suits against other state agencies in court, these agencies had their own powerful defense lawyers from the attorney general's office. Such lawyers often used politically persuasive arguments to legitimate the dam as serving the national interest. According to one MP bureaucrat, typical arguments put forth by the attorney general's office went something like: "Brazil needs this energy, [the dam] is the best source we have, if [we don't build it] we're not going to be able to have the World Cup, the Olympics" (quoted in Vilaça 2017: 55).

MP bureaucrats thus sought outside support for leverage in combatting opposition to their policy objectives from actors in other state agencies. Although they depended on various types of allies both inside and outside the state, they depended in particular on social-movement activists. One reason they sought the support of social-movement activists was to gain critical information to bolster their legal cases. According to one activist, "We're in the field, we have a much broader vision of what's happening in the community, the village, the quilombo, and we supply [the MP] with that information" (activist, cited in

Vilaça 2017: 67). The role of activists as informants was important in part because other local actors who had information relevant to MP investigations were often the very targets of these lawsuits and thus had motivations to hide or withhold information (Vilaça 2017: 63). According to one MP bureaucrat:

We're fighting against the government, so we knew we weren't going to get accurate information from FUNAI or IBAMA (state agencies ostensibly responsible for protecting indigenous populations and the environment), or the Federal Police ... But we needed that information in order to defend the environment and traditional populations ... The only way [to get it] was to go through that social movement in Altamira, which is the strongest social movement in all of the Amazon (MP bureaucrat, cited in Vilaça 2017: 64).

The role of activists as informants was also key because MP bureaucrats were unable to collect information from these communities on their own due to the extreme geographic isolation of these villages, which were often unreachable during the Amazonian winter (Vilaça 2017: 64).

Another reason MP bureaucrats sought alliances with activists was for the outside political pressure they could mobilize. Paradoxically, social-movement activists often aimed their political pressure at MP bureaucrats themselves, by demanding that MP bureaucrats follow up on their complaints and reports (Vilaça 2017: 67). Yet MP bureaucrats tended to interpret this pressure as a form of support for their broad policy goals. In the words of one bureaucrat, "We [in the MP] are limited in our interventions by the number of people we have [in our office]. So, certainly, if a social movement is always putting pressure on you, you're going to intervene more often, and, maybe, better" (MP bureaucrat, cited in Vilaça 2017: 67). In the words of another bureaucrat in the MP, their alliance with social movements "was strategic for us; it was a strategy of survival for the Ministério Público" (MP bureaucrat, cited in Vilaça 2017: 96). In turn, activists came to view MP bureaucrats as partners and allies. According to one environmental activist:

If the *Ministério Público* didn't exist, we wouldn't achieve a third of what we do ... We pressure the *Ministério Público*, and the *Ministério Público* pressures the environmental agency or goes after the problem itself – this is how stuff gets done. (quoted in McAllister 2008: 158)

In short, bureaucrats in the MP recognized that they depended on a mobilized and autonomous social movement to help them achieve their goals.

Whereas this study of AIDS policy in prior chapters contributed new hypotheses about the ways state actors influence civic organization and mobilization in the twenty-first century, these shadow cases provide evidence to suggest other cases of civic corporatism. Other recent studies of Brazilian politics capture dynamics of civic corporatism as well, such as in the areas of black rights (Paschel 2016), land reform (Tarlau 2019), in rural development, urban policy, and security (Abers, Serafim, and Tatagiba 2014), and in other environmental policy sectors (Abers 2019; Abers and Keck 2013; Hochstetler and Keck 2007). Civic corporatism also spread over time from the AIDS policy sector to other policy sectors, such as LGBT rights (Dehesa 2010; Facchini 2005), sex-worker rights (Murray 2015), and to other health policy areas such as tuberculosis (Rich and Gómez 2012). Certainly, we would expect civic corporatism is to take form in different ways across policy sectors, depending on the relative strength of state actors versus civil-society actors, and depending on the goals of social-movement actors. Together, however, these cases suggest the concept of civic corporatism captures a broad national phenomenon.

THE STATE, DEMOCRACY, AND POLITICAL PARTICIPATION

In conclusion, the model of civic corporatism offers a new perspective on the relationship between democracy and the state. It shows how increased diversity within the state alters the motivations of state actors in confronting civil society. Intra-state conflict motivates state actors to look outside the state for political leverage – and to support relatively independent forms of civic mobilization in pursuit of that goal.

Increased diversity within the state is not only a product of the neoliberal reforms that have fragmented existing institutions. Rather, diversity has also come from an *expansion* of the state. Democracy – and the civil liberties it entails – allowed citizens whose interests had long been neglected by government to demand inclusion through social-movement mobilization. Democratically elected politicians responded to their demands by creating new government programs. The bureaucrats who were recruited to administer these programs thus held objectives that differed fundamentally from the objectives of bureaucrats in the pre-democratization period: to build national policies that supported formerly marginalized interests. These bureaucrats form what we might think of as a new political class in Brazil – a new set of interests inside the state. As the size of this new policymaking elite grew, so did the likelihood of intra-state conflict – as well as the likelihood of new state-social movement alliances.

By calling attention to new state agencies and actors, civic corporatism also helps us understand the potential (and limitations) for Brazil's extraordinary democratic transition to expand political participation. For most of its modern political history, Brazil was known as a country of extreme political and economic inequality. Even among South American countries, Brazil was distinguished by its political conservatism. Whereas the rest of the region had important episodes of populism in the twentieth century, which "incorporated" segments of the lower classes into the political system (as well as legalized and regulated unions), in Brazil the lower classes continued to be largely excluded from the political system (Collier and Collier 1991). Yet in 1988, as if to make up for the past, Brazilian legislators forged the most progressive new constitution in Latin America at the time – committing the state to a set of new responsibilities just at a time when neoliberalism was spreading globally and states were in retreat. Similar to Mexico's historic 1917 document, Brazil's new constitution placed a strong central focus on social rights, with explicit social provisions incorporated into the text. Even further, Brazil's constitution opened the way for the creation of new political institutions with mechanisms to foster the direct participation of societal groups in the policy process. Far from its old reputation as a bastion of conservatism, Brazil began to be lauded by the international development community as a global model for civil-society participation in policymaking. What is clear about this transition is that for the first time in history, Brazil's formal political institutions were opening access to citizens beyond the elite minority. Less clear, however, has been whether, and under what conditions, Brazil's new participatory governance institutions have expanded participation in practice.

The concept of civic corporatism suggests that we cannot understand whether or how participatory governance institutions expand political participation to include new sectors of society without examining the motivations of the people who run them: bureaucrats. To be sure, the interests of politicians and political parties matter. Yet, the majority of participatory institutions in Brazil correspond to new government programs, driven by social-movement demands for political inclusion. These institutions are run not by politicians, but by Brazil's new political class of mid-level bureaucrats. More broadly, the most fundamental transformation of the Brazilian state was not just the electoral system and the structure of government institutions, but also the unelected actors who populate them.

Appendix

Survey and Catalog of Associations

THE BRAZILIAN SURVEY OF AIDS NGOS

The Brazilian survey of AIDS NGOs was carried out between February and May 2010 via the Internet in the states of Rio de Janeiro and São Paulo. In total 231 organizations were included in the sample and 123 organizations responded, yielding a response of 53 percent.

Sample Design

A sample was drawn from three registries of AIDS-related organizations in each state: the list of NGO forum members, the list of organizations that had received funding from the state-level AIDS program at any time over the four years prior to the survey, and the list of government-funded AIDS hospices.

My sampling procedure likely produced a selection of organizations that was more politically active than a random sample would have produced. Drawing such a sample was not possible, since no reliable registries existed from which to determine a population. At the same time, my analytic goal was not to make generalizations about the population of NGOs in Brazil but, rather, about the population of civic groups that are involved in political demand-making. At the same time, the bias of the survey toward more politically mobilized organizations supports some of my claims. For example, the survey shows that *even among* the most politically connected AIDS associations, the level of professionalization is fairly low and the level of financial dependence on the state remains quite high.

The Survey Instrument

I conducted the survey via the Internet. My response rate of 53 percent was high relative to the typically low returns on internet-based surveys.

THE NATIONAL CATALOG OF CIVIC AIDS ORGANIZATIONS

I constructed a national database of civic AIDS organizations in the years 2001 and 2002 using information from The National Catalog of HIV/AIDS Civil Society Organizations. This catalog of organizations is the product of an effort by the Ministry of Health to construct a comprehensive registry of AIDS associations in Brazil. The end result of this national questionnaire was a thick, hardcover book that contained two pages of information on every organization in their national sample. The responses of each organization are printed word-for-word, some of which were open-ended, and some of which were answers to multiple-choice questions. The focus of the questions was on their missions, activities, leadership, and organizational attributes. No electronic version of the catalog was available.

I constructed the database by hiring a data capturing company, Digital Divide, to enter all the information contained with the catalog into a spreadsheet that I could use to perform quantitative analyses of the survey responses.

This catalog serves two analytic purposes. First, the catalog data provide evidence to support claims about civic mobilization in the AIDS policy sector that extend beyond the Southeastern states of Rio de Janeiro and São Paulo, where I conducted the survey and where I conducted most of my interviews. Second, the data in the catalog provide a snapshot of civic organization and mobilization around AIDS in 2002 after federal funding for civic AIDS projects had produced a boom in the number of service-providing AIDS organizations across Brazil, but before the federal AIDS bureaucracy had begun to focus their resources on mobilizing these organizations as political advocates. Thus, the data in the national catalog provides evidence to support claims about the effect of donor funding on interest mobilization when it is *not* combined with other forms of support.

SURVEY OF COMMUNITY-BASED ASSOCIATIONS

I complemented the internet survey with a survey of forty-five community-based organizations that worked with AIDS in the state of Rio de Janeiro. This survey contained the same questions and the same basic format as the internet survey.

Sample Design

I drew the sample from the participant list of the conference "AIDS in the Community" held in the state of Rio de Janeiro in 2008. This conference brought together over one hundred representatives from community-based associations that worked with HIV prevention in the state of Rio.

Whereas my sample of AIDS associations in the internet survey was likely biased toward more professionalized and higher-SES associations, the sample of AIDS associations in the community-based survey was likely biased toward the least professionalized and lowest SES AIDS associations. I have not analyzed this data yet, but can use it as a base of comparison against the internet-survey respondents.

Survey Instrument

I trained four research assistants to assist me in implementing the survey during a two-day conference. A research assistant collected five more survey responses by following up with representatives who were unavailable during the conference.

References

2003, Jun 10. "Brazil Becomes Developing World Model for HIV/AIDS Treatment, Prevention Strategy." *Kaiser Health News Network*.

2005, Jul 28. "Science and Technology: Roll Out, Roll Out; AIDS in Brazil." *The Economist*.

2006. "Descentralização dá mais eficiência ao sistema, mas ainda causa problemas." *Valor Econômico*, April 12.

2008. "Ex-secretário de Saúde e mais nove são presos em operação." *O Globo*, July 15.

2009a. Fortalecimento do Associativismo e do Cooperativismo dos Catadores de Materiais Recicláveis: Formação para a Autogestão, Assistência Técnica e Mobilização. edited by Ministério do Trabalho e Emprego.

2009b. "Projeto sobre Aids provoca polêmica." *O Globo*, April 30.

2010a. "Falta de remédio para HIV causa protestos." *Gazeta do Povo*, April 29.

2010b. "Falta de remédios contra aids causa protestos." *O Estado de São Paulo*, April 28.

2012a. "ONGs acusam governo de discriminar gays." *Agência Estado*, February 11.

2012b. "ONGs/Aids divulgam protesto contra desmantelamento do controle social no Governo Dilma." *Agência AIDS*, March 22.

Abers, Rebecca. 2019. "Bureaucratic Activism: Pursuing Environmentalism Inside the Brazilian State." *Latin American Politics and Society* 61 (1).

Abers, Rebecca and Luciana Tatagiba. 2015. "Institutional Activism: Mobilizing for Women's Health from Inside the Brazilian Bureaucracy." In *Social Movement Dynamics: New Perspectives on Theory and Research from Latin America*, edited by Federico Rossi and Marisa von Bülow. Surrey, England: Ashgate.

Abers, Rebecca and Margaret Keck. 2013. *Practical Authority: Agency and Institutional Change in Brazilian Water Politics*. Oxford: Oxford University Press.

Abers, Rebecca and Marisa von Bülow. 2011. "Movimentos sociais na teoria e na prática: Como Estudar o Ativismo Através da Fronteira entre Estado e Sociedade?" *Sociologias* 13 (28): 52–84.

Abers, Rebecca, Lizandra Serafim, and Luciana Tatagiba. 2014. "Changing Repertoires of State–Society Interaction under Lula." In *Brazil under the Workers' Party: Continuity and Change from Lula to Dilma*. London: Palgrave MacMillan.

Abers, Rebecca Neara. 2000. *Inventing Local Democracy: Grassroots Politics in Brazil.* Boulder, CO: Lynne Rienner.

ABIA. 1989. "Entrevista com o dr. Álvaro Matida e a Doutora Regina Guedes, do Departamento de Vigilância Epidemiológica da Secretaria Estadual de Saúde/RJ." *Boletím ABIA.*

Abrucio, Fernando Luiz. 1998. *Os Barões da Federação: Os Governadores e a Redemocratização Brasileira.* São Paulo: Editora Hucitec.

Abrucio, Fernando, Maria Rita Loureiro, and Silvia Pacheco, eds. 2010. *Burocracia e Política no Brasil: Desafio para o Estado Democrático no Século XXI.* Rio de Janeiro: Editora de Fundação Getulio Vargas.

Alvarez, Sonia. 1990. *Engendering Democracy in Brazil: Women's Movements in Transition Politics.* Princeton, NJ: Princeton University Press.

Alvarez, Sonia E. 1999. "Advocating Feminism: The Latin American Feminist NGO 'Boom'." *International Feminist Journal of Politics* 1 (2):181–209. doi: 10.1080/146167499359880.

Alvarez, Sonia E., Evelina Dagnino, and Arturo Escobar. 1998. *Cultures of Politics/ Politics of Cultures: Re-visioning Latin American Social Movements.* Boulder, CO: Westview Press.

Amengual, Matthew. 2016. *Politicized Enforcement in Argentina: Labor and Environmental Regulation.* Cambridge: Cambridge University Press.

Amenta, Edwin. 2008. *When Movements Matter: The Townsend Plan and the Rise of Social Security.* Princeton and Oxford: Princeton University Press.

ANAIDS. 2011. Carta de Princípios.

Arce, Moises. 2008. "The Repoliticization of Collective Action after Neoliberalism in Peru." *Latin American Politics and Society* 50 (3):37–62.

Arce, Moises, and Paul T. Bellinger Jr. 2007. "Low-Intensity Democracy Revisited: The Effects of Economic Liberalization on Political Activity in Latin America." *World Politics* 60:97–121.

Arnquist, Sarah, Andrew Ellner, and Rebecca Weintraub. 2011. "Title." Questões relativas à Provisão Universal de Saúde.

Arretche, Marta. 2002. "Federalismo e Relações Intergovernamentais no Brasil: A Reforma de Programas Sociais." *Dados: Revista de Ciências Sociais* 45 (3):431–458.

Avritzer, Leonardo. 2009. *Participatory Institutions in Democratic Brazil.* Baltimore, MD: Johns Hopkins University Press.

Baldioti, Fernanda. 2010. "Pacientes com HIV enfrentam falta de remédios e médicos em postos do Rio, além da demora para realização de exames." *O Globo*, January 27, 2010.

Bano, Masooda. 2008. "Dangerous Correlations: Aid's Impact on NGOs' Performance and Ability to Mobilize Members in Pakistan." *World Development* 36 (11):2109–2562.

Barbieri, Cristiane. 2008. "No Brasil, acesso ao tratamento é tardio para mais de 40% dos pacientes." *Cadernos PELAVIDDA: Aids, tratamento e ativismo* XVII (46):18–19.

Barbieri, Cristiane and Raphael Ferrari. 2007. "Pesquisa revela a precária realidade dos CTAs em todo o Brasil." *Cadernos PELAVIDDA: Aids, tratamento e ativismo* 31:2297–2313.

Barboza, Renato. 2006. "Gestão do Programa Estadual DST/Aids de São Paulo: uma análise do processo de descentralização das ações no período de 1994 a 2003."

Mestrado, Saúde Coletiva, Coordenadoria de Controle de Doenças da Secretaria de Estado da Saúde de São Paulo (SES/CCD/CD-141/06).

Bennett, W. Lance and Alexandra Segerberg. 2013. The Logic of Connective Action: Digital Media and the Personalization of Contentious Politics. Cambridge Studies in Contentious Politics.

Biancarelli, Aureliano. 2012. 15 anos na promoção de Direitos: Fórum de ONG/Aids do Estado de São Paulo. 1st edn. São Paulo: Editora cuore.

Biehl, Joao. 2007. "Pharmaceuticalization: AIDS Treatment and Global Health Politics." Anthropological Quarterly 80 (4):1083–1126.

Biehl, João Guilherme and Torben Eskerod. 2007. Will to Live: AIDS Therapies and the Politics of Survival. Princeton, NJ: Princeton University Press.

Boyd, Barbara L. and John Garrison. 1999. NGO participation in HIV/AIDS Control Project in Brazil achieves results (English). Environmentally and Socially Sustainable Development network newsletter. Washington, DC: World Bank.

Brandão, Igor. 2018. "Governar o desperdício: a inclusão de catadores no regime brasileiro de políticas de resíduos." Instituto de Ciência Política, Universidade de Brasília.

Brandão, Igor, and Luiz Vilaça. n.d. Ativismo burocrático na construção de Belo Monte e na inclusão socioprodutiva de catadores de materiais recicláveis.

Brass, Jennifer N. 2016. Allies or Adversaries: NGOs and the State in Africa. Cambridge, UK: Cambridge University Press.

Bruera, Hernán F Gómez. 2013. Lula, the Workers' Party and the Governability Dilemma in Brazil. New York: Routledge.

Brysk, Alison. 2000. "Democratizing Civil Society in Latin America." Journal of Democracy 11 (3):151–165.

Cameron, Maxwell, Eric Hershberg, and Kenneth Sharpe. 2012. New Institutions for Participatory Democracy in Latin America: Voice and Consequence. Basingstoke: Palgrave Macmillan US.

Carpenter, Daniel. 2001. The Forging of Bureaucratic Autonomy: Reputations, Networks, and Policy Innovation in Executive Agencies, 1862–1928. Princeton, NJ: Princeton University Press.

Cartaxo, Mariana G. 2018. "Dez Anos de Política de Aids (2006–2016) Conflictos e Transformações." Instituto de Ciência Política, Universidade de Brasília.

Carvalho, Ana Paula Soares. 2007. "Reforma Urbana no Brasil: a intelligentzia e o Estatuto da Cidade." XIII Congresso Brasileiro de Sociologia.

Castells, Manuel. 1996. The Rise of the Network Society, Information Age. Cambridge, MA: Blackwell Publishers.

  2012. Networks of Outrage and Hope: Social Movements in the Internet Age. Cambridge, UK; Malden, MA: Polity.

Castilho, Euclides and Pedro Chequer. 1997. "Epidemiologia do HIV/AIDS no Brasil." In Políticas, Instituições e AIDS: Enfrentando a Epidemia no Brasil, edited by Richard Parker. Rio de Janeiro: ABIA.

Chalmers, Douglas A., Carlos M. Vilas, Katherine Hite, Scott B. Martin, Kerianne Piester, and Monique Segarra, eds. 1997. The New Politics of Inequality in Latin America: Rethinking Participation and Representation, 1st edn. Oxford, UK: Oxford University Press.

Chartock, Sarah. 2013. "Corporatism With Adjectives? Conceptualizing Civil Society Incorporation and Indigenous Participation in Latin America." Latin American Politics and Society 55 (2):52–76. doi: 10.1111/j.1548-2456.2013.00193.x.

Cohen, Cathy J. 1999. *The Boundaries of Blackness: AIDS and the Breakdown of Black Politics.* Chicago, IL: University of Chicago Press.

Collier, David. 1995. "Trajectory of a Concept: 'Corporatism' in the Study of Latin American Politics." In *Latin America in Comparative Perspective: New Approaches to Methods and Analysis,* edited by Peter H. Smith. Boulder, CO: Westview Press.

Collier, David, and Ruth Berins Collier. 1977. "Who Does What, to Whom, and How: Toward a Comparative Analysis of Latin American Corporatism." In *Authoritarianism and Corporatism in Latin America,* edited by James M. Malloy, 489–512. Pittsburgh, PA: University of Pittsburgh Press.

Collier, Ruth Berins, and David Collier. 1979. "Inducements versus Constraints: Disaggregating 'Corporatism'." *The American Political Science Review* 73 (4):967–986.

1991. *Shaping The Political Arena: Critical Junctures, the Labor Movement, and Regime Dynamics in Latin America.* Notre Dame, IN: University of Notre Dame Press.

Collier, Ruth Berins and Samuel Handlin. 2009a. "Logics of Collective Action, State Linkages, and Aggregate Traits: The UP-Hub versus the A-Net." In *Reorganizing Popular Politics: Participation and the New Interest Regime in Latin America,* 61–92. University Park, PA: Pennsylvania State University Press.

2009b. *Reorganizing Popular Politics: Participation and the New Interest Regime in Latin America.* University Park, PA: Penn State University Press.

Cook, Maria Lorena. 2010. *Politics of Labor Reform in Latin America: Between Flexibility and Rights.* University Park, PA: Penn State Press.

Cooley, Alexander, and James Ron. 2002. "The NGO Scramble: Organizational Insecurity and the Political Economy of Transnational Action." *International Security* 27 (1):5–39.

Coslovsky, Salo and Amit Nigam. 2015. Building Prosecutorial Autonomy from Within: The Transformation of the Ministério Público in Brazil. NYU Wagner Working Paper.

Câmara, Cristina and Ronaldo Lima. 2000. "Historica das ONGs/AIDS e sua contribuição no campo das lutas sociais." *Cadernos Abong* 28:29–74.

D'Argent, Eduardo. 2015. *Technocracy and Democracy in Latin America: The Experts Running Government.* Cambridge, UK: Cambridge University Press.

Dagnino, Evelina, Alberto Olivera, and Aldo Panfichi. 2006. *A disputa pela construção democrática na América Latina.* Rio de Janeiro: Paz e Terra.

Dahl, Robert A. 1961. *Who Governs? Democracy and Power in an American City, Yale Studies in Political Science.* New Haven, CT: Yale University Press.

Daniel, Herbert and Richard Parker. 1991. "A terceira epidemia: o exercício da solidariedade." In *AIDS: A Terceira Epidemia,* edited by Herbert Daniel and Richard Parker. São Paulo: Iglu Editora.

Daniel, Herbert, and Richard G. Parker. 1993. *Sexuality, Politics, and AIDS in Brazil: In Another World?, Social Aspects of AIDS.* London Washington, DC: Falmer Press.

Davis, Gordon J. and Amanda Hawes. 1967. "Toward an Understanding of Decision Making in the Office of Economic Opportunity." *Harvard Civil Rights-Civil Liberties Law Review* 2:259–297.

De la Dehesa, Rafael. 2010. *Queering the Public Sphere in Mexico and Brazil: Sexual Rights Movements in Emerging Democracies.* Durham, NC: Duke University Press.

Della Porta, Donatella, Massimillano Andretta, Lorenzo Mosca, and Herbert Reiter. 2006. *Globalization from Below: Transnational Activists and Protest Networks*. Minneapolis, MN: University of Minnesota Press.

Della Porta, Donatella, and Mario Diani. 2006. *Social Movements: An Introduction*. Oxford; Malden, MA: Blackwell.

Diani, Mario. 2003. "Networks and Social Movements: A Research Programme." In *Social Movements and Networks: Relational Approaches to Collective Action*, xix, 348 p. ill., map 24 cm, edited by M. Diani and D. McAdam. Oxford: Oxford University Press.

DiMaggio, Paul J., and Walter W. Powell. 1983. "The Iron Cage Revisited: Institutional Isomorphism and Collective Rationality in Organizational Fields." *American Sociological Review* 48 (2):147–160. doi: 10.2307/2095101.

Eaton, Kent. 2006. "Decentralization's Nondemocratic Roots: Authoritarianism and Subnational Reform in Latin America." *Latin American Politics & Society* 48 (1):1–26.

Eaton, Kent and Tyler Dickovick. 2004. "The Politics of Re-centralization in Argentina and Brazil." *Latin American Research Review* 39 (1):90–122.

Eckstein, Susan. 2001. *Power and Popular Protest: Latin American Social Movements*. 2nd edn. Berkeley, CA: University of California Press.

Elkins, Zachary, Tom Ginsburg, and Beth Simmons. 2013. "Getting to Rights: Treaty Ratification, Constitutional Convergence, and Human Rights Practice." *Harvard International Law Journal* 54 (1):61–94.

ENONG. 2007. "Proposta Final." Encontro Nacional de ONGs AIDS, Goiânia, Goiás. 2009. Documento Norteador. Rio de Janeiro.

Escobar, Arturo and Sonia Alvarez, eds. 1992. *The Making Of Social Movements In Latin America: Identity, Strategy, And Democracy* Boulder, CO: Westview.

Evans, Peter. 1979. *Dependent Development: The Alliance of Multinational, State, and Local Capital in Brazil*. Princeton, NJ: Princeton University Press.

Evans, Peter. 1996. "Government Action, Social Capital and Development: Creating Synergy across the Public-Private Divide." *World Development* 24 (6):1119–1132.

Ewig, Christina. 1999. "The Strengths and Limits of the NGO Women's Movement Model: Shaping Nicaragua's Democratic Institutions." *Latin American Research Review* 34 (3):75–102.

Facchini, Regina. 2005. *Sopa de letrinhas?: Movimento homossexual e produ√ß√£o de identidades coletivas nos anos 90*. Editora Garamond.

Fairfield, Tasha. 2015. *Private Wealth and Public Revenue in Latin America: Business Power and Tax Politics*. Cambridge, UK: Cambridge University Press.

Faleiros, Vicente de Paula, Jacinta de Fátima Senna da Silva, Luis Carlos Fadel de Vasconcellos, and Rosa Maria Godoy Silveira. 2006. *A Construção do SUS: Histórias da Reforma Sanitária e o Processo Participativo*. Brasília: Ministério da Saúde.

Falleti, Tulia. 2010. *Decentralization and Subnational Politics in Latin America*. Cambridge: Cambridge University Press.

Fenwick, Tracy Beck. 2009. "Avoiding Governors: The Success of Bolsa Família." *Latin American Research Review* 44 (1):102–131.

Flynn, Matthew. 2008. "Public Production of Anti-Retroviral Medicines in Brazil, 1990–2007." *Development and Change* 39 (4):513–536.

2015. *Pharmaceutical Autonomy and Public Health in Latin America: State, Society, and Industry in Brazil's AIDS Program, Routledge Studies in Latin American Politics*. New York: Routledge.

Fox, J. 1994. "The Difficult Transition from Clientelism to Citizenship: Lessons from Mexico." *World Politics* 46 (2):151–184.

Fox, Jonathan. 1993. *The Politics of Food in Mexico: State Power and Social Mobilization.* Ithaca, NY: Cornell University Press.

Frasca, Tim. 2005. *AIDS in Latin America.* New York: Palgrave Macmillan.

Friedman, Elisabeth Jay and Kathryn Hochstetler. 2002. "Assessing the Third Transition in Latin American Democratization: Representational Regimes and Civil society in Argentina and Brazil." *Comparative Politics*, 35(1):21–42.

Galvão, Jane. 2000. *AIDS no Brasil: a agenda de construção de uma epidemia.* 1st edn. Rio de Janeiro, RJ, Brasil São Paulo, SP, Brasil: Associação Brasileira Interdisciplinar de AIDS; Editora 34.

Galvão, Jane. 2008. "Betinho: A Celebration of Life." Chapter 12 in The Practice of International Health: a Case-Based Approach, edited by Daniel Perlman and Ananya Roy. Oxford: Oxford University Press.

Garay, Candelaria. 2007. "Social Policy and Collective Action: Unemployed Workers, Community Associations, and Protest in Argentina." *Politics & Society* 35 (2): 301–328. doi: 10.1177/0032329207300392.

2016. *Social Policy Expansion in Latin America.* New York, NY: Cambridge University Press.

Gauri, Varun and Evan Lieberman. 2006. "Boundary Institutions and HIV/AIDS Policy in Brazil and South Africa." *Studies in Comparative International Development* 41 (3):47–73.

Geddes, Barbara. 1990. "Building 'State' Autonomy in Brazil: 1930–1964." *Comparative Politics* 22 (2):217–235.

Goldfrank, Benjamin. 2011. *Deepening Local Democracy in Latin America: Participation, Decentralization, and the Left.* University Park, PA: Penn State Press.

Green, James. 1999. *Beyond Carnaval: Male Homosexuality in Twentieth-Century Brazil.* Chicago, IL: The University of Chicago Press.

Greenstone, J. David and Paul E. Peterson. 1973. *Race and Authority in Urban Politics: Community Participation and the War on Poverty.* Chicago, IL: The University of Chicago Press.

Grindle, Merilee S. 1980. *Politics and Policy Implementation in the Third World.* Princeton, NJ: Princeton University Press.

2004. "Good Enough Governance: Poverty Reduction and Reform in Developing Countries." *Governance* 17 (4):525–548. doi: 10.1111/j.0952-1895.2004 .00256.x.

Grindle, Merilee Serrill. 2007. *Going Local: Decentralization, Democratization, and the Promise of Good Governance.* Princeton, NJ: Princeton University Press.

Gupta, Akhil. 2012. *Red Tape: Bureaucracy, Structural Violence, and Poverty in India.* Durham, NC: Duke University Press.

Gurr, Ted Robert, and Woodrow Wilson School of Public and International Affairs. Center of International Studies. 1970. *Why Men Rebel.* Princeton, NJ: Published for the Center of International Studies, Princeton University by Princeton University Press.

Gurza Lavalle, Adrian, Arnab Acharya, and Peter Houtzager. 2005. "Beyond Comparative Anecdotalism: How Civil and Political Organizations Shape Participation in São Paulo, Brazil." *World Development* 33 (6):951–964.

Gurza Lavalle, Adrian, Peter Houtzager, and Graziela Castello. 2006. "Representação política e organizações civis: Novas instâncias de mediação e os desafios da legitimidade." *Revista Brasileira de Ciências Sociais* 21 (60):43–66.

Gurza Lavalle, Adrian, Jessica Voigt, and Lizandra Serafim. 2016. "O que fazem os conselhos e quando o fazem? Padrões decisórios e o debate dos efeitos das instituições participativas." *Dados – Revista de Ciências Sociais* 59 (3):609–650.

Hansen, John Mark. 1991. *Gaining Access: Congress and the Farm Lobby, 1919–1981.* Chicago, IL: University of Chicago Press.

Hochstetler, Kathryn. 2000. "Democratizing Pressures from Below? Social Movements in the New Brazilian Democracy." *Democratic Brazil: actors, institutions, and processes*, chapter 8, edited by Peter R. Kingstone and Timothy J. Power, 167–184. Pittsburgh, PA: University of Pittsburgh Press.

Hochstetler, Kathryn and Margaret E. Keck. 2007. *Greening Brazil: Environmental Activism in State and Society.* Durham, NC: Duke University Press.

Hochstetler, Kathy. 2008. "Organized Civil Society in Lula's Brazil." In *Democratic Brazil Revisited*, edited by Kingston Peter and Power Timothy J., 33–56. Pittsburgh, PA: University of Pittsburgh Press.

Hoffman, Florian and Fernando Bentes. 2008. "Accountability for Social and Economic Rights in Brazil." In *Judicial Enforcement of Social and Economic Rights in the Developing World*, edited by Varun Gauri and Daniel Brinks. Cambridge: Cambridge University Press.

Howard, Philip N. and Muzammil M. Hussain. 2013. *Democracy's Fourth Wave?: Digital Media and the Arab Spring, Oxford Studies in Digital Politics.* Oxford; New York, NY: Oxford University Press.

Htun, Mala and Laurel Weldon. 2018. *The Logics of Gender Justice: State Action and Women's Rights Around the World, Cambridge Studies in Gender and Politics.* Cambridge: Cambridge University Press.

Hunter, Wendy. 2010. *The Transformation of the Workers' Party in Brazil, 1989–2009.* New York and Cambridge: Cambridge University Press.

Jalali, Rita. 2013. "Financing Empowerment? How Foreign Aid to Southern Ngos and Social Movements Undermines Grass-Roots Mobilization." *Sociology Compass* 7 (1):55–73. doi: 10.1111/soc4.12007.

Jelin, Elizabeth. 1997. "Emergent Citizenship or Exclusion? Social Movements and Non-Governmental Organizations in the 1990s." In *Politics, Social Change, and Economic Restructuring in Latin America*, edited by William C. Smith and Roberto Patricio Korzeniewicz. Boulder, CO: Lynne Rienner.

Jones, Patrice M. 2003, Jun 08. "Brazil AIDS Program Touted as Model for World." Chicago Tribune.

Juris, Jeffrey S. 2008. *Networking Futures: The Movements against Corporate Globalization, Experimental Futures.* Durham, NC: Duke University Press.

Juris, Jeffrey S., and Alex Khasnabish. 2013. *Insurgent Encounters: Transnational Activism, Ethnography, and the Political.* Durham, NC; London: Duke University Press.

Kahler, Miles. 2009. *Networked Politics: Agency, Power, and Governance, Cornell Studies in Political Economy.* Ithaca, NY: Cornell University Press.

Kaufman, Robert and Joan Nelson, eds. 2004. *Crucial Needs, Weak Incentives: Social Sector Reform, Democratization, and Globalization in Latin America.* Baltimore, MD: The Johns Hopkins University Press.

Keck, M. E., and K. Sikkink. 1998. *Activists Beyond Borders: Advocacy Networks in International Politics*. Ithaca, NY: Cornell University Press.

Kingstone, Peter R. 1999. *Crafting Coalitions for Reform: Business Preferences, Political Institutions, and Neoliberal Reform in Brazil*. University Park, PA: Pennsylvania State University Press.

Kingstone, Peter, Joseph K. Young, and Rebecca Aubrey. 2013. "Resistance to Privatization: Why Protest Movements Succeed and Fail in Latin America." *Latin American Politics and Society* 55 (3):93–116.

Kriesi, Hanspeter. 1996. "The Organizational Structure of New Social Movements in a Political Context." In *Comparative Perspectives on Social Movements*, edited by Doug McAdam, John D. McCarthy, and Mayer N. Zald, 152–184. Cambridge: Cambridge University Press.

Kurtz, Marcus J. 2004. "Dilemmas of Democracy in the Open Economy Lessons From Latin America." *World Politics* 56:262–302.

Levitsky, Steve. 2003. *Transforming Labor-Based Parties in Latin America: Argentine Peronism in Comparative Perspective*. New York, NY: Cambridge University Press.

Levitsky, Steven and Kenneth Roberts, eds. 2011. *The Resurgence of the Latin American Left*. Baltimore, MD: Johns Hopkins University Press.

Lieberman, Evan S. 2009. *Boundaries of Contagion: How Ethnic Politics Have Shaped Government Responses to AIDS*. Princeton, NJ: Princeton University Press.

Loureiro, Maria Rita, Vinicius Macário, and Pedro Guerra. 2013. Democracia, arenas decisórias e políticas públicas: o Programa Minha Casa Minha Vida. Texto para Discussão, Instituto de Pesquisa Econômica Aplicada (IPEA).

Lucero, Jose Antonio. 2008. *Struggles of Voice: The Politics of Indigenous Representation in the Andes*. Pittsburg, PA: University of Pittsburgh Press

Lusa, Agência. 2010. "Brasil: Falta de antirretrovirais gera protestos em sete estados brasileiros." Agência Lusa, April 28.

Macrae, Edward. 1990. *A Construção da Igualdade*. Campinas: Editora Unicamp.

—— 1997. "Movimentos Sociais e os Direitos de Cidadania dos Homossexuais." In *Trabalho, cultura e cidadania – um balanço da história social brasileira*, edited by A. Araújo. São Paulo: Editora Scritta.

Malloy, James M. 1977. *Authoritarianism and Corporatism in Latin America*. Pittsburgh, PA: University of Pittsburgh Press.

Manuela, Massé. 2009. "From Cycles of Protest to Equilibrium: Explaining the Evolution of AIDS-related Non-governmental Organisations in Brazil." *Masters in Philosophy, Latin American Studies*. Oxford: Oxford University Press.

Maricato, Ermínia. 2000. "As idéias fora do lugar e o lugar fora das idéias." *A cidade do pensamento único: desmanchando consensos*. Petrópolis: Vozes:165.

Mayka, Lindsay. 2019a. *Building Participatory Institutions in Latin America*. New York, NY: Cambridge University Press.

—— 2019b. "The Origins of Strong Institutional Design: Policy Reform and Participatory Institutions in Brazil's Health Sector." *Comparative Politics*.

Mayka, Lindsay and Jessica Rich. n.d. "Brazil's Participatory Infrastructure: Opportunities and Limitations for Inclusion." In *The New Inclusion in Latin America*, edited by Diana Kapiszewski, Steve Levitsky, and Deborah Yashar.

McAdam, Doug. 1982. *Political Process and the Development of Black Insurgency, 1930–1970*. Chicago: University of Chicago Press.

McAdam, Doug, and W. Richard Scott. 2005. "Organizations and Movements." In *Social Movements and Organization Theory*, edited by Gerald F. Davis, Doug McAdam, W. Richard Scott and Mayer N. Zald, 4–40. Cambridge, UK: Cambridge University Press.

McAllister, Lesley K. 2008. *Making Law Matter: Environmental Protection and Legal Institutions in Brazil*. Stanford, CA: Stanford Law Books. Book.

McCarthy, John D. and Mayer N. Zald. 1977. "Resource Mobilization and Social Movements: A Partial Theory." *The American Journal of Sociology* 82 (6):1212–1241.

McGann, James and Mary Johnstone. 2006. "The Power Shift and the NGO Credibility Crisis." *The International Journal of Not-for-Profit Law* 8 (2):65–77.

McGuire, James W. 1997. *Peronism without Peron: Unions, Parties, and Democracy in Argentina*. Stanford, CA: Stanford University Press.

McNulty, Stephanie L. 2011. *Voice and Vote: Decentralization and Participation in Post-Fujimori Peru*. Stanford, CA: Stanford University Press.

Melo, Daniela Tranches de. 2015. *Movimentos Sociais e Institucionalizacao de Politicas Publicas de Saude no Brasil*. Rio de Janeiro: MAUAD.

Mericle, Kenneth S. 1977. "Corporatist Control of the Working Class: Authoritarian Brazil Since 1964." In *Authoritarianism and Corporatism in Latin America*, edited by James M. Malloy. Pittsburgh, PA: University of Pittsburgh Press.

Meyer, David S. 2004. "Protest and Political Opportunities." *Annual Review of Sociology*, 30:125–145.

Michels, Robert. 1949. *Political Parties: A Sociological Study of the Oligarchical Tendencies of Modern Democracy*. Illinois, IL: The Free Press.

Mills, C. Wright. 1956. *The Power Elite*. New York, NY: Oxford University Press.

Montero, Alfred and David Samuels. 2004. *Decentralization and Democracy in Latin America*. Notre Dame, IN: University of Notre Dame Press.

Montero, Alfred P. 1998. "State Interests and the New Industrial Policy in Brazil: The Privatization of Steel, 1990–1994." *Journal of Interamerican Studies and World Affairs* 40 (3):27–62.

2001. "Decentralizing Democracy: Spain and Brazil in Comparative Perspective." *Comparative Politics* 33 (2):149–169.

2002. *Shifting States in Global Markets: Subnational Industrial Policy in Contemporary Brazil and Spain*. University Park, PA: Penn State Press.

Murillo, Maria Victoria. 2001. *Labor Unions, Partisan Coalitions, and Market Reforms in Latin America*. New York, NY: Cambridge University Press.

Murray, Laura R. 2015. "Not Fooling Around: The Politics of Sex Worker Activism in Brazil." Doctorate of Philosophy, Graduate School of Arts and Sciences, Columbia University.

Needleman, Martin L. and Carolyn Emerson Needleman. 1974. *Guerrillas in the Bureaucracy: The Community Planning Experiment in the United States*. New York, NY: Wiley.

Nunes, Edson de Oliveira. 1997. *A gramática política do Brasil: Clientelismo e insulamento burocrático*. Brasília: Escola Nacional de Administração Pública.

Nunn, Amy. 2009. *The Politics and History of AIDS Treatment in Brazil*. New York, NY: Springer.

Oliveira, Claudio. 2006. "Religiões e AIDS: Uma agenda de desafios." *Boletim ABIA* 54:6–7.

Olson, Mancur. 1965. *The Logic of Collective Action*. Boston, MA: Harvard University Press.

Oxhorn, P. 2006. "Conceptualizing Civil Society from the Bottom Up: A Political Economy Perspective." In *Civil Society and Democracy in Latin America*, edited by R. Feinberg, C. H. Waisman and L. Zamosc, 59–84. York: Palgrave MacMillan.

Oxhorn, Philip and Graciela Ducatenzeiler. 1998. *What Kind of Democracy? What Kind of Market?: Latin America in the Age of Neoliberalism*. University Park, PA: Pennsylvania State University Press.

Page, Joshua. 2011. *The Toughest Beat: Politics, Punishment, and the Prison Officers' Union in California*. Oxford; New York, NY: Oxford University Press.

Parker, Richard. 1997. *Políticas, Instituições e AIDS: Enfrentando a Epidemia no Brasil*. Rio de Janeiro: ABIA.

1999. *Beneath the Equator: Cultures of Desire, Male Homosexuality, and Emerging Gay Communities in Brazil*. New York, NY: Routledge.

2003. "Building the Foundations for the Response to HIV/AIDS in Brazil: The Development of HIV/AIDS Policy, 1982 – 1996." *Divulgação em Saúde para Debate* 27:143–183.

2009. "Civil Society, Political Mobilization, and the Impact of HIV Scale-Up on Health Systems in Brazil." *JAIDS Journal of Acquired Immune Deficiency Syndrome* 52 (1):49–51.

Parker, Richard and Veriano Terto. 2001. *Solidariedade: A ABIA, Na virada do milenio*. Rio de Janeiro: ABIA.

Paschel, Tianna. 2016. *Becoming Black Political Subjects: Movements and Ethno-Racial Rights in Colombia and Brazil*. Princeton, NJ: Princeton University Press.

Pereira, Maria Cecília Gomes and Marco Antonio Carvalho Teixeira. 2011. "A inclusão de catadores em programas de coleta seletiva: da agenda local à nacional." *Cadernos EBAPE.br* 9 (3):895–913.

Phillips, Susan. 1991. "Meaning and Structure in Social Movements: Mapping the Network of National Canadian Women's Organizations." *Canadian Journal of Political Science* 24 (4):755–782.

Piven, Frances Fox, and Richard A. Cloward. 1979. *Poor People's Movements: Why They Succeed, How They Fail*. New York, NY: Vintage Books.

Pogrebinschi, Thamy and David Samuels. 2014. "The Impact of Participatory Democracy: Evidence from Brazil's National Public Policy Conferences." *Comparative Politics* 46 (3):313–332.

Putnam, Robert D., Robert Leonardi, and Raffaella Nanetti. 1993. *Making Democracy Work: Civic Traditions in Modern Italy*. Princeton, NJ: Princeton University Press.

Raizer, Elisabeth. 1997. "O estatal, o público e o privado e suas expressões na epidemia de Aids." Ph.D. Doctoral Dissertation, Pontífica Universidade.

Raxach, Juan Carlos. 2005. "As deficiências do atendimentos aos portadores de HIV/AIDS." *Boletim ABIA* (53):4–5.

Rich, Jessica. 2019. "Making National Participatory Institutions Work: Bureaucrats, Activists, and AIDS Policy in Brazil." *Latin American Politics and Society* 61 (1).

Rich, Jessica A. J. 2013. "Grassroots Bureaucracy: Intergovernmental Relations and Popular Mobilization in Brazil's AIDS Policy Sector." *Latin American Politics and Society* 55 (2):1–25.

Rich, Jessica A. J. and Eduardo J. Gómez. 2012. "Centralizing Decentralized Governance in Brazil." *Publius: The Journal of Federalism* 2012. doi: 10.1093/publius/pjs002.

Rich, Jessica A. J., Lindsay Mayka, and Alfred Montero. 2019. "The Politics of Participation in Latin America: New Actors and Institutions. *Latin American Politics and Society* 61 (1).

Rios, Roger Rapp. 2003. "Legal responses to the AIDS epidemic in Brazil." *Divulgação Em Saúde Para Debate* 27:228–238.

Roberts, Andrew. 2005. "The Quality of Democracy." *Comparative Politics*, 37 (3):357–376.

Roberts, Kenneth M. 2008. "The Mobilization of Opposition to Economic Liberalization." *Annual Review of Political Science* 11 (1):327–349.

Rolnik, Raquel. 2011. "Desafios para a implementação do direito à moradia no Brasil." In *Quintas urbanas: Cidades e possibilidades*, edited by César Augusto Ávila Martins, Susana Maria Veleda da Silva, and Solismar Fraga Martins. Rio Grande: Editora e Gráfica da FURG: 13–23.

Rossi, Federico M. 2015. "The Second Wave of Incorporation in Latin America: A Conceptualization of the Quest for Inclusion Applied to Argentina." *Latin American Politics and Society* 57 (1):1–28.

2017. *The Poor's Struggle for Political Incorporation: The Piquetero Movement in Argentina*. Cambridge: Cambridge University Press.

Rossi, Federico M. and Eduardo Silva. 2018. "*Reshaping the Political Arena in Latin America: From Resisting Neoliberalism to the Second Incorporation.*" In *Pitt Latin American series*. Pittsburgh, PA: University of Pittsburgh Press. https://muse.jhu.edu/book/59058/.

Rossi, Federico M., and Marisa Von Bülow. 2016. *Social Movement Dynamics: New Perspectives on Theory and Research from Latin America*. Farnham: Ashgate Publishing, Ltd.

Rossi, Federico and Marisa Von Bülow. 2015. "Introduction: Theory-Building Beyond Borders." In *Social Movement Dynamics: New Perspectives on Theory and Research from Latin America*, edited by Federico Rossi and Marisa Von Bülow. Surrey: United Kingdom: Ashgate.

Samuels, David J. and Fernando Luiz Abrucio. 2000. "Federalism and Democratic Transitions: The 'New' Politics of the Governors in Brazil." *Publius: The Journal of Federalism* 30 (2):43–61.

Samuels, David J. and Cesar Zucco. 2018. *Partisans, Antipartisans, and Nonpartisans: Voting Behavior in Brazil*. United Kingdom: Cambridge University Press.

Saúde, Ministério da. 2003. Catálogo de organizações da sociedade civil HIV/AIDS 2001/2002. edited by Ministério da Saúde.

Schattschneider, E. E. 1960. *The Semisovereign People: A Realist's View of Democracy in America*. New York, NY: Holt, Rinehart and Winston.

Schlozman, Kay Lehman, Sidney Verba, and Henry E. Brady. 2012. *The Unheavenly Chorus: Unequal Political Voice and the Broken Promise of American Democracy*. Princeton, NJ: Princeton University Press.

Schmitter, Philippe C. 2015. "Will The Present Crisis Revive the Neo-Corporatist Sisyphus?" In *Complex Democracy: Varieties, Crises, and Transformations*. Edited by Volker Schneider and Burkard Eberlein. 155–163. Switzerland: Springer International Publishing.

1974. "Still the Century of Corporatism?" *The Review of Politics* 36 (1):85–131.

1971. *Interest Conflict and Political Change in Brazil*. Stanford, CA: Stanford University Press.

Schneider, Ben Ross. 1991. *Politics within the State: Elite Bureaucrats and Industrial Policy in Authoritarian Brazil*. Pittsburgh, PA: University of Pittsburgh Press.

2004. *Business Politics and the State in Twentieth-Century Latin America*. New York and Cambridge: Cambridge University Press.

Sekles, Flavia. 2001. "Brazil's Needle-Exchange Programs Reduced HIV Risks for Drug Users," *Population Reference Bureau*.

Selee, Andrew D. and Enrique Peruzzotti. 2009. *Participatory Innovation and Representative Democracy in Latin America*. Washington, DC; Baltimore, MD: Woodrow Wilson Center Press; Johns Hopkins University Press.

Serafim, Lizandra. 2013. "Participação no governo Lula: as pautas da reforma urbana no Ministério das Cidades (2003–2010)."

Shadlen, Kenneth C. 2002. "Orphaned by Democracy: Small Industry in Contemporary Mexico." *Comparative Politics* 35 (1):43–62.

2017. *Coalitions and Compliance: The Political Economy of Pharmaceutical Patents in Latin America*. Oxford: Oxford University Press.

Silva, Eduardo. 2009. *Challenging Neoliberalism in Latin America*. New York and Cambridge: Cambridge University Press.

2013. "Transnational Activism and National Movements in Latin America: Concepts, Theories, and Expectations." In *Transnational Activism and National Movements in Latin America: Bridging the Divide*, edited by Eduardo Silva, 232. New York, NY: Routledge.

Silva, Eduardo and Federico M. Rossi. 2018. *Reshaping the Political Arena in Latin America: From Resisting Neoliberalism to the Second Incorporation*. Pittsburgh, PA: University of Pittsburgh Press.

Smelser, Neil J. 1962. *Theory of Collective Behavior, International Library of Sociology and Social Reconstruction*. London: Routledge & Paul.

Smith, Jackie. 2008. *Social Movements for Global Democracy*. Baltimore, MD: Johns Hopkins University Press.

Solano, Nelson. 2000. "As organizações não-governamentais e a coordenação nacional de DST/AIDS." *Cadernos ABONG* 28:75–130.

Souza, Celina. 1997. *Constitutional Engineering in Brazil: The Politics of Federalism and Decentralization*. London: Palgrave Macmillan.

1998. "Intermediação de Interesses Regionais no Brasil: O Impacto do Federalismo e da Descentralização." *Dados* 41 (3).

2008a. "Regras e contexto: as reformas da Constituição de 1988." *Dados* 51 (4).

Souza, Paula de Oliveira e. 2008b. "AIDS, Religiões, e Políticas Públicas." *Boletim ABIA* (56): 8–9.

Spink, Mary Jane Paris. 2003. *A Comissão Nacional de Aids: a presença do passado na construção do futuro*. Brasília: Ministério da Saúde.

Spires, Anthony J. 2011. "Contingent Symbiosis and Civil Society in an Authoritarian State: Understanding the Survival of China's Grassroots NGOs." *American Journal of Sociology* 117 (1):1–45.

Steinberg, Paul F. 2001. *Environmental Leadership in Developing Countries: Transnational Relations and Biodiversity Policy in Costa Rica and Bolivia*. Cambridge, MA: MIT Press.

Stepan, Alfred. 1978. *The State and Society: Peru in Comparative Perspective*. Princeton, NJ: Princeton University Press.

Stern, Elliot. 2005. Evaluation of UNESCO Brazil's Contribution to AIDS II. edited by Unesco.

Swidler, Ann, and Susan Cotts Watkins. 2017. *A Fraught Embrace: The Romance and Reality of AIDS Altruism in Africa*. Princeton, NJ: Princeton University Press.

Tarlau, Rebecca. 2013. "Coproducing Rural Public Schools in Brazil Contestation, Clientelism, and the Landless Workers, Äô Movement." *Politics & Society* 41 (3): 395–424. doi: 10.1177/0032329213493753.

2019. *Occupying Schools, Occupying Land: How the Landless Workers Movement Transformed Brazilian Education, Global and Comparative Ethnography*. Oxford: Oxford University Press.

Tarrow, Sidney G. 1998. Power in Movement: Social Movements and Contentious Politics. 2nd edn, *Cambridge Studies in Comparative Politics*. Cambridge England; New York, NY: Cambridge University Press.

2005. *The New Transnational Activism, Cambridge Studies in Contentious Politics*. New York, NY: Cambridge University Press.

Teixeira, Paulo. 1997. "Políticas públicas em Aids." In *Políticas, instituicões e Aids: enfrentando a epidemia no Brasil*, chapter 5, edited by Richard Parker. Rio de Janiero: ABIA.

Tendler, Judith. 1997. *Good Government in the Tropics*. Baltimore, MD: Johns Hopkins University Press.

Terto Jr., Veriano. 1997. "A AIDS e o local de trabalho no Brasil." In *Políticas, Instituições e AIDS: Enfrentando a Epidemia no Brasil*, chapter 5, edited by Richard Parker. Rio de Janeiro: ABIA.

Thayer, Millie. 2010. *Making Transnational Feminism: Rural Women, NGO Activists, and Northern Donors in Brazil*. New York: Routledge.

Trevisan, João Silverio. 1986. *Devassos no paraiso*. Rio de Janeiro: Editora Record.

Truman, David B. 1951. *The Governmental Process: Political Interests and Public Opinion*. New York, NY: Alfred A. Knopf.

Tulchin, Joseph S., and Andrew Selee, eds. 2004. *Decentralization and Democratic Governance in Latin America*. Washington, DC: Woodrow Wilson International Center for Scholars.

Van Cott, Donna Lee. 2005. *From Movements to Parties in Latin America*. New York and Cambridge: Cambridge University Press.

Ventura, Miriam. 2003. "Strategies to promote and guarantee the rights of people living with HIV/AIDS." *Divulgação Em Saúde Para Debate* 27:239–246.

Viana, Rafael R. 2017. "Programa Minha Casa Minha Vida-Entidades: Um Olhar Para A Ação Dos Atores Em Torno Das Controvérsias." Instituto de Ciência Política, Universidade de Brasília.

Vilaça, Luiz. 2017. "Costuras, deslocamentos e bricolagens: a atuação de procuradores no Ministério Público Federal no caso de Belo Monte." Masters, Ciência Política, Universidade de Brasília.

Von Bülow, Marisa. 2010. *Building Transnational Networks: Civil Society and the Politics of Trade in the Americas*. Cambridge, UK: Cambridge University Press.

Walker, Lucy, Joãn Jardim, and Karen Harley. 2010. Waste Land. Midas Filmes.

Wampler, Brian. 2007. *Participatory Budgeting in Brazil: Contestation, Cooperation, and Accountability*. University Park, PA: Penn State Press.

Wampler, Brian, and Leonardo Avritzer. 2004. "Participatory Publics: Civil Society and New Institutions in Democratic Brazil." *Comparative Politics* 36 (3):297–312.

Wampler, Brian, and Stephanie L. McNulty. 2011. *Does Participatory Governance Matter?: Exploring the Nature and Impact of Participatory Reforms.* The Woodrow Wilson Center.

Watkins, Susan Cotts, Ann Swidler, and Thomas Hannan. 2012. "Outsourcing Social Transformation: Development NGOs as Organizations." *Annual Review of Sociology* 38 (1):285–315. doi: 10.1146/annurev-soc-071811-145516.

Weir, Margaret. 1999. "Power, Money, and Politics in Community Development." In *Urban Problems and Community Development*, edited by Ronald F. Ferguson and William T. Dickens. Washington, DC: Brookings Institution Press.

Weyland, K. 1995. "Social Movements and the State: The Politics of Health Reform in Brazil." *World Development* 23 (10):1699–1712.

Wiarda, Howard J. 1973. "Toward a Framework for the Study of Political Change in the Iberic-Latin Tradition: The Corporative Model." *World Politics* 25 (02):206–235. doi: 10.2307/2010494.

Wolford, Wendy. 2010. *This Land Is Ours Now: Social Mobilization and the Meanings of Land in Brazil.* Durham, NC: Duke University Press.

World Bank. 1998. Implementation Completion Report: AIDS and STD Control Project (Loan 3659-BR). The World Bank.

2004. *Brazil First and Second AIDS and STD Control Projects: Project Performance Assessment Report.* Washington, DC: The World Bank.

2005a. *Evaluation of the World Bank's Assistance in Responding to the AIDS Epidemic: Brazil Case Study.* Washington, DC: Operations Evaluation Department.

2005b. Improving healthcare and quality of life for people living with HIV and AIDS in Brazil." Document brief.

2007. *Governance in Brazil's Unified Health System (SUS): Raising the Quality of Public Spending and Resource Management.* Washington, DC: The World Bank.

2010. *Project Appraisal Document on a Proposed Loan in the Amount of US$67 Million to the Federative Republic of Brazil for the AIDS-SUS Project (National AIDS Program – National Health Service).* Washington, DC: The World Bank.

Yashar, Deborah J. 2005. *Contesting Citizenship in Latin America: The Rise of Indigenous Movements and the Postliberal Challenge.* New York and Cambridge: Cambridge University Press.

Zayani, Mohamed. 2015. *Networked Publics and Digital Contention: The Politics of Everyday Life in Tunisia.* Oxford: Oxford University Press.

Index

CPSIA information can be obtained
at www.ICGtesting.com
Printed in the USA
LVHW042249270821
696290LV00010B/673